ASSESSING
ASSESSMENT

'GOOD SCHOOL,
BAD SCHOOL'

ASSESSING ASSESSMENT

Series Editor:
Harry Torrance, University of Sussex

The aim of this series is to take a longer term view of current developments in assessment and to interrogate them in terms of research evidence deriving from both theoretical and empirical work. The intention is to provide a basis for testing the rhetoric of current policy and for the development of well-founded practice.

Current titles

ASSESSING
ASSESSMENT

'GOOD SCHOOL, BAD SCHOOL'

EVALUATING PERFORMANCE AND ENCOURAGING IMPROVEMENT

John Gray and Brian Wilcox

Open University Press
Buckingham · Philadelphia

Open University Press
Celtic Court
22 Ballmoor
Buckingham
MK18 1XW

and

1900 Frost Road, Suite 101
Bristol, PA 19007, USA

First Published 1995

A catalogue record of this book is available from the British Library

ISBN 0 335 19489 3 (pb)   0 335 19490 7 (hb)

Library of Congress Cataloging-in-Publication Data
'Good school, bad school' / Evaluating performance and encouraging improvement / John Gray and Brian Wilcox.
    p.   cm. — (Assessing assessment)
  Includes bibliographical references and index.
  ISBN 0–335–19490–7. — ISBN 0–335–19489–3 (pbk.)
    1. Education—Great Britain—Evaluation.   2. Educational accountability—Great Britain.   3. School improvement programs—Great Britain.   4. Educational change—Great Britain.   I. Gray, John (John Michael), 1948– .   II. Wilcox, B. (Brian)   III. Series.
LA632.G52   1995
370'.941—dc20   94–45442
                                                     CIP

Typeset by Colset Pte Ltd, Singapore
Printed in Great Britain by Biddles Ltd, Guildford and King's Lynn

To Jean and Julia

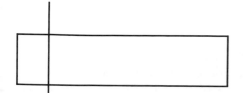

CONTENTS

SERIES EDITOR'S INTRODUCTION

Changing theories and methods of assessment have been the focus of significant attention for some years now, not only in the UK, but also in many other western industrial countries and many developing countries. Curriculum developers have realized that real change will not take place in schools if traditional paper-and-pencil tests, be they essay or multiple choice, remain unchanged to exert a constraining influence on how teachers and pupils approach new curricula. Similarly, examiners have wanted to develop more valid or 'authentic' ways of assessing the changes which have been introduced into school syllabuses over recent years – more practical work, more oral work, more problem solving. In turn psychologists and sociologists have become concerned with the impact of assessment on learning and motivation, and how that impact can be developed more positively. This has led to a myriad of developments in the field of assessment. They often involve an increasing role for the teacher in school-based assessment, as more relevant and challenging tasks are devised by examination agencies for administration by teachers in schools, and as the role and status of more routine teacher assessment of coursework, practical work, and groupwork has become enhanced.

However, educationists have not been alone in focusing much more closely on the interrelation of curriculum, pedagogy and assessment. Governments around the world, but particularly in the UK, have also begun to take a close interest in the ways in which assessment can influence and even control teaching, as well as in the changes in curriculum and teaching which could be brought about by changes in assessment. This interest has not been wholly coherent. Government intervention in the UK has sometimes initiated, sometimes reinforced, the move towards a more practical and vocationally oriented curriculum and thus the move towards more practical, school-based assessment. But government has also acted to inhibit such developments at various times when the political debate has instead centred on issues of accountability and the maintenance of what might be called traditional academic standards, through the use of externally set tests.

Developing in tandem with such concerns has been an interest in measuring school effectiveness, particularly through focusing on test and examination results. However, this concern has been pursued as much by researchers interested in enhancing school effectiveness as policy-makers interested in narrow approaches to evaluation and accountability. Thus the uneasy association of research, development and policy-making continues.

It is precisely because of this complexity and confusion that this series of books on assessment has been developed. Many claims are being made with respect to the efficacy of new approaches to assessment which require careful review and investigation. Likewise many changes are being required by government intervention which may lead to hurried and poorly understood developments being implemented in schools. The aim of this series is to take a longer-term view of the changes which are occurring, to move beyond the immediate problems of implementation and to explore the claims and the changes in terms of broader research evidence which derives from both theoretical and empirical work. In reviewing the field in this way the intention of the series is thus to highlight relevant research evidence; identify key factors and principles which should underpin the developments taking place; as well as provide teachers and administrators with a basis for informed decision-making which takes the educational issues seriously and goes beyond simply accommodating the latest policy imperative.

John Gray and Brian Wilcox's book adds a further dimension to the series, taking it beyond analyses of trends, issues and problems in the design and conduct of assessment *per se*, to address the uses to which the *results* of assessment are being put, with respect to both school accountability and school improvement. Gray and Wilcox present the results of a broad range of research on school effectiveness and school improvement, undertaken by themselves and colleagues over a number of years. Many of the chapters have appeared in one form or another before, but have been gathered together and redrafted to form a comprehensive and coherent review of current knowledge in the field. Some new material also appears for the first time, as Gray and Wilcox draw together research findings from different sources and different methodological perspectives in order to try to establish what makes a difference to school performance and how improvement can be engendered.

The novelty and timeliness of the book resides in this drawing together of their own research, their reading of others' research, and their concern to integrate debates about how to measure school effectiveness with practical approaches to school improvement. They review research on how to measure the performance of schools, fairly and accurately, along with the substantive findings of such research on the extent to which schools can and do make a difference to pupil achievement. In so doing they draw attention to the nature and methods of the 'value-added' debate, demonstrating that it should not be, and indeed is not, too complicated a procedure for government to take on board when determining policy on the publication of exam results. Beyond this debate, Gray and Wilcox also then look at the lessons learned from more detailed case studies of effective (and ineffective) schools, both in this country and the USA, and at the literature of school management and development. Their review does not stop at research studies however. They also examine the process and products of school inspections and the way in which inspection reports have an impact on individual schools, or, in some cases, do not.

The contribution of the book lies in its combination of an authoritative analysis of research, with detailed descriptions of how particular approaches to 'value-added' methods and feedback from inspections can be utilized by local education authorities and individual schools. The book demonstrates the strength of a team approach to such complex issues, the contribution that differing research traditions and sources of evidence can make to understanding and helping bring about the process of improvement, and the need for a longer-term perspective on the possibility of change (years rather than months). The authors also recognize that distilling evidence of what appears to be the necessary conditions for school improvement does not always describe what is sufficient; there is no easy 'cookbook' approach and what works in one set of circumstances may not work in another. As Gray and Wilcox point out, 'How an "ineffective" school improves may well differ from the ways in which more effective schools maintain their effectiveness.'

Harry Torrance

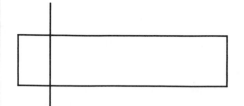

ACKNOWLEDGEMENTS

This book brings together a number of pieces of our research which we have written in recent years. Some of the contributions have been specifically prepared for this volume but the majority have already been published elsewhere.

We should especially like to thank our co-authors for their contributions. David Jesson has worked with one of us (John Gray) for many years and the fruits of this collaboration can be seen in a number of the chapters (see Chapters 2, 6 and 11). Our other co-authors of particular chapters, to whom we are also extremely grateful, are: Valerie Hannon (Chapter 3), Nicholas Sime (Chapters 2 and 6) and Harvey Goldstein, Keith Hedger and Jon Rasbash (Chapter 11). Jean Booker, Louisa Chapman and Brenda Finney helped, at various stages, with the preparation of the manuscript whilst other colleagues within QQSE offered ideas and advice.

Much of the research reported here was conducted with the assistance of the Economic and Social Research Council (ESRC) which we should like to acknowledge. Back in the mid-1980s they funded the Contexts Project, directed by John Gray, David Jesson and Stewart Ranson; this allowed us to pioneer many of the techniques which are now used in assessing 'value-added'. The two of us are, at the same time, grateful to the ESRC for supporting our more recent project, Programmes to Assess the Quality of Schooling (R00023322701), which has allowed us to look at various aspects of inspection and school evaluation. They also provided the resources for John Gray, David Reynolds, Carol Fitz-Gibbon and David Jesson to organize a series of research seminars on school effectiveness and school improvement (R452126400519) from which our most recent thinking has undoubtedly benefited. In addition, Shropshire, Nottinghamshire and Leicestershire LEAs provided significant resources and assistance for our research at various points.

A number of copyright holders have kindly given us permission to reproduce work in whole or in part in this volume. We should like to acknowledge their cooperation. They are: *The British Journal of Educational Studies* and Basil Blackwell (Chapter 1); The Scottish Office Education Department and HMSO (Chapter 2); *The Journal of Education Policy* and Taylor & Francis (Chapter 3); K. Riley and Falmer Press (Chapter 4); HM Inspectors of Schools, Audit Unit, Scottish Office Education Department (Chapter 5); *The Oxford Review of Education* and Carfax Publishing (Chapter 6); *The Cambridge Journal of Education* and Carfax Publishing (Chapter 8).

Finally, a very large number of teachers, LEA officers and other researchers have helped us over the years. Much of our work is facilitated on the basis of offering anonymity and confidentiality to our respondents. We feel it would be invidious to name some (for whom anonymity was not an issue) and ignore others (for whom, for one reason or another, it was). We should none the less like to thank them all most sincerely for their willing and, in many cases, continuing collaboration.

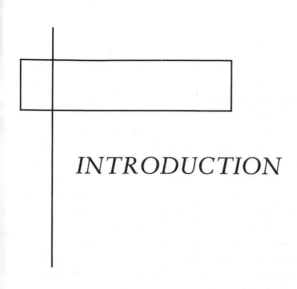

INTRODUCTION

Interest amongst policy-makers, the public and researchers in the quality, effectiveness and improvement of schools continues to grow. How is this interest – obsession even – to be explained?

School reputations

The character of schools has always, of course, been of interest to the discerning parent. Parents often talk to others about the merits of local schools, particularly at those crucial times when their off-spring are about to start formal education or to transfer from one stage of schooling to another. Schools sometimes acquire 'reputations' for being 'good' or 'bad' in general or specific terms. The keen interest shown in such reputations indicates that parents firmly believe that schools can confer advantages or disadvantages on those who attend them. In other words, parents are generally of the view that schools can have effects for good or ill. Choice of school matters.

In the days of selective education, despite the rhetoric of 'parity of esteem', the public generally regarded grammar schools as 'better' than secondary moderns. A minority of the age group, considered the more 'academic', attended the former while the majority were consigned to the latter. For many parents therefore 'reputation' was embodied in the two broad types of secondary school available. The decision as to which type of school a pupil attended was taken in the final year of the primary school. Consequently some primary schools acquired a reputation for being better at getting children through the 'eleven plus' selection examination than others.

The notion of the superiority of grammar school education persisted into the early days of the development of comprehensive schools in the late 1950s and early 1960s. A popular slogan at that time for comprehensive schools was that they would provide 'a grammar school education for all'. The move towards comprehensivization was a slow process, which took place over three decades and which, nevertheless, left a selective system virtually untouched in a small minority of local education authorities (LEAs). Comprehensive schools never really shook off the air of controversy which surrounded their emergence. Consequently, it was easy for some policy-makers to argue that the public's attitude towards these schools was equivocal and disenchanted.

Anxieties about education – schools 'in the dock'

Growing anxiety about the supposed quality of education provided by the comprehensive school was articulated in a series of so-called 'Black Papers' on education which appeared at the end of the 1960s (Cox and Dyson, 1969a, 1969b, 1970). The Black Papers consisted of contributions from academics, writers and others and attacked not only the educational standards of comprehensive schools but also 'progressive' methods of education, particularly those associated with some primary schools. A common theme running through the papers was the claim that standards of literacy and numeracy had deteriorated significantly since the 1950s. The Black Papers were taken up by influential members of the media and this helped, in turn, to influence the public's views of schooling.

The new decade of the 1970s inaugurated a period of sustained hostility in the media towards the public education system and its methods, which continued into the 1980s and beyond. The William Tyndale school, an Inner London Education Authority (ILEA) primary school, provided a *cause célèbre* in the mid-1970s. The school was pilloried in the national press for its poor standards of education and its ideologically motivated teachers. It was the subject of an official enquiry (Auld 1976) and the subsequent press coverage did much to demonize the idea of progressive education.

The condition of the public education system became a key political priority and resulted in the first major prime ministerial contribution on the subject for many years. This was delivered by the then Labour Prime Minister Jim Callaghan in a speech given at Ruskin College, Oxford in 1976. His speech drew on the contents of a privately circulated paper, prepared by officials at the Department of Education and Science (DES), which was heavily critical of recent educational developments. One consequence of the Ruskin speech was to initiate a so-called 'Great Debate' on education conducted throughout the country in a series of regional conferences.

With the benefit of hindsight, this series of events can be seen as a curtain-raiser to one of the most intensive periods of change in the history of the education system following the return to power of the Conservatives in 1979. Change has continued unabated through successive Conservative governments to the present day. It has resulted, *inter alia*, in the centralization of the curriculum, national testing programmes, the creation of alternative types of school outside the maintained sector, and a dramatic reduction in the responsibilities of LEAs, which may yet lead to their total demise. Driving the reforms has been a sense that teachers and other educationists have been failing both the young people in our schools and the nation as a whole and that radical reforms were required to transform the situation. Some critics went as far as to argue for the breaking up of LEAs (and similar 'bureaucratic' organizations) and their replacement by a full-blown 'market' system (see, for example, Chubb and Moe 1990 for a widely read analysis). Government policy in education can be seen, in part at least, as a series of responses to economic and moral panic.

It is not our intention here to provide a detailed critique of the events that constitute this most politicized period of educational change (see Ball 1990 and Knight 1990 for extended accounts). Rather it is to focus on a particular consequence, which we explore in the chapters to follow. Schools have clearly become the focus of intensified surveillance and interest. A major aim has been to assess the quality of education which schools provide, to identify

in particular those schools where standards are seen to be inadequate, and to hold up as models those whose performance is more
exemplary – as in the HMI study of *Ten Good Schools* (HMI 1977).
In brief, a major development in the last 20 or so years has been the
attempt to pin down definitively the characteristics of schools, to
move beyond the vague notion of school 'reputations' towards more
precise and reliable descriptions, and – perhaps in more populist
language – to identify 'good' and particularly 'bad' schools.

The move towards more precise judgements about schools

Initial justifications for this enhanced interest in schools' performance were couched in terms of 'accountability'. Schools, it was
argued, should be held accountable for the quality of the education
which they provided. This raised the question 'to whom are schools
accountable?' The answers given to this question in the late 1970s,
a period which saw the emergence of a modestly burgeoning literature on educational accountability (see, for example, Lello 1979),
tended to be rather unclear. Was it accountability to the Secretary of
State, the LEA, the school governors, the parents or even the pupils?
    Accountability, the notion of rendering an account, implies the
presentation of information in some form to those with 'a right to
know'. The issue of 'who has a right to know?' has effectively been
answered by government's insistence that relevant information
should be published and therefore available to all. This particularly
includes parents, who are increasingly conceptualized as consumers
operating within an educational market. The key concept here is
'choice'. It is argued that it is essential for parents to have appropriate information if they are to make rational decisions in the
market, for example in the choice of schools for their children. This
'right' is enshrined in a 'Parent's Charter' (Department for Education
1994a), which effectively brings together the notion of accountability and standards with that of information and choice.

> But everyone, not just parents, should benefit from improved
> standards and choice. The Charter reforms are also the key to
> making the country more competitive . . .
>
> Under the Government's reforms you should get all the

information you need to keep track of your child's progress, to find out how the school is being run, and to compare all local schools . . .

Better information about schools is also important for raising standards. For example, publishing tables which compare the performance of schools has encouraged many schools to take a hard look at the examination results their pupils achieve and how the school can help the pupils to do better.

(DFE 1994a: 1–3)

The Parent's Charter guarantees that parents will have access to five key documents:

- reports about their children;
- regular reports on schools from inspectors;
- performance tables for all local schools;
- a prospectus or brochure about individual schools;
- an annual report from governors of the school(s) attended by their child(ren).

All but the first of these are descriptions of schools in one form or another. Together they add up to an unprecedented initiative in making publicly available details of the characteristics and achievements of individual schools. In this book our interest is particularly with the second and third items in this list. Essentially we focus on the attempts which have been made in recent years to judge the quality of schools using, on the one hand, statistically based information related to pupil performance and, on the other, descriptive accounts of schools derived from inspections. The chapters which follow describe our own efforts in both of these fields and our concern with the methodological and other challenges posed by these approaches.

An overview of the book

Before proceeding further the reader may welcome some orienting comments. The first point that should be made is that the developments outlined above, although described within the English scene, have their parallels in other countries not only in the United Kingdom but also in Europe, Australasia and North

America. This apparently worldwide fascination with schools is undoubtedly influenced by common concerns: the spiralling costs of mass education and the consequent emphasis on 'value for money', the belief that education is an essential condition for achieving a competitive edge in the global economy, the need to meet the greater educational expectations of parents and a measure of disenchantment with some of the methods of education and some of its modes of organization. There is also a growing awareness that, in a post-modern era, the school remains as perhaps the only institution for moral socialization which virtually all young people will encounter. The responsibilities which are placed on the school and the expectations which society has of it have never been greater.

The second point to emphasize is that these developments have attracted the attention of a growing body of educational researchers. Their activities have helped to clarify and address the issues involved in assessing the characteristics and effects of schools, as well as how to improve them. Our aim in this book is to help the reader understand these developments by encountering a series of separate but related studies which we have carried out in recent years.

Our final point is an extension of the second and provides an initial overview of the kind of research which features in the chapters to follow. This generally falls under two broad approaches. The first is essentially quantitative in nature and is concerned with the collection and analysis of 'hard' evidence. The aim here is basically to test the commonsense belief that some schools are 'better' or more effective than others in improving the performance of pupils. Much of the story we tell is about developing better methods of analysing schools' results in order to distinguish between the effectiveness of individual schools or groups of schools.

A major concern here has been an insistence on the importance of 'contextualizing' results so that comparisons between schools are fairer. To put the issue starkly – the direct comparison of the examination results (e.g. in terms of numbers or percentages of specific grades obtained) achieved by a school with a high proportion of able and socially advantaged pupils with those of a school with a small proportion of such pupils is unjustifiable. Methods of contextualization basically take account of such differences in pupil intake either directly, by using measures of prior attainment, or indirectly, and less satisfactorily, by using related measures such as social class. Central to such contextualization is the use of appropriate statistical techniques. The chapters in Part 2 of the book record some of our experiences of applying increasingly sophisticated techniques to the examination results of large samples of schools from a range of LEAs.

The crucial issue which runs through this part of the book is whether or not some schools do better or worse by their pupils than would be expected from knowledge of their intakes. This can be more succinctly expressed in the current language of quality management as 'value-added'. Our research confirms that some schools do, indeed, add more value than others, and also indicates the order of magnitude that can be expected.

The use of examination results has been at the centre of the government's interest in the performance measurement of schools. There have, however, been several government-inspired initiatives to develop other possible performance indicators. Since 1992 the government has published performance tables of local schools. One version of these for secondary schools includes rates of absence and length of the taught week, as well as examination results and vocational qualifications (DFE 1994b). Although the government has made some concessions to the arguments of researchers (for example, the inclusion of LEA and national averages in the tables) the presentation of information falls well short of the requirements we would want to see. Our story is therefore not only statistical and methodological but also, in part, political.

The second approach to assessing the quality of schools is broader in scope. While it may utilize quantitative data where appropriate its methods are essentially qualitative. The aim is to provide an account of the school as a whole. As a research approach this has often taken the form of case studies of individual schools (see, for example, Ball 1981; Lightfoot 1983; Reynolds *et al.* 1987). Although much of our thinking has been influenced by studies of this kind it is to another variant of the approach that we turn in Part 3. We focus there on the accounts of schools provided by inspection.

In the past inspection has been the responsibility of Her Majesty's Inspectorate (HMI) and, to a lesser extent, the inspectorates and advisory services of LEAs. Inspection and the accounts of schools which it produces have been woefully neglected by the research community. This is all the more surprising when it is recognized that the number of school studies produced each year by inspectors far outnumber those from researchers. This is even more the case with the introduction of the inspection arrangements arising from the 1992 Education (Schools) Act, which set up an annual target of inspecting a quarter of all schools. In other words, each year individual studies (inspection reports) of some 6000 schools will be generated.

Every inspection claims to 'identify strengths and weaknesses in schools so that they may improve the quality of education offered and raise the standards achieved by their pupils' (OFSTED 1994a: 2, 5). 'Good' schools identified in this way will be lauded. 'Bad' schools, or those described as 'requiring special measures', will no doubt incur the opprobrium of the public and the media. If such schools are unable to convince the Secretary of State that they are able to remedy their deficiencies they can, in the last resort, face closure. Thus will institutional virtue and its opposite be rewarded and punished.

Inspection effectively makes two substantial claims: first, to assess the effectiveness and the quality of a school; and second, to provide an agenda for its improvement. Neither of these claims has been subjected systematically to the scrutiny of research. We address both in the four empirical studies which constitute Part 3 of the book.

The book has a simple structure. What we have described so far forms the broad middle section. A brief comment is required on the remaining parts. The two chapters of Part 1 provide an overview of the field – its broad political context, the range of practices available and its relationship to educational research, particularly that on school effectiveness.

The concluding part looks to the future, accepts the argument that the focus should be on improvement and attempts to identify some of the most promising strategies. Chapter 11 refers to a rare study in which examination results of a large sample of schools have been investigated over successive years. This revealed different dynamic patterns of performance improvement and deterioration. We offer some explanations of these patterns and suggest ways in which these might be further explored by situated case studies.

These and other possibilities for bringing together the approaches of quantitatively-oriented school effectiveness research and the more qualitatively inclined school improvement movement are considered in the final chapter. Suggestions are also offered on how such a rapprochement might also inform a more efficient and potent inspection model in the future.

PART 1

SETTING FRAMEWORKS

1

THE QUALITY OF SCHOOLING: FRAMEWORKS FOR JUDGEMENT

Introduction

Those of you who like to review the health of the nation's schooling over breakfast will have noted that something is amiss. The *Daily Express* did not mince words. Commenting on a recent report from the then HM Senior Chief Inspector of Schools, Eric Bolton, it 'exposed' the 'Scandal of our rotten schools'. Even the *Guardian* was concerned: 'Schools must do better' was the line it took. It was left to *The Times Educational Supplement* to put a somewhat different gloss on the Inspectorate's conclusions: 'Less able most likely to be have-nots.'

With the passage of the 1988 Education Reform Act a concern with 'quality' in the education service has become something of an obsession. In the late 1980s we had:

- the Coopers & Lybrand report on local management of schools (LMS);
- the CIPFA 'Blue Book' on Performance Indicators;
- a pilot project from the Department of Education and Science (DES) in eight local education authorities (LEAs);
- a lengthy *aide-mémoire* from the Minister.

Since that time other bodies have made their contributions too. As a direct result of the Act many LEA personnel see their main role in the future as monitoring and evaluating schools. It is a source of some concern, as LEA after LEA starts establishing frameworks for judgement. In the rush to have something up and running quickly they run the risk of failing the very institutions such procedures are intended to protect.

'Quality' in educational circles is a potentially elusive concept. It undoubtedly has something of the 'best buy' features so assiduously researched and celebrated in *Which* magazine in relation to washing machines, TV sets and electric food mixers. Few people, however, would be happy with definitions that were restricted to these kinds of 'qualities'. They are undoubtedly looking for more. Articulating what that 'more' is remains a major challenge but will come, one hopes, to form the cornerstone of how schools find themselves judged over the next decade.

Different groups have different criteria for judging a school's quality. Rhodes Boyson, former headteacher and Tory Education Minister, is reported to have had three 'instant tests'. The first was the amount of litter in the playgrounds. The second was the amount and quality of graffiti in the loos. And the third was the angle at which children hold their heads, forty-five degrees being the optimum. Below that, they were clearly fast asleep; beyond it, in open revolution!

Some quantitative indicators of quality

In the attempt to understand quality many people turn to such traditional indicators of educational outcomes as exam results and staying-on rates. Using the Youth Cohort Study of England and Wales, some relevant statistics for a period in the mid-1980s have been picked out (Gray *et al.* 1990). Two of these are also available from official sources but the other two (the proportions of pupils truanting and pupils' attitudes) are not.

Whichever of the four measures are employed things do not seem to have changed very much during the 1980s. This conclusion applies to: (1) the percentage obtaining one or more 'higher grade' passes; (2) the percentage staying on at this time; (3) the percentage truanting; or (4) the percentage saying 'school was a waste of time'.

Whatever the 'quality' in absolute terms of the education on offer in the secondary system, its quality (as judged by small and steady improvements over time) does not appear to have altered much despite press reports to the contrary.

The view from HM inspectors

National responsibility for monitoring the quality of what goes on in schools was vested till the early 1990s in members of Her Majesty's Inspectorate (HMI). It was their report which provoked the outburst in both the press and parliament.

HMI follow events more closely than statisticians ever could. They visit institutions which are directly affected by events, both intended and unintended. Not surprisingly, their account is of a system which has had a bumpier ride. Policy initiatives actually affect what is happening.

So what did HMI actually say in their report regarding quality? They reported that:

> Across schools and colleges around 70%–80% of the work seen was judged to be satisfactory or better: roughly one-third of it at all levels was adjudged good or very good. That is *not* a profile of a service in great difficulty about its general standards of work. But . . . there are serious problems of low and under-achievement; of poor teaching; and of inadequate provision. It is particularly troubling that in schools some 30% . . . of what HMI saw was judged poor or very poor. Those figures, if replicated throughout the system, represent a large number of pupils . . . getting a raw deal.
>
> (DES 1990a)

These conclusions are undoubtedly disturbing and merit urgent attention. But what do the reports tell us about how quality has been changing over time? To establish this one needs to look at the annual reports from previous years.

Anyone embarking on such a venture needs to be aware that comparing HMI judgements over time is not an easy matter. There are several reasons for this. The most obvious is that, in attempting to capture the complete strengths and weaknesses of the educational system as a whole within a few pages of a report, much of the detailed basis for the judgements is inevitably omitted. But the difficulties are further compounded by the fact that HMI have, in fact, been using three summary judgements when they visit a school rather than just one. The report on the 1986 academic session provides the clearest discussion of this point (DES 1987):

- the first measure is an assessment of 'the overall quality of work in schools visited';
- the second is an assessment of 'the quality of provision for each class (or lesson) seen';
- the third is an assessment of 'pupils' response for each class (or lesson) seen'.

Interestingly, HMI nowhere commented on secondary schools' exam results in their annual report. The focus was truly on the processes of teaching and learning!

The 1986 HMI report suggests that for:

- 'overall quality' a figure of around 80 per cent satisfactory or better is to be expected;
- for 'quality of provision' around 70 per cent;
- for 'pupils' response' around 80 per cent – to their credit the pupils are apparently achieving in spite of the odds and the provision!

The evidence for the first of these three measures is assembled in Table 1.1. This was not always easy to do. The report on 1987–8, for example, refers to 'most of the work seen by HMI' rather than a specific percentage and the figure 'four lessons out of five', the only quantified statement about secondary schools offered, relates in fact to their report on GCSE and is accompanied by the statement that this was 'a higher proportion than is usually reported in our inspection findings' (DES 1989a).

By way of complete contrast the previous year's results (that is, 1986–7) were quoted to a satisfyingly precise single decimal place. Such confusions were shared by one or two HMI as well. Probably the only useful conclusion to be drawn is that, over the years, HMI have consistently found that somewhere between 70 and 80 per cent of the schools they have visited have been of 'satisfactory or better' quality.

In practice, as will be argued later, broad judgements of this kind are the only useful ones to be made. What is important, when

Table 1.1   HMI's judgements of school quality

Year	Proportion judged to be 'satisfactory or better'*
1988–9	'70% to 80% of work seen'
1987–8	'Four lessons out of five'
1986–7	'83% of work seen'
1985–6	'81% of work seen'
1982–6	'Nearly three-quarters of schools'

* 'Satisfactory' is the mid-point on a five-point scale running from 'excellent to poor'. Sources were as follows: 1988–9: DES report published in 1990a; 1987–8: DES 1989a; 1985–6 and 1986–7: DES 1987; 1982–6: DES 1988a.

judging the quality of schools, is to note those occasions on which there are marked variations from the expected norms. Small fluctuations, one way or the other, are neither here nor there. At the national level at least, things do not appear to have changed very much over the years whether one is looking at the quantitative indicators or the qualitative ones.

A 'poor' school by any yardstick

This is not to deny that there are marked variations in the quality of different schools, a point forcibly brought home by HMI's report on a Hackney secondary school. 'Only 20 per cent of the lessons seen reached satisfactory standards of teaching and learning . . . As many as 50 per cent were of the poorest quality, lacking a clear sense of purpose, pace, progression or direction' (DES 1990b).

The gap between the national picture and the local one presented here is so stark that the apparent precision offered by the statistics is unnecessary. The school's 'overall standards' would surely be recognized as 'exceptionally low' by anyone. The environment in the upper school was 'squalid', the graffiti 'very offensive' and the toilets 'insanitary'. 'Many lessons failed to start on time' and 'pupils' attendance and punctuality gave serious cause for concern'. 'Teacher–pupil relationships . . . varied from the kindly, supportive, interested and positive to the distant, aggressive and, on occasions, the verbally abusive.' Many teachers did not have the classroom management skills to maintain discipline. 'Overall the school [was] not managed effectively and in some respects it was badly managed.'

Even by the standards of the measured language of evaluation employed by HMI it is clear that something had gone very wrong indeed. The 1983 HMI report on the Liverpool Institute for Boys was the last occasion on which one could read about a similarly neglected institution. On this latter occasion, after almost 18 years of increasing neglect, the LEA eventually closed it down.

The national position

How many secondary schools might be like these two nationally? The honest answer is that it is hard to say. The Hackney and Liverpool schools are doubtless at one extreme. There are none the less several pointers.

In their report on secondary schools in the early to mid-1980s, HMI reported that 'fewer than one in ten was judged poor or very poor overall' (DES 1988a). We ourselves noted, in our research for the Elton Enquiry into Discipline, that 'teachers in fewer than one in ten [8%] schools thought that the discipline problems in their school were verging on the "serious"' (Gray and Sime 1988).

Again, the national picture may well mask local differences. Back in 1986 the Inner London Education Authority (ILEA) declared that the academic performance of almost one in four of its secondary schools gave 'cause for concern' (London *Evening Standard*, 20 March 1986). The performance of the Hackney school, as it turns out, was at issue even then although it was not, it should be pointed out, one of the bottom ten which were 'carpeted' at that time. Of course, part of the answer to our question lies in how you choose to draw the line between the 'good' and the 'not so good'. To those who would maintain that the 'figures speak for themselves' we would merely observe that we have yet to find a single figure that could speak, let alone for itself.

Over the years a number of different strategies for 'drawing the line' may be noted. HMI's preference, using a five-point scale running from 'excellent' to 'poor', has been to draw the line below the third category; hence 80 per cent of lessons are 'satisfactory' (the mid-point) or 'better' (good or excellent). By way of contrast, most LEAs have liked to draw the line half-way down the list; this enables them to offer the insight that half the schools in the authority are above the LEA average and half below it.

Our preference is to draw two lines on the assumption that the majority of schools are performing at or around the average. One is looking, therefore, for ways in which schools may be said to differ from this average as well as for reasons; either they are a good deal above it or, alternatively, a good deal below. Most of the time there is nothing exceptional about their performance. They achieve what one would expect.

The politics of school evaluation

Setting the line is not just a matter of statistics or personal preference. As those who have tried to introduce improved strategies for schools' evaluation have found, more is at stake. In any system for evaluating schools there will be winners and losers. In selecting the overall approaches and the particular criteria this needs to be borne in mind. However, we could scarcely have a system more unfair than that which exists at present. By insisting that schools and LEAs publish their 'raw' exam or test results we run the distinct risk of rewarding schools for the 'quality' of the intakes they can attract rather than what they actually do with pupils.

Research on school effectiveness has something to contribute here. There are basically two ways in which the quality of a school's performance can be judged. The easiest way is to compare this year's performance with last year's and the year before that and so on. On the assumption that the intake has remained much the same over the years, how do the results compare?

The second approach is to compare like with like. How much progress have the pupils in this school made compared with pupils at similar starting points in other schools?

Ideally, one would use both approaches at the same time (see Chapter 11). In practice, most school effectiveness studies have concentrated on comparing like with like, whilst giving scant attention to trends over time.

How much difference do schools make?

The debate about whether schools 'make a difference' has raged since the 1960s. Like most such debates there has been ample scope for misunderstanding. The simple and unequivocal answer to the question whether they make a difference is a positive one – of course they do! The crucial questions are how much? and why?

Back in the early 1970s, Christopher Jencks argued that at least half the differences in pupils' performances in their late teens were due to differences in their social backgrounds and prior attainments; the remaining unexplained half he attributed to 'other factors' (Jencks *et al.* 1972). Whilst these 'other factors' undoubtedly included the schools young people attended, he maintained that no-one could actually identify which were the more effective schools, prior to the event, or what precisely made them more effective. As far as predicting outcomes was concerned, schools, to all intents and purposes, made only rather small differences to life-chances.

Jencks' overall analysis of the relative importance of home and school continues to be one of the most comprehensive available and his conclusion that, relatively speaking, what pupils bring to school with them is considerably more important than what schools can do to or with them has scarcely been quarrelled with since.

Our own most recent work confirms the sorts of estimates that have been made up until now (see Chapter 6). Working with data from six different LEAs, and using the most sophisticated statistical techniques currently available (multi-level modelling), we found that when differences in schools' intakes were taken into account the differences between schools' results were roughly halved. We have seen this happen so frequently with the datasets we have analysed that we have come to refer to this phenomenon as the 'rule of half'.

None the less, there were differences in the results of pupils attending schools of differing 'effectiveness'. In some LEAs these differences were quite small; in one or two cases they were rather larger. In all cases, however, differences in schools' effectiveness were a great deal smaller than differences in their 'raw' results.

What causes the differences? Jencks himself was adamant that none of the things that policy-makers could directly influence 'made a difference'. 'We can see no evidence', he declared, 'that either school administrators or educational experts know how to raise test scores, even when they have vast resources at their disposal. Certainly we do not know how to do so' (Jencks *et al.* 1972: 95).

When discussing the effects of policies and resources on pupil outcomes Jencks confined his attention to those 'school policies and resources that could be directly controlled by legislators, school boards and administrators'. In a brief but key paragraph he remarked:

> We did not look in any detail at things like morale, teacher expectations, school traditions and school 'climate'. While these things may well be associated with unusually rapid or slow cognitive development, policy-makers cannot usually measure them . . . and no one can be sure whether they cause achievement or only result from it.
>
> (Jencks *et al.* 1972: 95)

Factors which seem to make a difference

Two decades have passed since Jencks was formulating his conclusions, and it is a decade and a half since Rutter and colleagues (1979) published *Fifteen Thousand Hours*. Some of Jencks' conclusions have withstood the test of time, others have been modified. Crucially, somewhat more is now understood about the nexus of relationships which Jencks was quick, perhaps too quick, to dismiss.

Whichever account one reads of research on school effectiveness, a prominent place is given to the centrality of the institution's values. In a nutshell, the more effective or successful schools seem to know what they are about and where they are going. They have, as Lightfoot (1983) puts it in her account of six 'good' American High Schools, visible and explicit ideologies. The particularly interesting (and, with hindsight, not unexpected) feature, however, is that staff and pupils alike can provide a reasonably good account of what the school is all about as well; the schools' aims and objectives are not merely the creation of, and confined to, their heads and senior teachers.

Teaching and learning are, of course, at the heart of any school's activities. What particularly distinguishes the more effective ones, Oakes (1989) argued in her wide-ranging review of the literature, is their 'press for achievement'. Teachers expect their pupils to achieve and pupils, in turn, find themselves stretched and challenged in the classroom. Again, there appears to be some mutuality of perceptions between pupils and teachers.

A third area in which the more effective schools make their contribution is in terms of relationships (Goodlad 1984). Certainly, there is an absence of conflict between pupils and teachers; frequently there is some kind of mutual respect or 'rapport'. But crucially, at least in Lightfoot's study, there are plentiful opportunities for pupils to make good or, as she puts it, 'vital' relationships with one or more adults.

These sorts of things do not, of course, just happen; they are managed. Each of the various studies underlines, to a greater or lesser extent, the role of the school's leadership. Indeed, we are still looking for a research study which demonstrates convincingly that the headteacher was not at the centre of things and yet the school, for which they were responsible, still functioned effectively.

More recently, studies have gone beyond the headteacher to emphasize the role of senior management, the strategies that they implement and the ways in which they seek to support their more junior colleagues. A constant search for ways of evaluating and improving their institution's current performance also seems to be characteristic of the leaders of successful schools.

All four of these areas are ones to which Jencks paid scant attention. He would doubtless argue that the later research had given insufficient attention to the question of causal directions and there could be some truth in this charge. Taken collectively, however (and bearing in mind the qualitative accounts of how teachers and pupils actually behaved in the more successful schools) the balance of probabilities is that these things happened directly *because* of efforts made by the heads and their staffs. The most convincing demonstration would probably be to see how these factors were developed in a school over a period of time; but to date few researchers have been in a position to follow a school's development over this longer sort of period (see Chapter 11 for a start in this direction).

There is one area in which Jencks' conclusions have had to be modified a little, namely in relation to resourcing schools. This is the single area in which those responsible for a school, but none the less outside it, can influence matters directly. For much of the 1970s it was fashionable amongst researchers and policy-makers to assert that resources could not buy success. Class sizes did not make a difference; indeed researchers frequently reported that children did better in larger ones!

With hindsight nearly all the studies cited in support of these conclusions have been shown to be seriously flawed from the point of view of research design. One or two more recent studies (and notably the ILEA's Junior School Project) have shown that smaller classes do make some difference, although the effects have not been startling (Mortimore *et al.* 1988). Pupil–teacher ratios within any one LEA are not usually allowed to vary by very much.

Adequate levels of resourcing, then, seem to be a necessary but not sufficient condition for a school to be effective; quite wide mixes of resources seem to be associated (and one should emphasize the word associated) with success. Several caveats are, however, necessary.

1 In 20 years of reading research on the characteristics of effective schools we have only once come across a case of an 'excellent' school where the physical environment left something to be desired; interestingly, in that particular case, working on the environment of the school had been one of the new principal's first priorities, as indeed it appears to be with most new headteachers.
2 In many years of reading HMI's published reports on secondary schools we can only remember two or three occasions where their overall rating was highly favourable and the roof (or something similar) was in need of repair; and someone was always in the process of doing something about it.
3 We have never read an account of a 'good' school which had serious staffing difficulties.

One further point needs to be made about the current research on school effectiveness. In general terms it provides a relatively good introductory guide to the factors that make a difference. As a rule, schools which do the kinds of things the research suggests make a difference: they tend to get better results (however these are measured or assessed). The problem is that these are tendencies, not certainties. In betting terms the research would be right around seven out of ten times, especially if it could be supported by professional assessments.

Around three out of ten times, however, schools seem to achieve 'good' results without scoring particularly highly on all the 'key factors' identified by researchers' blueprints. The collective wisdom of researchers and experienced practitioners is quite simply not good enough to hold individual institutions to account. To do so would be to run the risk of hampering, perhaps even damaging, them.

The focus has tended to turn, as a result, from assertions about what schools must *do* to what schools must *achieve*. In particular, rather a lot of time has been spent debating the frameworks within which schools' performance will be judged.

Performance indicators: some lessons from North America

As we consider the introduction of performance indicators into this country we can learn something from experiences in North America. During 1987, Secretary Bennett of the US Department of Education introduced his infamous 'Wallchart'. This summarized, for the benefit of State superintendents, key features of pupils' performance in each of the states on certain nationally administered attainment tests, as well as providing information about their respective levels of resourcing. In addition it included columns specifying the improvements or gains in pupils' performance that would be needed 'to meet President Reagan's 1990 challenge'. Controversially, these targets seem to have been the same for states as diverse as Massachusetts and Mississippi.

During the 1980s the USA began to take the whole business of monitoring test performance fairly seriously as one major strategy for raising standards. Individual states have increasingly been administering nationally normed standardized achievement tests (of one kind or another) and reporting the results to their communities. However, little in the British experience, apart from the dodges of car manufacturers' mpg claims, could have prepared us for what has come to be known as the Cannell controversy (cf. Shepard 1989).

Cannell (1987) looked at the reports all 50 states had provided on their test results. According to him all 50 claimed to be above the national average and around 70 per cent of all students across the nation were told they were achieving at 'above average' levels. Cannell found this hard to believe. Surely there was some mistake?

In the subsequent debates some qualifications in relation to Cannell's conclusions were put forward. But, surprisingly, it emerged that he was essentially right. In a situation where each state had some freedom to determine which particular tests they would use as yardsticks it was perfectly possible for all or most to report 'above average' levels of performance.

There were several reasons for this but they mostly involved forms of 'teaching to the test'. In many states the testing environment was a 'high-stakes' one; pupils, teachers and their schools simply could not afford to do badly because life-chances were at stake. In others the schools' curricula were either aligned to the tests or, rather more frequently, the tests were aligned to the schools' curricula. Pupils were prepared more frequently for testing situations. There were also some doubts about what were euphemistically referred to as 'test security' and 'familiarity'. Clearly some part of the gains states were reporting was illusory. But then, in a situation where there was no national body taking responsibility for maintaining some kind of overall perspective, there was scope for quite a few unintended consequences.

Some early initiatives in relation to performance indicators

The initial push for the introduction of performance indicators in Great Britain came from the Audit Commission during the early 1980s. Auditors are usually accountants by training and inclination. Naturally, therefore, they asked to see the accounts. The education service provided them with some fairly promptly. It was only several months later that it became clear that the education services' 'accounts' lacked the structure that a modern, performance-driven accountant might be seeking.

The accountant's dream that every educational activity and outcome could be allocated to a cost heading and given a precise cost was some way off becoming reality. To an accountant such imprecision is disconcerting. Before much progress could be made the education service needed to determine where it was headed and to establish some performance indicators by which it could be judged.

Much of the work that has gone on to date in relation to performance indicators is best described as 'ground-clearing'. The Coopers & Lybrand report (1988), the CIPFA 'Blue Book' (1988) and, more recently, the DES's own Pilot Project involving eight LEAs, have all produced lengthy lists of criteria which *might* be used to judge a school's performance (DES 1989b).

Even if the DES had ever contemplated a 'grand design' for judging schools, it is clear that the experience of trying to orchestrate consensus during the pilot project contributed to the view that, in

the context of the National Curriculum and other major developments, a single set of recommendations was not appropriate.
Schools were to be free to construct their own yardsticks. Whilst
presenting the case for performance indicators, the Minister confined herself to the observation that each school should decide on
'a relatively small range of indicators for judging whether it is
achieving its goals'.

Unfortunately, to date, schools have been given little advice about
how they might make such decisions and, in the absence of such
advice, they are not likely to find information about their own performance, in isolation from other schools, very helpful. Judgements
about performance require a context within which they can be
located. Equally importantly, given the firmly embedded nature of
some existing approaches to school evaluation, they require some
overall coordination, if publicly credible judgements that have the
power to challenge existing assumptions and prejudices are to be
produced. Orchestrating such 'agreements' is not merely a technical
activity but involves influencing the social organization of 'educational knowledge' as well.

Developing some principles

Colleagues have worked on these issues with members of about one
in five of the English LEAs. A number of problems have emerged in
our discussions about how their LEAs are responding to the new
demands of the 1988 Education Reform Act, and things are a bit
muddled.

First, few LEAs have sophisticated procedures already in place for
judging the performance of their schools; indeed, as one HMI report
confirmed, a majority of LEAs had not yet got round to establishing
suitable procedures for interpreting schools' examination results
(DES 1989c). Lacking such approaches, LEAs and their schools
have found themselves falling victim to individuals or pressure
groups who have been prepared to employ whatever crude yardsticks were to hand.

Second, LEAs have only recently begun to develop procedures for
systematically sharing information about schools' performances, let
alone judging them. Few LEAs to date can rely on a consensus
amongst their officers and advisers about what it is important to

concentrate on. Should they, for example, look at outcomes as well as processes? And, in either case, which particular ones?

Third, even where the beginnings of some consensus have begun to emerge, there is considerable uncertainty about what precise evidence to collect. There is mounting pressure in many LEAs to use whatever happens to be on the shelf because time is short. But there is also widespread unease that what may currently be readily available or easily measurable is not necessarily central to the educational enterprise. Data collected for one purpose may not lend themselves to others.

Fourth, and most important of all, there is a need to establish some general principles for the construction of performance indicators. Table 1.2 represents an attempt to introduce some coherence to the debate by developing some general principles (Gray and Jesson 1991). The most important consideration relating to the construction of performance indicators is that they should *directly measure or assess schools' performance*. Many of the proposals we have encountered to date seem only indirectly related to actual performance. Performance indicators should:

- be *central to the process of teaching and learning* which we take to be schools' prime objectives;
- *cover significant parts of schools' activities* but not necessarily (and certainly not to begin with) all or even most of them;
- be chosen to *reflect the existence of competing educational priorities*; a school which did well in terms of one of them would not necessarily be expected (or found) to do well in terms of the others;
- be *capable of being assessed*: we distinguish assessment here from measurement, which implies a greater degree of precision than we intend;
- *allow meaningful comparisons* to be made over time and between schools.
- be couched in terms that would *allow schools, by dint of their own efforts* and the ways in which they choose to organize themselves, *to be seen to have changed their levels of performance*; that is to have improved or, alternatively, to have deteriorated relative to previous performance and other schools.
- be *few in number*; three or four might be enough to begin with. After some experimentation over a period of years one might end

Table 1.2 Some general principles for the construction of performance indicators

---

Performance indicators should:
  be about the school's performance
  be central to the process of teaching and learning
  cover significant parts of the school's activities (but not all)
  reflect competing educational priorities
  be capable of being assessed
  allow meaningful comparisons: over time and between schools
  allow schools to be seen to have changed their levels of performance
  by dint of their own efforts
  be few in number

---

up with a few more. The processes that establish the wider credibility of the first ones will lend themselves to development if required.

The three performance indicators

We have come to recognize that there is an inverse relationship between the number of questions one chooses to ask and the quality of the evidence that can be collected in relation to each. The Law of Performance Indicators states that 'too many questions drive out good answers'. As 'good answers' are fundamental to the task of setting agendas for schools' further development it follows that we felt we ought to confine ourselves accordingly.

In the interests of economy, efficiency and effectiveness we have therefore restricted ourselves to the three questions listed in Table 1.3. The choice of 'academic progress' as one focus strikes us as largely unproblematic although, in the context of a national curriculum and related attainment testing in as many as ten subjects, it may be necessary to impose some restrictions.

Our second and third choices (relating to pupil satisfaction and pupil–teacher relationships) have been heavily influenced by our reading of the literature on school effectiveness.

In sum, we are arguing that a 'good' school is one where high proportions of pupils:

- make above average levels of academic progress;
- are satisfied with the education they are receiving;

Table 1.3 The three performance indicators

Academic progress
What proportion of pupils have made above average levels of progress over the relevant time-period?

Pupil satisfaction
What proportion of pupils in the school are satisfied with the education they are receiving?

Pupil–teacher relationships
What proportion of pupils in the school have a good or 'vital' relationship with one or more teachers?

Answer categories for all three questions

All or most	Well over half	About half	Well under half	Few

- have formed a good or 'vital' relationship with one or more of their teachers.

We would agree with those who argue that these are not sufficient conditions for 'excellence'. As pragmatists we would argue, however, that it would be hard to imagine a 'good' school where these things did not happen in reasonable measure and, furthermore, that where they happened frequently, the odds would be on the institution being a 'good' one. The concern that all aspects of schools' activities must somehow be brought in to complete the picture (and for justice to be done) needs to be resisted.

The methodology of school assessments

The cynic will ask how these assessments can be made. The answer is a brief one.

First, the technology for undertaking sophisticated analyses of pupils' academic progress is largely in place. We ourselves have been involved in the routine application of statistical techniques whose complexity was defeating statisticians and the largest computers a few years ago.

Second, the assessments that are required in the other two areas (of pupil satisfaction and pupil–teacher relationships) are no more complex than those which HMI have made on a routine basis. If they can do it convincingly, then surely other experienced practitioners can as well.

The quality of a judgement rests in part on the evidence that has actually been collected in relation to it and, in part, on the way in which that evidence is marshalled to support the judgement. Having a group of 'judges' who are, by and large, in agreement also helps, especially if they can provide a collective articulation of the reasons why they reached the conclusions they did.

The missing dimension

It has been argued that the complexities of the routines and practices which go to make up contemporary schooling can be reduced to just three questions about their 'quality'. None the less, we would be the first to admit that something is missing. Education is about more than the mundane and the everyday. There are frequently 'lows' and there are, more occasionally perhaps, 'highs'. When people remember their educational experiences it is often these latter 'moments' that they particularly emphasize, moments when something of significance has been learnt or experienced.

In brief, a fourth question, or probe, is required to cover those parts of the educational experience that performance indicators cannot reach.

Two examples of such 'moments of quality' will help to make the point. The first is an example of pupils as scientists, drawn from the archives of the Children's Learning in Science Project (see Wightman 1986; Driver 1989).

After a number of initial activities relating to change of state, a class of 13-year-olds, working in groups, were asked by their teacher to explore and explain the properties of ice, water and steam. In particular, how precisely does ice turn into water and then water turn back again into ice?

One group starts by talking about molecules, then turns its attention to the question of bonding. They explore the idea of the bonds being somehow 'broken'. But if the bonds are broken, how are they subsequently remade?

The teacher intervenes and asks how they imagine 'bonding'.

The interactions amongst the group quicken as the pupils dig into the depths of their own understanding of scientific principles, each contributing their bit.

And then they begin to fly! Magnetism, electricity, the effects of heat on the 'vibrations' of the bond are all raised . . . and built on.

The pace of the discussion falters. And then one of them, taking a different tack, arrives at a fundamental insight. Perhaps the force is actually 'there' all the time.

The outcome of this discussion is a considerable achievement. The pupils (13-year-olds) have brought together their knowledge that particles are in constant motion and that this motion increases with temperature with the idea of the force between the particles being present all the time to explain the apparent 'making and breaking' of the bonds.

A second example is of pupils as poets. It is taken from the film *Dead Poets' Society.*

The new English teacher in a boys' school has challenged a lot of his pupil's assumptions as he tries to help them value poetry for what it can say about their own lives.

On this occasion he has set them, for homework, the task of actually writing some poetry. Some find it easier than others.

The teacher asks the boys to read to the class what they have written. One boy, in love for the first time, is carried through what he might otherwise have seen as an embarrassing requirement by the strength of his feelings. He reads, he affirms himself, he feels good.

Later the teacher invites a boy, who generally lacks confidence in his own abilities, to take his turn.

He draws him to the front of the class, covers the boy's eyes with his hands and moves him round whilst, at the same time, suggesting words and phrases that evoke a brief response.

The movement quickens. The boy's responses become longer. They build to a powerful personal crescendo.

The teacher releases the boy and the spell is broken. The boy is visibly shaken but emotionally liberated; his classmates stunned, but respectful.

In these two examples we see how young people need space and stimulus if they are to fulfil the potential of their minds and their imaginations.

There's a lot in good teaching and good learning that can't be captured by a checklist or a calculator. Schools and teachers must be encouraged to identify and celebrate *their* moments of excellence.

The role of the critic in judging performance

Some comments from Raymond Williams (quoted in Hare 1989) can help to bring this opening chapter to a close. He is discussing the problems facing a critic who is trying to write about the modern novel. The analogy is with inspectors trying to make judgements about schools.

The critic's task is not easy. 'There's too much going on! It all looks out of control! How do I deal with it?' The critic's first instinct is to reject so much energy, for energy is the enemy of order, and order is the critic's job. How does the critic deal with it? asks Raymond Williams. By embracing it. Let's not just peddle all that tired old stuff about standards in the name of quality. Let's celebrate what we have and what we, as experienced practitioners, know is good.

2

DEVELOPING LEA FRAME-WORKS FOR MONITORING AND EVALUATION FROM RESEARCH ON SCHOOL EFFECTIVENESS

Introduction

The vigour and enthusiasm with which LEAs in England and Wales have begun setting up systems for monitoring and evaluating the quality of education on offer in their schools is striking. Even the more laggardly have found the pressures imposed by the 1988 Education Reform Act something of a catalyst. The reports they have produced, outlining how they intend to proceed, constitute a mountain of documentation. Most of these reports represent statements of intent rather than developed practices. None the less, there is evidence of considerable determination in many LEAs to have more comprehensive systems up and running than anything that has previously been known. How is policy being turned into practice?

As much of the impetus for developing frameworks for evaluation has come from the LEAs, rather than from individual schools, we shall concentrate most of our attention on the LEAs' activities. An LEA which ignores the various contributions of its schools to the shaping of its evaluation agenda, however, does so at its peril. Systems which have been too one-sided in terms of the interests they have represented have already run into difficulties.

In this chapter we shall attempt to summarize the stages various LEAs have reached in England and Wales. As there are now over 100 of them, and as these are responsible between them for almost 5000 secondary schools and roughly four times as many primaries, this is no easy task. Developments are very much in progress. Some LEAs have systems in operation. Others (the majority) have made their plans and set about putting them into practice. Quite a few, however, have barely got started. In the short term this may be no bad thing; there are quite a lot of lessons to be learned from the efforts of the front runners. In debates about 'quality' much is at stake, especially when the futures of individual schools are potentially on the line.

Sources and traditions for establishing frameworks

LEAs have rapidly discovered that there are few ready-made schemes available off-the-shelf. Where have they turned, then, for ideas? Two immediate sources spring to mind: the inspections carried out by members of HMI and OFSTED, and the efforts to support self-evaluation and review launched in many LEAs during the late 1970s and the early 1980s.

At first glance the 'full inspections' of schools undertaken by HMI have had much to commend them. There is a fairly widespread understanding around in the system about what they involve, especially since the decision that they should be made publicly available. Two obvious strengths are HMI's efforts to capture the fullest range of activities going on in a particular institution and their capacity to place these in some comparative (and usually national) context. It is not surprising that quite a few LEAs have found the idea of continuing or (more often) developing HMI-type inspections, albeit modified to take account of local circumstances and constraints, quite attractive. And these initiatives have been given further impetus by the OFSTED developments.

The investments made by LEAs to support schools in their own self-evaluation activities have also proved relevant. It is frequently the case that the most impressive educational practices seem to occur in institutions which have developed the capacity to think about themselves. The correlation between the two activities is often compelling. In brief, the rhetoric of schools taking responsibility for evaluating themselves is well established in many LEAs, even if the practice is more variable.

Both traditions, then, have something to offer to the efforts of LEAs to establish more wide-ranging and systematic approaches to school evaluation. But each, in turn, has its problems. HMI-type inspections are very labour-intensive for all concerned, both schools and LEAs; this in itself is likely to make them infrequent. They tend, whatever HMI's intentions, to be one-off; the subsequent problems of helping an institution to develop are not to the fore. And the difficulties for LEAs' officers and advisers of sustaining relationships with schools after authoritative (and possibly damaging) judgements have been delivered are considerable (Wilcox 1989).

At the same time, most LEAs have not been seduced by their own rhetoric in regard to self-motivation. They recognize that part of the justification for such approaches has been pragmatic; they simply lacked the resources to carry out ambitious programmes of evaluation by themselves and have had to leave it to their schools (see Clift *et al.* 1987 for a fuller discussion). Crucially, they have had to come to terms with the fact that failing institutions are not always aware of their own weaknesses.

Inspection and self-evaluation have represented the dominant ports of call, but interest has also been expressed in approaches which have been developed in industrial and commercial settings. The potential role of performance indicators has generated a good deal of activity (see, for example, CIPFA 1988; DES 1989b; Fitz-Gibbon 1990) whilst the value of so-called quality assurance strategies has also been debated (see Audit Commission 1989).

Recognizing the potential contribution of these various approaches, some LEAs have attempted to draw on all of them (for a schematic overview see SCIA 1990). By requiring inspection teams to 'negotiate' their agendas for enquiry with schools and by 'encouraging' schools to devote some part of their self-evaluation activities to the LEAs' agendas it may be possible to enhance the system's evaluation capacity; whether this is what actually results, however, remains to be seen (for further discussion see Wilcox 1992). What is clear is that, to date, LEAs have put a good deal of thought into the mechanics of the processes by which they will organize their monitoring and evaluation activities; they are still developing the substantive areas and concerns that they hope to address. During the early 1990s a further problem and potential opportunity has emerged. The OFSTED inspection procedures require every school to be inspected once every 4 years. In theory, after a year or two's inspections have been conducted, LEAs will be in a position to assemble an 'independent' picture from this source. Whether OFSTED reports will lend themselves to comparisons of this kind remains, however, to be seen.

Shaping the agenda for evaluation: contributions from research

Research on school effectiveness has not, of course, been the only source of insight into the substantive issues that LEAs have sought to consider. None the less, it is abundantly clear that the various studies, both individually and collectively, have made considerable contributions to shaping their agendas for evaluation. Indeed, there has probably been a moment in most LEAs' discussions when they have looked to the research to offer a 'blueprint', followed quickly by the realization that what they were looking for wasn't really there or likely to be. To obtain the kinds of evidence that are currently being sought someone would have had to have had the foresight several years ago to fund a number of major studies.

The main findings of research on school effectiveness were reported in Chapter 1, so we shall not summarize them in any detail here. However, it is worthwhile noting some of the studies that have been mentioned more frequently as they provide shorthand ways of describing how people's thinking has been developing.

Many practitioners seem to have found ILEA's study of pupils' progress in some 50 primary schools timely (for a fuller account see Mortimore *et al.* 1988). Others have returned to the study known as *Fifteen Thousand Hours* of 12 Inner London secondary schools (Rutter *et al.* 1979). Both have been prominent landmarks in the development of quantitatively-focused research in Britain. It is also probably no accident that they were both conducted in an LEA which, from the mid-1970s, had been forcibly reminded on numerous occasions of the importance of monitoring and evaluating the quality of education on offer in its schools, as well as of the need to take corrective action.

School effectiveness research has been predominantly quantitative. On the other hand, many of the strategies which LEA inspectors have employed (and been favourably disposed towards) have been of a more qualitative nature. There has, therefore, been some interest in alternative approaches. One American study in particular, entitled *The Good High School*, is noteworthy in this respect (Lightfoot 1983). It offers in-depth 'portraits' or case studies of six 'excellent' secondary schools, drawing together some of their common concerns, approaches and strategies in a closing chapter. There are interesting parallels between the themes it addresses and those put forward in a much earlier study of *Ten Good Schools* undertaken by members of HMI (DES 1977).

In shaping their frameworks for evaluation, both practitioners and researchers have been quick to identify the missing dimensions of these various studies. The quantitative studies have tended to concentrate on the more easily measurable and the cognitive; other important aspects of schools' activities have been, relatively speaking, neglected. The difficulties of generalizing across the qualitative studies have, at the same time, been evident. Some studies have attempted to fuse both traditions. Goodlad's (1984) study *A Place Called School* is a major attempt to look at the quality of pupils' lives in American classrooms during the early 1980s. It considerably extends the range of concerns typically addressed in most school effectiveness studies. Another American study, known as *The Shopping Mall High School*, also challenges the conventional focus, raising fundamental questions in relation to what American schools are all about (Powell *et al.* 1985).

There is much to be learnt, then, from the school effectiveness literature. However, turning the research into practical strategies has presented considerable problems. The sheer range of studies, the plethora of findings and the continuing preoccupation with methodological issues all present problems when time-spans are short and evaluation budgets severely limited. Put bluntly, it is simply impossible for most LEAs (and probably all) to follow the research paradigms very closely. The research needs to be seen as offering a menu of questions and strategies from which to choose. LEAs have had to learn to be highly selective in building their overall frameworks for monitoring and evaluation.

The enduring questions: what should get asked?

Over the past two decades the school effectiveness literature has become relatively well established. Consequently it offers some useful guidance as to: (1) the questions it might be worthwhile including in any monitoring and evaluation framework; (2) some examples of how such questions might be asked; as well as (3) some evidence as to what the answers might look like.

We have outlined the key questions in Table 2.1, deliberately keeping the overall number down to those we view as absolutely essential (for an alternative selection, based on a review of the American research, see Oakes 1987). Questions like these are to be found in most of the LEA policy documents we have seen to date. They are not, however, usually formulated in quite this way. This

Table 2.1   Key questions for monitoring and evaluating secondary schools derived from research on school effectiveness

Core area	Key question
Clarification of values	What are our schools fundamentally about? What concerns do they share in common and in what ways do they differ significantly?
Academic progress	What is the extent of variation between schools in terms of the academic progress their pupils are making?
Other outcomes and forms of progress	What is the extent of variation between schools in terms of other aspects of pupils' experiences and development?
Teaching processes	What is the extent of variation between schools in terms of pupils' experiences of teaching and learning?
Key resources	What is the extent of variation between schools in terms of pupils' access to key resources known to be associated with growth in learning?
Equal opportunities	To what extent are differences in the above experiences related to pupils' characteristics or the context of the particular school they attend?

is partly a matter of differences in language, style and experience. It is also partly a matter of differences in perspective – research imposes its own distinctive strategies. The questions LEAs are asking are also rarely so clearly highlighted. Often this is because LEAs have not yet had time to prioritize their concerns. Sometimes it is because they have not considered it politic to do so – a long list has more chance of containing something for everyone than a short one!

There is one other respect in which the list differs from those put forward by most LEAs. The focus on differences in effectiveness between schools is made quite explicit. The literature is emphatic on this matter. There are differences between schools in their effectiveness; a few of them are sufficiently large to be worrying. The central strategy available to LEAs and their schools for enhancing their collective performance is to identify the extent of these differences and to understand some of the reasons for them. How the resultant knowledge is handled (who is informed, who is held accountable, and so on) is, of course, another matter. Better knowledge, by itself, about how schools in the system are performing is not sufficient to initiate school improvement. LEAs (and central government) need to find ways of encouraging schools themselves to take responsibility for understanding what the main messages for action are and for negotiating the routes that they appear to entail. Systems which fail to engage those closest to the point of action in initiating and sustaining change are likely to be doomed.

The frameworks in practice: what actually gets asked?

The litmus test for any policy document is how it is put into practice. What parts of their agendas have LEAs succeeded in turning into activities with practical outcomes? The honest answer to date, if one takes any one LEA, is not much. The size of the tasks is immense when placed alongside the resources that are currently being devoted to them. Most LEAs have only begun to develop an explicit evaluation capacity comparatively recently. Consequently the framework of evaluation activities outlined in Table 2.2 is culled from the collective experiences of the various LEAs rather than any particular one. In practice, any single LEA will probably have embarked on just two or three of them.

Possibly the biggest steps to date have been made in the area of

Table 2.2 A framework of activities for monitoring and evaluating secondary schools

Core area	Focused questions	Nature of	Frequency
		Evidence to be collected	
Clarification of values	General aims; distinctive concerns	Discussion groups/workshops; interviews with (samples of) staff across schools	Every 3–5 years; all (or most) schools
Academic progress	Exam results: – overall – English – maths – science – other 'core' subjects National Attainment Testing	Data on (large) samples of individual pupils passing through system allowing progress to be tracked, trends over time and like-with-like comparisons to be made	At least every 2 years; all schools Focus each time on specific curriculum area; most schools
Other outcomes: and forms of progress	Pupil's attendance; pupils' post-16 destinations	Data on (large) samples of individual pupils, preferably linked directly to academic progress and contextualized	At least every 2 years; all schools

	Pupils': – behaviour – satisfactions – attitudes to school – extra-curricular participation	Combinations of techniques, including small surveys, interviews and direct observation	Focus on specific area each time; some schools
Teaching processes	Pupils' experiences of: – 'active' learning – other innovative styles – relationships with teachers	Interviews and direct observation	One focus each year; some schools each time
Key resources	Class sizes; teachers' experience	Data from routine administrative sources	At least every 2 years; all schools
	Use of time; teachers' expectations	Interviews and direct observation	One focus each year; some schools
Equal opportunities	Gender; ethnicity; social background; entry level attainment; social context of school	Analyses of all above by gender; specific enquiries into other four, sometimes involving collection of additional data	Gender: each year; all schools Others: one focus each year; some schools

monitoring academic progress, particularly in relation to the interpretation of schools' examination results. One HMI report observed
that only a minority of LEAs were making systematic efforts to interpret the information they had assembled (DES 1989c). Compared
with some of the other areas outlined in Table 2.2 the substantive
and statistical issues in this area are relatively well understood and
have been for some time. The need to undertake comparisons over
a number of years and on a like-with-like basis is widely recognized.
A few LEAs, recognizing how much is at stake, have begun to put
in place procedures for collecting data on (samples of) individual
pupils, tracking their progress through their schools (see Chapter 5).
Furthermore, the most up-to-date and sophisticated statistical procedures can also be used fairly rapidly on the resultant data (see, for
example, Chapter 6 and Fitz-Gibbon 1992). Even in this area,
however, it is relatively easy to get bogged down in detail and tech-
nicalities. This is one of the reasons why we have suggested that,
initially at least, LEAs might care to opt for a 2-yearly pattern of
data collection (see final column of Table 2.2). Most, it has to be
said, have felt compelled to go for an annual pattern. The fact that
the development of this part of the LEA agenda has already taken
the better part of a decade to materialize needs to be borne in mind
when considering progress in the other areas.

Over the past 2 or 3 years there has been increasing interest in
gathering data on pupils' attendance. Interestingly the research tradition in this area also goes back for more than a decade (see, for
example, Rutter *et al.* 1979; Gray *et al.* 1983; and, in particular,
Reynolds 1976 for a detailed study which combines evidence of the
differences between schools with observational data on why some
of them may have occurred). All the small number of LEA analyses
we have seen to date, however, have been fairly crude, confining
themselves to overall LEA-wide averages, perhaps broken down
separately by year-groups and gender. Occasionally there have been
some comments on the position in certain socially deprived areas of
the authority, but, in general, nothing systematic. It is clear, from
the limited evidence available, that data on attendance should be
contextualized by taking into account differences in schools' intakes
in much the same way as for academic progress and performance.
Evidence on the extent to which differences in attendance patterns
(and especially truancy) relate to other aspects of schools' effectiveness is conflicting. The current interest in LEAs in monitoring

attendance patterns may well lead on this occasion to better answers to the researchers' questions.

Collecting data on pupils' attitudes towards their education is another area in which LEAs have been actively engaged. The catalysts have been the local evaluations of Technical and Vocational Education Initiative (TVEI) projects in which pupil questionnaires have been employed. A few of the evaluation reports have broken down the resulting evidence on a school-by-school basis. It would be a relatively small step for LEAs to incorporate these kinds of data systematically into their monitoring exercises.

The challenge of moving beyond the more easily measurable

There is an understandable worry that if LEAs concentrate their initial data-gathering activities on those areas where the procedures are relatively well tried and tested they will give out inappropriate and unbalanced messages about what is valued. Much is at stake (Ranson *et al.* 1986). Exam results matter – but so do other things. LEAs' early efforts to develop strategies in the other general areas of Table 2.2 are therefore of especial interest.

In order to redress the potential imbalance some LEAs have deliberately focused their initial approaches in the area called 'teaching processes'. For example, most advisory and inspection services have had particular responsibilities for fostering curriculum developments over the past decade. Concepts such as 'active learning' and 'pupil engagement in the learning process' have represented frequent focuses of interest for them. Consequently an element of continuity with previous activities and concerns has been perceived here. The opportunity to combine monitoring with a little curriculum development has proved too good to pass up.

Much of this work is still at a stage where there have been few written reports to digest. Most have also been undertaken on some quasi-confidential basis, often within the context of 'inspections', although we doubt whether they contain any very embarrassing evidence. We have only seen a handful. They have been primarily descriptive, tentative rather than assertive in tone, concerned to explicate key concepts and to ground them in the kinds of school and classroom realities which participants can recognize and discuss.

They derive as much from the traditions of the 'good practice' guide, which many LEAs have tried to develop over the years, as to any other source. The challenge over the next few years is to give them the kind of critical bite that researchers in this field have begun to achieve in describing what goes on in classrooms.

Activities of this kind will strike those who think of monitoring and evaluation in predominantly statistical terms as a bit 'soft'. Certainly those who are undertaking them seem to recognize that they have some way to go before they can be made to fulfil the same sorts of purposes as statistical data. In this respect, however, practitioners are merely playing out the kinds of debates that school effectiveness researchers have experienced in reconciling the quantitative and qualitative. Few statistics in educational evaluation ever turn out to be quite as 'hard' as their proponents originally imagined.

Traps and pitfalls for unwary LEAs

Whilst it is probably too early to say much about how the products of monitoring and evaluation exercises are being used, it is by no means difficult to describe the kinds of problems LEAs have been encountering. Some of these may well be of interest to others whose plans are less well-developed.

The first problem, not surprisingly, has been getting agreement on what the overall framework should look like. After initial discussions have taken place with their schools, LEAs' agendas have almost invariably tended to mushroom. This is perfectly proper – schools have more right than most to influence the criteria being used to judge them. What seems more difficult to manage is the way in which increasingly lengthy lists are reduced to agendas for action. Too often what seems to get done is what can be done most easily (perhaps because it is already on the shelf) rather than most advantageously. We have argued elsewhere that the crucial questions about what constitutes 'effective' schooling demand that LEAs become actively involved in creating new knowledge as well as merely confirming what is already known (see Chapter 1).

A second problem has emerged from LEAs' relative inexperience of systematic data-collection activities of a non-routine nature. They have, for example, locked themselves into exercises which have been heavily dependent on all parts of the system playing their part at roughly the same time. In practice, schools have their own time-tables and priorities; these do not always match with their LEA's. There is undoubtedly a learning curve in relation to what constitutes appropriate demands and timescales for all concerned. In the same vein, many LEAs have committed themselves to unrealistically brief timetables for writing up and interpreting the evidence they have planned to assemble.

The problem of accountabilities

The most intractable problem to date remains that of sorting out how monitoring and evaluation systems are to be used. Who is accountable to whom? For what? And with what results? In a situation of uncertainties myths are easily created.

An obvious myth is that of the 'all-knowing' LEA. By developing wide-ranging frameworks covering virtually every conceivable aspect of schooling, LEAs may give the impression that they want to gather information about everything and, by implication, have a right to do so. Few LEAs, in our experience, think like this; many headteachers, however, seem to suspect them of doing so.

Alternatively, by virtue of deliberate attempts to ensure that there is something in their frameworks for everyone, LEAs may give the impression that they will lift the burden of evaluation activities off schools almost completely. Often, collaborative activity is a more appropriate way forward than separate, uncoordinated efforts. However, in a largely devolved system of responsibilities, head-teachers will always need to have their own evaluation agendas. They may be able to gain insights from the LEA's activities; they may indeed find themselves at the sharp end of them; but the one is never likely to be a complete substitute for the other. By making clear to their schools exactly what they do (and equally do not) plan to cover, as well as something about how they intend to do it, LEAs can make the tasks facing schools less daunting and burdensome. Clinging to agendas that are either too vague or, alternatively, too comprehensive to be credible merely discredits everyone's efforts.

Judging the evidence

There is one obvious omission in the documentation prepared by LEAs on their evaluation plans; depending on one's point of view it is either curious or striking. We have yet to read an account (even a brief one) of how LEAs propose to judge the evidence they have accumulated. Their answer may, of course, be that they simply do not know how they want to proceed. This may be too innocent a position to maintain, however. In many LEAs the 'LEA average' (and schools' individual positions in relation to it) looms large in the collective memory. Unless LEAs take deliberate steps to allay fears it will be assumed that evaluation will be conducted 'on the usual terms'.

Research on school effectiveness has something to offer in this respect as regards changing and challenging such assumptions. When systematic efforts are made to place schools' results in some kind of appropriate context the great majority of schools are found, not altogether surprisingly, to be performing around the levels that might be expected, given knowledge of their intakes. Some schools may be doing a little better; others a little worse.

In the early days of school effectiveness research a good deal of time was spent trying to explain and make sense of what were probably relatively small differences in performance. More recently researchers have tended to pose their questions in a rather different way. Which are the schools that are doing a *good deal* better or worse than might be expected? What can others learn from what they are or are not doing?

If a school were to fall a long way below expectations, both across a number of criteria and over a period of years, then there would be legitimate cause for concern about its performance. The monitoring and evaluation framework should prompt action both on the part of those in charge of the school and those responsible for its position in the wider world. In practice, the evidence suggests that only a very small number of schools in any one LEA consistently under-perform. By the same token, only a small number of schools appear consistently to over-perform; what they are doing may provide a natural laboratory for other schools in the system to learn from if some of the strategies and tactics they have employed can be unlocked (but also see Chapter 11 for some of the problems posed).

It needs to be recognized that the 'winners' and 'losers' in evaluation systems based on the procedures of school effectiveness research differ from those thrown up by most LEAs' approaches. Such procedures are certainly fairer than any of the apparent alternatives. Perhaps LEAs ought to grasp this particular nettle and declare: first, that they believe that the great majority of their schools will be found, at the end of the day, to be doing a perfectly satisfactory job across various fronts; and second, that they see one major function of any monitoring and evaluation system as helping them to prove it.

LEAs are engaged in a sustained attempt to monitor the nation's schools. They cannot afford to be passive or complacent about national efforts which may do an injustice in their particular neck of the woods. The introduction of systematic strategies is based on the belief that they will strengthen patterns of accountability and simultaneously provide a means of facilitating school improvement. The challenge is to ensure that the two are kept in balance.

PART 2

GATHERING
'HARD EVIDENCE'

3

HMI's INTERPRETATIONS OF SCHOOLS' EXAMINATION RESULTS (WITH POSTSCRIPTS FOR THE 1990s)

The [fifth year] examination results, taking into account the ability range of the pupils, [were] in the main reasonably satisfactory, except at O level.

(HMI Report on Benfield School, Newcastle upon Tyne)

Introduction

The 1980 Education Act required schools to publish their examination results; it did not, however, require them to interpret them. As one of the supporters of the legislation maintained in the parliamentary debate, 'examination results speak for themselves' (Hansard 1979). Others were less convinced. 'League tables' and inappropriate interpretations would, they believed, abound. As the Secondary Heads Association (SHA) put it: 'Hospitals are not required to publish annual reports of the proportions of their admissions who, after stated periods as inmates, die. Common sense tells us that such statistics would be a very crude measure of the skill and devotion of hospital staff' (SHA 1980). So why should schools be required to publish equally misleading 'results', ran the argument.

The problem was further compounded by the absence of any publicly agreed procedures for evaluating schools' examination results: earlier controversies had merely served to emphasize the difficulties.

Furthermore, there were many who maintained that to confine the evaluation of schools' performance largely to examination results was unduly narrow; a broader, more embracing account was required, if the full range of schools' activities were to be captured and valued.

The publication of reports by HMI on the individual schools they had visited offered a partial answer to both these concerns. From the beginning of 1983, authoritative and professional judgements on schools' performance were made public for the first time. However, as this chapter will show, debates about how to judge exam results have dragged on; in the mid-1990s it was still not clear that agreement had been secured about how best to proceed.

HMI's judgements are of central interest because they provide a set of criteria that are publicly visible; as such, they should provide a model for others. They are also important because their observations are placed in the wider framework of the work of the whole school. As former Senior Chief Inspector Sheila Browne put it:

> The basic principle has always been close observation exercised with an open mind by persons with appropriate experience and a framework of relevant principles. HMI's first duty is to record what is and to seek to understand why it is as it is. The second step is to try to answer the question whether or not it is good enough. To do so, HMI uses as a first set of measures the school's – or other institution's – own aims; and, as a second, those which derive from practice across the country and from public demand or aspiration.
>
> (Browne 1979)

HMI's involvement in the assessment of schools' examination results, then, would appear to offer some prospect of judgements which are professionally credible. At the same time, because HMIs have themselves been recruited from amongst experienced practitioners, their procedures offer some purchase on how the teaching profession might itself judge its performance.

In this chapter we explore some of the ways in which HMIs have assessed the examination performances of individual secondary schools and ask the question whether they adopt strategies that are equally 'fair' to all schools. Can any school, in other words, given its particular intake of pupils, be seen to be doing well? Or do the procedures run the risk of favouring some kinds of schools at the expense of others? The reports on which the analysis was originally conducted are now rather dated but, as the two Postscripts show, the issues that the analysis throws up have yet to be properly and fully resolved. Constructing more appropriate frameworks for school evaluation is clearly a task which should be measured in decades rather than years!

Frameworks for interpretation

As we have seen from previous chapters, the view that examination results somehow 'speak for themselves' needs to be challenged. Any set of statistics embodies more or less explicit views about what it is important to present and what requires interpretation. Such inter-pretations, in turn, depend crucially on the evaluative frameworks which underly them.

It is not our intention here to suggest in any great detail how a school's examination results might be evaluated; such discussions already exist elsewhere (see, for example, Chapters 5 and 6). Rather, our concern is to explore the broader evaluative frame-works that have been employed and their underlying assumptions.

We have obtained a good deal of experience in understanding how local authorities and schools evaluate their own performance through our work on the ESRC-funded Contexts Project. We worked in a research and/or consultancy role with some dozen local authorities and, as a direct result, began to establish the essential features of their evaluative strategies.

From our work we discerned four basic approaches to the assess-ment of a school's performance. These can be based on: (1) com-parisons with national or local averages; (2) 'pass rates'; (3) comparisons of the school's performance over time; and (4) com-parisons with schools with comparable intakes. We shall now dis-cuss each approach briefly in turn.

1 *National or local averages:* In this approach the individual school's performance is compared with national or local averages for relevant nationally-available statistics and its position in rela-tion to them serves as the focus for evaluative comment.
2 *'Pass rates':* The focus here is on the percentages of candidates who were entered for an examination and 'passed' it. A pass is

typically taken as a grade A, B or C at O level or GCSE; there was more variability as regards what counts as meriting attention at CSE but, typically, candidates obtaining grade 1's were emphasized. Comparisons are often made with the norms for candidates from the relevant examination boards.

3 *Comparisons over time:* The school's performance one year is compared with its performance on the same measures in previous years; trends are noted.

4 *Comparisons with pupils of comparable ability levels or schools with comparable intakes:* In this approach the school's performance is judged against other schools serving pupils of similar abilities or from similar socio-economic circumstances; it is, in other words, an approach that takes account of the school's context. Although the approach is relevant to all schools, several local authorities, to our knowledge, make particular use of this approach with respect to their 'social priority' schools.

It is tempting to argue that all four approaches should be considered in any overall assessment of a school's examination performance. However, such a strategy is likely to produce certain kinds of inconsistencies that, we argue below, are unhelpful. The potential conflict between a judgement based on (1) – the 'standards' model – which relates judgements to the national average compared with (4) – the 'contextual' model – which takes account of intakes, is outlined in Figure 3.1. In theory, someone who was consistently employing the former model to judge schools' performance would reach a different judgement from someone consistently employing the latter in 50 per cent of the total cases. In practice, given that many schools in both models would be performing around the average, the actual conflicts would probably be fewer in number than this theoretical limit suggests; the example indicates that they would, none the less, occur quite frequently.

The database and our methodology

The analyses which follow are based on the set of 35 long reports (i.e. those based on 'full' inspections) published in 1983. Schools inspected included those with different age ranges, comprehensive and selective schools. Although the 'short' reports often included

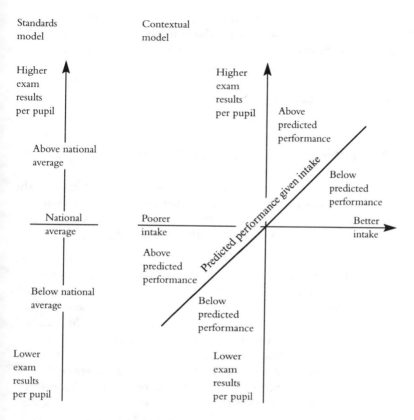

Figure 3.1 The standards and contextual models for interpreting schools' exam results.

comments on schools' examination results, they did not usually pro-vide much by way of supporting evidence. 'Full' reports, in contrast, usually contained one or more pages of appendices, providing sum-mary statistics of examination results and breakdowns of grades subject-by-subject. It is, therefore, possible to make some indepen-dent checks on the HMI's assessments in the light of the available data.

As not all the schools for which reports were available contained sixth forms with A level candidates, we confined our study to fifth-year examination results (which included O level, CSE and com-bined 16-plus examinations). We also confined ourselves, for the purposes of this chapter, to those sections of the reports which dealt with summary evaluations of the schools' examination results, rather than the detailed breakdowns of the results in terms of individual subjects. The task of determining how HMIs have proceeded is a complex one, even at the level of summary assessments; subject-by-subject comparisons must await further analyses.

Which evaluative frameworks did HMI employ?

Our reading of the reports enabled us to identify for each of the individual schools which of the four evaluative frameworks outlined earlier HMI were employing. The kinds of comments which contributed to our judgements are outlined briefly below.

1 *National averages:* In such evaluations the individual school's performance would be compared with the national average for the same measure. Thus HMIs first remarked of Beal High School, in the London Borough of Redbridge, that nearly 30 per cent of pupils obtained five or more O level (or CSE grade 1 equivalent) passes and that this was 'well above the national average'. The comment in respect of the same school that '79 per cent of pupils obtained above grade 4 at CSE or grade A–E at O level in five or more subjects' is also relevant in this respect. Sometimes we found that the way in which such statistics were presented and discussed did not always make the basis of comparison fully explicit but, in such cases, the context usually made the implicit evaluation clearer. At Kirk Hallam School in Derbyshire, for example, the comparison with the national average was left implicit – 'only' nine pupils (6.3 per cent of the year group) gained five or more passes at O level.

2 *'Pass' rates:* These assumptions appeared to be based on judgements of the 'success' or otherwise of those who were entered as candidates for public examinations. Again some kind of norm was usually implicit; this norm appeared to be the 'success' rates of all candidates who were entered for the examination(s), such as are provided on a subject-by-subject basis in the annual reports of examination boards. At Copley High School in Tameside, for example, the fact that in 1982 'less than 50 per cent of O level entries achieved grades A–C' evoked the negative comment that

'the entry policy may be too ambitious'. The results of Kirk Hallam School for the same year were described as 'disappointing' because '55 per cent of entries achieved grades below grade C and most subjects' results were below the norm of the examination boards'. Liverpool Institute for Boys came in for similar criticism. The fact that only 33 per cent of entries for O level in 1981 and 46 per cent of entries for O level in 1982 obtained A–C grades was seen as 'suggesting either that pupils were entered for inappropriate exams, or that the preparation of pupils was inadequate, or both'.

As many of these comments were essentially about the appropriateness or otherwise of schools' policies for entering pupils for public examination, we also judged comments about the extent to which pupils were 'double-entered' for both O level and CSE examinations in the same subjects to fall into this category as well. Hainault High School in Redbridge, for example, appeared to have had 'difficulty in judging appropriate target exams for pupils'. There was an excessively high double entry policy for O level and CSE. Ormesby School in Cleveland, on the other hand, was described as having a 'generally sound policy for exam entries. Double entry was avoided unless a strong case was made on educational grounds.'

3 *Comparisons of performance over time:* Examples of comments falling into this category included the judgement that Ormesby's results were 'good' and 'showed noticeable improvement over the last three years'; that at Beal the number of O level A–C or CSE grade 1 passes per pupil went up 'from 2.4 to 2.9 per pupil over the last two years'; whilst at Kirk Hallam the overall 'CSE results in 1982 were marginally better than those in 1981 and in some subjects markedly improved'.

4 *Comparisons with pupils of comparable ability levels or schools with comparable intakes:* A number of different types of comments, which indicated that the school's results had been placed in the context of the ability levels of the pupils or catchment area the school was serving were included in this category. Often this was indicated by a phrase or comment that implied that such factors should be taken into consideration. At Benfield School in Newcastle, for example, the report commented that 'the exam results, taking into account the ability range of the pupils, were in the main reasonably satisfactory, except at O level'. Kirk

Hallam's most recent results were described as 'disappointing' but this judgement was qualified by the remark that these results were obtained by the school's 'first comprehensive intake [which] probably included fewer able pupils than might be expected when compared with the national distribution'. The results of the Liverpool Institute were described as 'generally disappointing'; however, the Inspectors found the CSE results 'more satisfactory, with the exception of the numbers who were absent or ungraded'. They remark that evidence on the ability range of the intake suggests that these latter (absent and ungraded) results were 'unduly high'.

In making judgements about which framework(s) were being employed we occasionally found it necessary to infer the approach from relatively brief comments. With respect to making decisions about approaches (1) and (2), relating respectively to 'national averages' and 'pass rates', this was rarely a problem; however, in relation to approaches (3) and (4), relating respectively to 'comparisons over time' and 'comparisons taking account of intakes', we sometimes encountered difficulties. In these cases we recorded passing references as evidence that the framework was being employed to a greater or lesser extent.

In Table 3.1 we report on the evaluative frameworks being employed by HMI to judge the examination results of the 35 schools whose reports we reviewed. From this it is clear that the most commonly employed criterion was that of 'pass rates', which we found to have been used in 86 per cent of cases. By contrast attempts to evaluate exam results by contextualizing them (i.e. by reference to

Table 3.1 Incidence of criteria used to judge results in 35 schools for which full inspection reports were available

Criteria	National average	'Pass rates'	Comparison over time	Contextualized in terms of intake
Times employed	23	30	13	6
as percentage of total	66%	86%	37%	17%

the ability level of a school's intake) were found in only 17 per cent of the reports.

Table 3.2, which analyses the combinations of criteria employed for each report, reveals a particularly interesting picture. This shows that the context-based evaluative framework was never employed on its own: it was either used in conjunction with all three other criteria (three times), with a combination of 'national average' and 'pass rate' criteria (once), or in conjunction with the 'pass rate' criterion (twice). We have argued above that attempts to combine a 'standards model' (i.e. one based on 'national averages') with a contexts-based framework are likely to lead to inconsistencies. Yet our findings suggest that this is what the Inspectorate did in four out of the six instances in which they appeared to make contextualized judgements. We turn now to look in detail at those examples where there was some evidence of contextualized evaluation.

Table 3.2 Numbers and combinations of criteria employed in judging results

Number of criteria employed	Number of school reports	Totals
Four		
All	3	3
Three		
National average + Pass rate + Time	7	
National average + Pass rate + Context	1	8
Two		
National average + Pass rate	8	
National average + Time	1	
Pass rate + Time	1	
Pass rate + Context	2	12
One		
National average	3	
Pass rate	8	
Time	1	
Context	0	12
		35

A context-based model of evaluation

It is perhaps unsurprising that context-based evaluative frameworks were more likely to be brought into play in situations of pronounced disadvantage/advantage in terms of intake abilities.

Table 3.3 shows that of the six schools which we found had had their exam results evaluated in contextual terms, three were clearly identifiable as being at the extremes in terms of the ability of their intake. Of course, the Inspectorate is to some extent dependent on the data that a school makes available. Often, in the absence of accurate information about the prior ability levels and attainments, some informed 'guesswork' is required; but other information that could assist in the process of forming a contextualized judgement (e.g. that the school served a social priority area) is frequently available. This explanation, however, cannot account for the absence of contextualized judgements for, in the majority of reports which we found lacked the contextual dimension, some information about the abilities of the intake *was* available; it was simply unrelated to the judgement made about exam results. For example, of Range High School, Formby, HMI reported that: 'on the basis of standardized tests administered in the school, the intake received, while giving a fully comprehensive span, represents an ability range slightly above the national average'. But this fairly precise knowledge was not referred to or, apparently, utilized when the school's exam performance was assessed. Later in the same report, results were judged to be 'very satisfactory' on the basis of data on pass rates, without reference to the known features of the intake.

Table 3.3 Inspected schools categorized according to intake and nature of criteria used to judge examination performance

Category of school in terms of ability of intake	Numbers of schools in each category	Number of schools where evaluation of exam results was contextualized
Disadvantaged	5	2
Advantaged	3	1
Average/unspecified	27	3

Other reports in contrast illustrate that, on occasions, HMI did look very carefully at the available information on intake, and took it into account when evaluating a school's efforts. For example, the results of standardized tests carried out on the intake of Moreton School, Wolverhampton, showed that over the 5 years preceding the date of inspection the school received a first year intake with significantly lower scores than some 80 per cent of the other secondary schools in Wolverhampton. The report linked this information explicitly to exam results in the following way: 'If these [standardized test] scores are used as indicators of pupils' potential exam success at 16+ one might expect that some two to ten pupils each year would achieve 5 or more O level grades A–C or CSE grade 1. Using these criteria, pupils' achievements are satisfactory.'

The comment exemplifies the context-based model as employed by HMI: a school's exam performance was judged on the basis of whether it performed better or worse than what it would have been reasonable to predict on the basis of the measured ability of the pupils at intake. In the report on Moreton, however, as in all the other cases where a context-based model was employed, such judgements were not allowed to stand alone. Hence, on the basis of pass-rate measures, the O level results were dubbed 'generally poor'.

Chelmsford High School, by contrast (the only grammar school in an area with nine 'comprehensives') had an intake consisting of 'a very narrow band from the top of the ability range'. A contextualized assessment of performance was presented: 'Public exam results are, in general, highly satisfactory in relation to the intake.'

However, data were then reported making implicit comparison with the national average: 'the mean number of O level grades per pupil was 8.29'. These figures 'show highly commendable results in GCE examinations'. It is interesting to note how these conclusions were reported in the press. An article in the *Sunday Times*, summarizing some findings from HMI reports, described Chelmsford High School as 'Top Exam School' (Wilby 1983). The figure of 8.29 O level passes was quoted, and there was no reference to the ability of the intake. Arguably, in relation to the kind of selective intake it had received, the school was doing no more than would be reasonably expected. HMI's conclusion on the school must, however, be said to be ultimately standards-based: 'the school enjoys a record of achievement of which it may justifiably be proud'.

A thorough-going context-based model of assessment for exam

results would permit of the possibility that a school with relatively 'poor' results (i.e. in terms of comparisons with national averages and pass rates) could none the less also be said to enjoy a record 'of which it might justifiably be proud'. We found, however, a marked difference between the language employed in the description of the performance of disadvantaged schools as against that used in relation to schools clearly identified as advantaged. In Table 3.4 we compare the summary evaluations of exam performance in respect of three advantaged and three disadvantaged schools. The contrast is clear. Irrespective of the degree of deprivation, disadvantaged schools merited no more than a 'satisfactory' to sum up their performance.

Now it could be, of course, that the Inspectors had not, in fact, visited any 'disadvantaged' schools whose performance merited higher praise than that in Table 3.4; but it seems odd that this should be the case with these three disadvantaged schools and yet not apply to even one of the three advantaged ones. And we wonder what the Inspectors actually meant when they commented of Benfield's exam results that the 'exam results were, in the main, reasonably satisfactory *except at O level*' (our emphasis)? Did they mean that the school's CSE results were 'reasonably satisfactory'? Equivocal evaluations of this kind abound in the reports.

None of these pieces of evidence is fully convincing as regards the HMI's use of contextualized approaches to evaluation. However, the genuine assimilation of such a model should result in the language of excellence being as frequently applied to disadvantaged schools as to more advantaged ones. This does not appear to have been the case.

Discussion

In the introduction to this analysis we quoted former Senior Chief Inspector Sheila Browne's comments on the criteria HMI employed to answer the question whether or not a school's performance was 'good enough'. To recap in her own words, 'as a first set of measures [they use] the school's own aims and, as a second, those which derive from practice across the country'. Browne was, of course, referring to the whole spectrum of a school's aims, objectives and activities, and not just those which lend themselves to public examination.

Table 3.4 Summary evaluations of the exam performances of three advantaged and three disadvantaged schools

School	Intake descriptions	Exam performance summary
Advantaged schools		
Chelmsford High	'Intake consists of a very narrow band from the top of the ability range.' 'Certain that the majority of the pupils are from relatively prosperous homes'	'Highly commendable' 'Highly satisfactory'
King Edward VI	'Apparent that there are few pupils with serious learning difficulties and many with above average potential'	'Very good'
Beal High	'Rather more of above average academic aptitude than below.' 'Significant numbers for whom a high academic expectation is entirely appropriate'	'Very good' 'Generally sound' 'A good degree of success'
Disadvantaged schools		
Moreton	'Intake with significantly lower (VR) scores than some 80% of the other secondary schools in Wolverhampton' serving area 'suffering multiple and intense deprivation'	'Satisfactory'
Ruffwood	In LEA with 'the highest proportion of disadvantaged children in socio-economic terms'. This is 'reflected in the ability range of the school population, which is skewed downward. Average attainment on entry is about one year below the national average . . .'	'In about all cases satisfactory rather than good'
Benfield	'3/4 of pupils from inner city areas in which there is considerable deprivation.' 'Full ability range, but pupils of below average ability are over-represented. The proportion of pupils with reading age of less than nine years on entry has averaged 10% over the past seven years'	'In the main reasonably satisfactory except at O level'

Furthermore, in our experience to date, secondary schools rarely set out explicitly their objectives in the field of public examinations. If we were to impose an interpretation upon their aspirations in this area, however, we suspect it would take the form that: (1) they would wish their performance to be at least as good as that of schools with comparable intakes of pupils; and (2) they would hope to improve it over the years. Such objectives would, of course, correspond to the third and fourth criteria we identified HMI employing, namely comparisons over time and the contextualization of performance.

In practice, we have found that, to date and in the reports we have examined in detail, HMI have placed emphasis on the second set of measures to which Browne refers. Whilst our four categories of criteria do not exhaust those employed, we found that in no fewer than 34 of the 35 schools comments were made in terms of criteria that made reference to standards 'derived from across the country', either based on national averages, pass rates (see Table 3.2) or both. In contrast, only 16 of the 35 schools were evaluated in terms of what we take to be the schools' 'own aims', namely comparisons over time, on a contextualized basis, or both. Whilst 19 of the 35 schools were evaluated exclusively in terms of a model based on national averages, pass rates or both, just one school was evaluated exclusively in terms of the alternative, on comparisons over time or context (again see Table 3.2). Furthermore, whereas Browne's comments would lead one to suppose that aspects of both sets of approaches would be used, in the group of reports we have examined here we found this to be the case in fewer than half (15 out of 35). In brief, a standards-based approach seems to have predominated.

We asked in our introductory remarks whether HMI had developed an approach to evaluating schools' examination results which was equally fair to all schools. We indicated that, given the demonstrably strong relationship between schools' intakes and subsequent outcomes in terms of exam results (see, for example, Rutter *et al.* 1979; Gray and Jones 1983), a standards-based approach could not achieve this objective. In so far as our analysis has suggested that HMI have, in practice, adopted such an approach, we must conclude that schools were unlikely to be treated on an equal footing. Indeed, it follows logically that the less favoured a school was in terms of the ability levels of its intake, the more likely it was to receive a relatively less favourable evaluation. None the less, there were some potentially interesting exceptions. We found the fullest interpretation of a school's results, taking account of its intake, in a 'short' report rather than a 'full' one. Archbishop Tenison's School was part of the ILEA. As a direct consequence of the Authority's policies, it undertook analyses of its examination performance broken down in terms of the ability levels of its pupils which were presented in some detail in the HMI's report on the school! Because this was a 'short' report, however, we did not include it in our analysis.

In conclusion, we have found very considerable variation between reports on individual schools in respect of which combinations of evaluative approaches were employed, and what supporting evidence was provided for their judgements. We have not attempted to address in this chapter the question of how much weight should be attached to schools' examination results as against other forms of achievement, nor how HMI appear to us to have balanced these in their reports. However, we find it a matter for concern that, on the single dimension of examination results, three schools in our sample were evaluated in terms of all four criteria identified, but twelve were evaluated exclusively in terms of one. A more rigorous and consistent application of an agreed framework, from the professional body best placed to operate it, would surely be of service to the schools inspected, and ultimately to the school system as a whole.

Postscript one: at the end of the 1980s

In 1990 John Gray and Susan Harris took a fresh look at HMI's reports on schools' examination results. They selected ten reports at random from amongst those full inspections conducted in 1989 on state-maintained secondary schools. In the process several changes from the position which had been identified in 1983 were noted:

1 More of the four criteria were usually employed in each report than had previously been the case.
2 There was more frequent evidence of attempts to compare schools' results over time (although usually just for 2 years) and

to contextualize them in terms of pupils' backgrounds and prior attainments.

3 There was less emphasis placed on 'pass rate' statistics.

On all three grounds there were signs of appropriate development towards the more sensitive interpretation of schools' results. The fourth change, however, created some doubts in this respect.

It turned out that the change which was most frequently noted was that all schools' results were compared with the national average, regardless of the kind of school they were or the kind of pupils they served. Consistency would appear to have been achieved at the expense of appropriateness.

A sample size of ten was, of course, on the low side even though the findings were so clear-cut. John Gray therefore invited various Masters students on courses at Sheffield to replicate the findings on different (albeit small) samples of reports from the period at the end of the 1980s. They tackled the task in slightly different ways and reported some differences in the extent to which they believed 'contextualizing' strategies were driving HMI's analyses. All of them, however, replicated the finding with respect to consistency. The only yardstick against which all schools were compared was the 'national average'.

Postscript two: prospects for the mid-1990s

We have not attempted a systematic analysis of the reports emerging from HMI and OFSTED during the 1990s. When we have dipped into schools' reports, however, we have noted some spectacular lapses from the general trend towards greater consistency and contextualization.

The case of Newall Green

Newall Green High School in Manchester is one such example. It was inspected by HMI in October 1991. In the third paragraph of the report the school is described as being located on the Wythenshawe local authority estate:

> The estate, one of the largest in Europe, is in an area of socio-economic deformation with comparatively high rates of long-

term (32.5 per cent) of youth (16 per cent) unemployment. Very few pupils come from ethnic minority groups but more than a third of pupils in Year 7 and a quarter in Year 8 have been identified as needing extra help with reading comprehension.

(Newall Green 1991: para 3.)

Clearly, from the description, we are dealing with a school serving a very disadvantaged area. HMI usually choose their words with care. Use of the term socio-economic 'deformation' suggests an alienated community on the verge of break-up (although it is just possible this could have been a misprint for 'deprivation'); and whilst a number of schools will have been serving areas where the adult unemployment rates were averaging one-third of the adult population few, anywhere in the country, will have had long-term rates running at this level.

As in previous reports on which we have commented in this chapter, the stage seems set for a contextualized analysis of the school's examination results. What was written, therefore, seems both stark and inappropriate. HMI simply reported: 'There has been a slight dip in examination performance between 1990 and 1991, and results are below national and Manchester LEA averages' (Newall Green 1991: para 42). The dominant comparison, in other words, was still with the 'national average'. Yet the circumstances of the school seem no different to those other disadvantaged schools described earlier in this chapter, some of which at least benefited from a contextualized analysis of their performance.

In the event things did not turn out quite so badly for Newall Green as might have been anticipated from the adverse report on its performance. HMI had identified a strong management team as one of the strengths of the school and, 3 years later, it was singled out for praise in an OFSTED publication on school improvement (OFSTED 1994c). Newall Green seemed to have made impressive progress over a relatively short period of time.

OFSTED on value-added

The decision to set up the Office for Standards in Education (OFSTED) heralded a potentially new era for school evaluation. In particular, it was possible to interrogate publicly the criteria being used to judge schools for the first time as they were now reproduced in the Inspectors' *Handbook for the Inspection of Schools* (OFSTED 1992b, 1993b).

Probably the most important feature of the Handbook as regards value-added discussions was the recognition that, for the time being, schools themselves would need to be involved in providing the necessary data: 'Schools should be asked to provide any quantified data on the intake's ability or attainment. Standardized test results . . . may give inspectors some insight into the value added by the school as shown in its overall GCSE results' (OFSTED 1993b: 5:33).

At the same time inspectors were encouraged to consider, when making their judgements, 'the areas from which most pupils are drawn . . . and the school's perceptions of the backgrounds of the pupils' (OFSTED 1993b: 7:57). In addition, they were counselled to 'bear in mind the limitations inherent in comparisons of the results of individual schools with local and national data'. There were, in other words, distinct signs that the strictures and caveats made earlier in this chapter had been taken on board. The Handbook concluded: 'It may be possible to make cautious comments on value-added aspects of a school's results, based on the data [the school has provided]' (OFSTED 1993b: 5:36).

The tentative manner in which some of this advice is couched deserves comment and is of some significance. If schools were in a position to provide data on value-added aspects of their performance, then the inspectors were enjoined to make use of them. If such data were not available, then they were expected to use the Pre-Inspection Context and School Indicators (known as PICSI's) schools had provided, which included judgements regarding the socio-economic backgrounds of a school's intake. Unfortunately the Handbook, at least in its earliest version, did not appear to contain much explicit advice about what to expect by way of performance from schools drawing pupils from different socio-economic backgrounds. Inspectors were required, it appears, to use their own judgement and experience. The case for contextualizing judgements appears to have been recognized, but the means by which to do it appears to have lagged behind.

In practice, these general trends mask a more fundamental debate which surfaces at various points in the Handbook about how to judge schools. The sticking-point seems to have been the criteria for identifying so-called 'failing schools'.

The 'failing' school

When the *Framework for the Inspection of Schools* (OFSTED 1992a) was published for the purposes of consultation it listed four criteria for determining whether a school was 'at risk'. These were:

- the achievements of pupils;
- behaviour;
- staff and teaching;
- management.

The criteria for judging the achievements of pupils in such schools are of particular interest here. These were listed as: 'low standards and achievement among the majority of pupils or consistently among particular groups of pupils; poor examination results and levels of attainment in relation to those of children in comparable schools' (OFSTED 1992a: 7).

The inclusion of the phrase 'in relation to those of children in comparable schools' was a clear sign that the case for contextualization had been recognized. However, when the first edition of the inspection Handbook appeared there was a significant omission. The four criteria for identifying an 'at risk' school were identically worded but the phrase 'in relation to those of children in comparable schools' had been struck out (OFSTED 1992b: p. viii, para. 13). The criterion now read simply as 'poor examination results and levels of attainment'. Someone's nerve seems to have (temporarily) failed.

The next edition of the Handbook (OFSTED 1993b) talked of the criteria for judging whether a school is 'failing' rather than whether it is 'at risk'. Each of the four criteria had become longer and more detailed. Much of the original wording of the four criteria was, however, retained and the phrase 'in relation to those of children in comparable schools' remained deleted, a position that remained the same in the 1994 version (OFSTED 1994a: 5:96).

Simply focusing on the criteria for 'failing' schools does not provide quite the whole story. In a later section some advice is given to the Registered Inspector (RI), who must make the judgement that a school is, in fact, 'failing'. This advice takes the following form:

Where there is substantial under-achievement – that is where standards are either well below the national averages for schools of that type, or consistently well below pupils' demonstrable capability, or both – the RI must consider whether the school is failing. Under-achievement may be present in any type of school including those which select on entry. A judgement that the school is failing on these grounds will need to take into account the intake to the school and the school's circumstances and be supported by evidence using a range of indicators including test results and external examination results.

(OFSTED 1993b: Part 5, p. 94, para. 11)

Clearly much of this advice was based on a 'standards' dimension in which performance is compared with the national average. However, the phrase 'for schools of that type' admits the possibility of a contextualized judgement and this impression is reinforced by the comment that 'under-achievement may be present in any type of school, including those which select on entry'. Interpretation, inevitably, hangs on what is meant by 'type of school'. In practice, to judge from other references in the text, this seemed to mean 'organizational' type (grammar, secondary modern, comprehensive, etc.). Schools that 'select on entry' are a type of school. The possibility of a school that serves a disadvantaged area or community being a 'type of school' is not directly addressed. In the context of advice that was trying to make explicit what might otherwise be inexplicit the consequences would seem to be clear – ultimately 'failing' schools were to be judged against standards-based criteria.

The final phase?

In the course of this discussion we have charted some of the debates about whether schools' examination results should be contextualized. Progress towards more appropriate judgements has been slow. Regardless of whether the intellectual case for contextualizing or value-added approaches has been accepted, however, there has been one major stumbling-block – inspectors have not had national data made available to them on what to expect by way of performance from schools serving different communities. Even if they have wanted to place schools' performance in context, they will have found this difficult to bring about.

In the autumn of 1993, OFSTED asked researchers to tender for a contract to provide evidence which would permit inspectors to make more informed comments on schools' examination results. A team from the London Institute of Education was awarded the contract. There was some debate within the research community as to whether the national data already available (and various restrictions on the new data which could be collected) would permit the construction of a framework that was up to the task. At the time of writing it is too early to say, but obviously any attempt to secure a firmer basis for contextualized judgements is to be welcomed. More than a decade after disadvantaged schools were first exposed to the public glare of inappropriately based judgements there is some real prospect that they can expect a fairer deal.

4

PERFORMANCE INDICATORS: FLOURISH OR PERISH?

Introduction

Interest in performance indicators, and optimism about their potential, probably reached a peak amongst English LEAs in the late 1980s. In the wake of the Education Reform Act the case for their introduction was made in several influential reports including one by a prestigious accountancy firm which had been asked to explore the local management of schools (Coopers & Lybrand 1988) and another by the Audit Commission, the local authority 'watch-dog' (Audit Commission 1989). Performance indicators would become, it was argued, one of the key mechanisms through which the monitoring and accountability of schools would be assured. The time seemed particularly propitious for their development and imaginative use within the school system.

The case for the introduction of performance indicators flows from the model of the school that is implicit in government educational policy. This seeks to describe schools in terms that refer directly to their 'performance' or 'effectiveness'. Such terms are applied to the achievements of the school, and especially those associated with the pupils. Pupil achievements are expressed most frequently as the knowledge, skills, characteristics and specific accomplishments acquired by individuals (often assessed in the form of examination results, test scores or behavioural measures); these are then aggregated into appropriate indicators of a statistical nature. The use of such indicators reinforces the popular tendency to see standards, targets and performance as unproblematic entities, 'out-there', measurable and (in the popular sense of the word) 'objective'. The fact that they are essentially abstractions, which have been socially constructed and which arise from attempts to make sense of some parts of the complex realities of 'schooling', is often forgotten.

From the experience of the early 1990s it is clear that progress on the development of performance indicators has been slow and, at least in terms of the aspirations of enthusiasts, somewhat disappointing. They do not appear, as yet, to have become influential tools for management or evaluation purposes. The view of one LEA chief adviser we interviewed in early 1992 is not untypical. 'We set up a working group in 1988–9. There has been a lot of ink spilt on performance indicators since then and I don't know that we're much further forward.'

Why is it then that performance indicators have still to live up to their promise? What problems have to be surmounted before relevant and useful ones can be developed? These and related questions are considered below in the context of some recent initiatives.

Brainstorming the agenda

Towards the end of 1989 Mrs Rumbold, an Education Minister at that time, presented a long-awaited list of performance indicators for schools at a conference of the Industrial Society. This list, referred to as an *aide-mémoire* (DES, 1989b), was one of the major outcomes of a year-long study involving some eight LEAs and some 40 of their schools.

In introducing the list the Minister argued that it was intended to take debates about schools' effectiveness beyond merely looking at examination results. She is quoted as saying that: 'It is our job to make sure that parents recognize that there are other things going on in schools to prepare pupils for the world of work and life after school'; and later on that: 'The more we put across the fact that performance indicators go a lot further than exam results – important though they are – the better we shall be.' Each school was to be urged to decide on 'a relatively small range of indicators for judging whether it is achieving its goals' (Rumbold 1989).

In practice any other advice about how to use the *aide-mémoire* would have been implausible. The various working groups had produced a dauntingly long list of items (50 in all) many of which had been subdivided into several parts. The items listed were also very heterogeneous. Some were expressed in specific and explicitly quantifiable forms such as: 'the overall pupil–teacher ratio' (item 4) and 'the percentages of (Year 11) pupils who continued into the sixth form or entered sixth form/tertiary college' (item 28). Others consisted of descriptive statements or questions such as: 'organization of the curriculum' (item 6) or 'School's objectives for community links? Are these being achieved? How does the school assess the local community's perception of its work? How does the school receive visitors?' (item 20).

Closer analysis of the items on the list reveals that 20 were descriptive whilst only 12 could be regarded as explicitly quantifiable. Another 11 could be regarded as implicitly quantifiable in cases where the quantifying categories were given in general rather than specific terms. Examples would include 'socio-economic factors affecting the pupil population such as incomes, housing and employment' (item 14). Of the remaining seven items, five were a mixture of descriptive and explicit/implicit quantitative statements and two were just questions requiring a simple yes/no answer; for example, 'Does the school have a delegated budget under an approved LMS scheme?' (item 13). Seven of the items had trend-style questions appended to them implying access to data or experiences across several years; an example would be the question: 'Are such incidents of internal vandalism increasing or decreasing?' (item 35).

Several other features of the list are worthy of comment. First, its length was justified on the grounds that it provided a comprehensive set of indicators from which schools would be able to select a smaller subset for their own use. Potential users, however, would probably not find the list very helpful as, in most cases, they would be left with the difficult task of translating general descriptive statements into more specific and usable forms.

Second, the compilers of the *aide-mémoire* would probably justify the high proportion of descriptive statements on the grounds that they were 'keen to make it a priority to develop qualitative indicators and . . . did not consider that [schools'] success could be judged adequately by a few statistics' (Rumbold 1989). Again, however, the difficult task of turning so-called qualitative indicators into usable categories was left to the individual user.

Third, perhaps the most striking feature of the *aide-mémoire* is its atheoretical nature. In launching it the Minister drew attention to the recently published report by HMI on effective school management (DES 1988a). Whilst commending the HMI's report, however, it is not obvious how its criteria were related to the structure of the *aide-mémoire*, which was simply organized under a number of conventional and minimalist headings: basic data, context, pupil achievement, pupil attitudes and management.

Overall, then, the *aide-mémoire* seems to be a rather diffuse collection of statements representing, in the main, what heads, inspectors, LEA officers, teachers and DES officials collectively understood to be some of the features of 'effective schools'. It reflected many of the compromises that emerge when committees of educators sit down together to share views about what it is important to manage and assess.

It is easy to single out the DES project for comment because its products were amongst the most visible of the various attempts that were made at the turn of the decade to 'brainstorm' possible lists of performance indicators. It is important to stress, however, that similar comments and criticisms could have been applied just as easily to the lists and reports various other bodies produced around this time. These would include the so-called 'Blue Book' produced by a working party of LEA officials (CIPFA 1988) and any number of locally generated reports by heads and LEA officers.

Listing the multiple criteria by which schools might be judged seems to be endemic to the process of constructing performance indicators. It is a process which bears a notable resemblance to efforts in an earlier decade to construct lists of questions which schools might wish to ask themselves in the course of undertaking self-evaluative reviews (Clift *et al.* 1987).

Assembling some evidence

We have already hinted at some of the difficulties to be overcome in beginning to establish a framework for monitoring performance. None the less, over a relatively short period of time there are indications that many LEAs had begun to make progress in putting something in place. As part of our Programmes to Assess the Quality of Schooling (PAQS) project, we asked chief inspectors and advisers in England and Wales to tell us about the position in their own LEA in the year 1990–1. Did they have quantitative measures available to them to assist in forming judgements about schools? And, if they did, which ones?

The PAQS questionnaire presented respondents with a list of ten items and additional space to write in further items if they wished. Chief advisers and inspectors of 99 of the 115 English and Welsh LEAs provided answers. Their responses in relation to secondary schools in their LEAs are listed in Table 4.1.

Not surprisingly, measures of public examinations results dominated the picture. Over three out of four reported that they had this measure available. It is of interest, given the then impending requirement for the publication of results, that one in four did not appear to be in this position during 1990–1. Roughly half the LEAs also had information available to them about pupils' post-16 destinations and attendance.

Amongst items relating to the contextual circumstances of individual schools, and the communities they served, two items of information emerged as particularly prominent – the incidence of free school meals and of special needs. In both cases just under half the LEAs had this information. It is likely that, in both cases, this information would have been needed for other administrative purposes within the authority and that ready availability was a by-product of these other demands. Evidence on other aspects of pupils' performance, at the point of entry to secondary school or relating to their background circumstances, was a good deal more limited. For each such item listed in Table 4.1 only around one in ten LEAs claimed to have something available during 1990–1. Systematically quantified information on other aspects of schools' characteristics also appeared to be in rather short supply.

It is perhaps important to stress that the position described in Table 4.1 reflects the respondents' views of what was available for

Table 4.1 Quantitative measures reported by LEAs as being available to them in 1990–1 to inform the judgement of secondary schools' performance

	% of all LEAs
Possible outcome measures	
Public examination results	78
Post-16 destinations	55
Attendance	52
Exclusions	4
Possible contextual measures	
Incidence of free school meals	42
Incidence of special needs	44
Reading tests	12
English tests	9
Arithmetic/mathematics	8
Verbal reasoning tests	8
Non-verbal reasoning tests	5
Ethnic backgrounds of pupils	7
Other measures of pupil attainment	5
Other pupil characteristics	8
Possible school characteristics	
Staff	10
School	6
Finance/resources	3
Parents/community	3

Based on 99 responses out of 115 English and Welsh LEAs to the PAQS questionnaire.

use; other information may have been to hand in other parts of their authorities. None the less, the overall picture presented by the table is a patchy one. By the end of the 1980s many LEAs (and perhaps a majority) did not appear to have had a systematically organized database containing pertinent information of a quantitative kind available to them for ready use. Sometimes this was because they simply lacked the information; in other instances it was because the organizational conditions that would have facilitated their construction had yet to materialize. It is a situation which many LEAs are still taking steps to redress.

The evidence in Table 4.1 reveals a number of problems for those who are seeking to establish a national framework for judging schools' performances. As the position stood in 1990–1 it would not have been possible to construct (through the medium of LEAs' databases) a comprehensive national picture of schools' achievements for any outcome measure other than examination results – and even in this case it would have been an incomplete one. Some sense of the patterns relating to post-16 destinations and attendance would also have been possible but, in both cases, the picture would have been still more incomplete. In only around half the LEAs in the country could any analysis contextualizing schools' results have been attempted. In a rather small number of LEAs (and in some individual schools) a fuller picture would have been possible. By whatever standards one employs, however, the position revealed in Table 4.1 offers no more than the rudimentary outlines of a possible national framework.

Turning exam results into a convincing account

The pressure on schools and LEAs to give a convincing account of their performance, as evinced by their pupils' examination results, has been on since the early 1980s. Over the intervening period, however, the stakes have increased. What started as a requirement for schools to include details of their own results in the backs of their prospectuses developed into a demand that LEAs publish the results of all schools in their localities in their local newspapers and, finally, the decision by the DFE to publish national lists in late 1992.

There have been some changes over this period in the nature of the information about pupils' performances which schools were expected to publish. Certain kinds of comparative information about national and local averages, as well as performance in the previous year, now have to be included and some figures have to be calculated as a percentage of the pupils on the school roll rather than the number of candidates. But, essentially, these have been matters of refinement rather than fundamental reconstruction – when one is dealing with examination results the raw figures are somehow still assumed to 'speak for themselves'.

In tandem with the debates about what exactly is to be published a fierce debate has been raging about what, if anything, it all appears to mean. In brief, can one legitimately infer anything from the examination results of the pupils about the performance of their schools? Do the figures, in practice, tell one any more about the school than what kinds of pupils it was in a position to attract in the first place? Knowing how pupils actually performed is an important part of the information one would require to make this judgement but few educators have thought it sufficient.

Although practitioners have drawn heavily on the findings of research on school effectiveness, research perspectives have been noticeably absent from most of the debates about performance indicators. There has been one exception to this general pattern. Attempts to contextualize schools' examination results have drawn heavily on statistical techniques adopted by researchers and have continued to develop in relation to them. In the early 1980s various attempts were made to contextualize schools' results using information about the social background characteristics of their intakes (see Gray 1981a for an early account). Interestingly, more recent developments in the underlying statistical theories have been taken up as understanding of the potential of so-called 'value-added' approaches has increased (Aitkin and Longford 1986; Gray *et al.* 1986).

Most surprisingly of all, perhaps, certain LEAs have sought out researchers capable of undertaking analyses using the most sophisticated statistical techniques. In particular, there has been heightened interest in the potential of multi-level approaches and their application (see, for example, Chapter 6; and Nuttall *et al.*1989). Indeed, we ourselves have collaborated with several LEAs where such ideas have already been disseminated to head-teachers and begun to inform their practice (see Chapter 5 and also Hedger 1992). In brief, sophisticated analytical and statistical approaches have begun to become part of the evaluation armoury in a number of LEAs.

Extending the account

Whilst there is widespread agreement that schools' examination results could be important indicators of performance, few LEAs seem to be happy with the idea that they are sufficient. Consequently, in one way or another, most have begun to develop their own 'criteria for judgement'.

'Criteria for judgement' have emerged in many LEAs as part of their programmes for monitoring and evaluating schools introduced in the wake of the 1988 Education Reform Act. Whilst they share some features in common with performance indicators, however, their development has often occurred alongside, and often separately, from them. A distinction needs to be maintained between the two, although this is essentially a matter of degree. Performance indicators tend to be quantitative measures of organizational aspects, often characterized in input and output terms. In contrast, criteria are usually more specific, qualitative statements describing the processes which are assumed to mediate inputs and outputs.

The *Criteria for School Evaluation* developed by Suffolk LEA are a good example of the kind of approach LEAs have adopted (Suffolk LEA 1990). These criteria are organized on an essentially hierarchical basis. A total of 183 'success criteria' are grouped under 63 criterial statements. These, in turn, are organized under 18 broad statements about effectiveness in five key areas of the school's operation: (1) school aims; (2) the ethos of the school; (3) curriculum organization and assessment; (4) curriculum implementation; and (5) management and administration.

An example may help to clarify the nature of the exercise:

Resources and tasks are differentiated to take account of pupils' abilities and needs

is one of three success criteria which fall under the broader criterion:

The pace and scope of work provides a real and continuous challenge to pupils

which, in turn, is one of six items related to the effectiveness statement:

Learning activities are purposeful.

The latter, together with a further five statements, constitute the key area of 'curriculum implementation'.

There are at least three important questions that can be asked of such criterial lists. Why and how have they been produced? How are they used in practice? And in what ways do they relate to performance indicators?

The pressure to produce criterial lists has largely emerged, we suspect, from the perceived need to make inspection and external evaluation more credible and acceptable both to schools and other users. Credibility, in turn, has been linked with the requirements of 'objectivity'. In the words of the influential Audit Commission report, 'The observations on which reports to an institution are based should be made against pre-stated criteria of judgement' (Audit Commission 1989: 18). Criteria have typically been made available to schools and, in some cases, developed in conjunction with them through the agency of working parties composed of teachers and LEA staff. In many LEAs this way of working has tended to be seen as overt expression of the LEA's commitment to partnership with its schools.

The actual content of criterial lists has been influenced by at least three sources. The practices of HMI have been particularly prominent. Traditionally HMI did not publish their criteria for inspecting schools. However, as a result of increased interaction between HMI and LEA inspectorates, much of their practice became fairly common knowledge. Finally, all was revealed to all intents and purposes when OFSTED's inspection manuals were published (OFSTED 1992b). A second source has been generally agreed notions of so-called 'good practice'. Finally, claims are sometimes made that the choice of criteria has been influenced by research into school effectiveness. Research findings emphasizing the leadership role of the headteacher, for example, are sometimes reflected in such criteria as: 'The headteacher and senior staff maintain a clear, positive and consistent sense of direction; staff and pupils are motivated by the headteacher's personal interest, encouragement and concern; the headteacher gets directly involved in improvements, particularly in the early stages' (Salford LEA 1991).

Rather little is known about how such criteria are used in the various kinds of reviews and evaluations commonly carried out in LEAs. Although a lot of effort has gone into the compilation of criteria, little seems to have been devoted to specifying exactly how these criteria should be used in observing school and classroom processes and constructing the notes and reports which inspectors subsequently make. In addition, few if any inspectorates, including HMI, have been able to offer evidence that their criteria are, in fact, applied consistently from occasion to occasion and from inspector to inspector (for further discussion see Wilcox 1992: 191–6).

One method of using criteria is to combine them with rating scales. This strategy offers a means through which criteria can be developed into performance indicators. HMI have contributed more than most groups to developments in this respect, applying five-point scales to a variety of key areas of school and classroom life. The ratings are designed to accompany the descriptive and evaluative notes made by the inspectors and the scale is defined in terms of the retrievability value of the associated text. A rating of 1, therefore, corresponds to: 'generally good, or with some outstanding features; very useful for retrievers of good practice'. At the other end of the scale a rating of 5 indicates: 'many shortcomings, generally poor; very useful for retrievers of examples of bad conditions, unsound practice, etc.' (HMI 1988).

If separate ratings are made of similar aspects in a variety of circumstances these can then be aggregated into percentages falling into particular categories. HMI's ratings of schools' performance were summarized in the following terms, for example, in their Annual Report on the state of the nation's schooling:

> In the 18,000 lessons seen in over 2,400 secondary schools work was satisfactory or better in 73%, including 31% where it was good.
>
> (HMI 1992: 16)

Similar kinds of evidence were in the process of being prepared for the annual reports of the Chief Inspector of ILEA, prior to its demise. Since that time a small number of other LEA inspectorates have also adopted variants of HMI's approach. In Wandsworth, for example, a system was trialled in which features of particular lessons were observed and rated on a scale defined by three points: E (exemplary); A (acceptable); and D (requires further development). Lessons were rated in five major areas: (1) planning; (2) clarity of purpose; (3) teaching approaches; (4) pupils' conduct and involvement; and (5) evidence of learning. From these various pieces of information a summary score was then derived using a four-point scale on which a 1, for example, denoted an 'exemplary' rating on all five aspects of performance.

The combination of rating scales and criteria would appear to offer a promising method of generating performance indicators that goes beyond the easily measurable to embrace some aspects of the quality of educational experiences and provision. However, before indicators derived in this manner can be expected to become publicly credible, it is essential that inspectorates demonstrate that they can achieve acceptable levels of consistency. To date few seem to have accepted this particular challenge.

The agenda for the 1990s

Will the 1990s see the coming of age of performance indicators or will they continue to languish as a specialist interest, having only a rather marginal effect on school management and planning? The position, in our view, is finely poised. Performance indicators could easily join the scrap-heap of 'good ideas'. If the momentum of earlier developments is to be sustained various steps will need to be taken fairly soon.

From the perspective of those whose job it is to report on (or provide information about) the quality of the nation's schooling, there is a compelling logic to the development of performance indicators. How can a school be run effectively and efficiently, they ask, if the areas in which it is trying to perform are not known and evaluated systematically? And surely, if those involved in running a school have sorted out what it is they are trying to achieve and how to evaluate it, don't they then stand a better chance of succeeding? From this perspective, the introduction of some kind of system of performance assessment seems to be an obvious step in managing the development of the institution.

On the other hand, from the perspective of the practitioner, it seems to have been perfectly possible to run an institution without any elaborate system of performance indicators at all. Furthermore, although there is evidence in the literature that 'good schools' often know fairly precisely what their objectives are and whether they are achieving them (see, for example, Lightfoot 1983), there is a noticeable dearth of evidence that they have actually been assisted in reaching their position by virtue of putting (systems of) performance indicators into place. It is not difficult to see how the innovation can have come to be perceived, in many situations, as serving someone's interests – but not necessarily the school's!

The impetus for the introduction of performance indicators frequently stems from a particular view of how schools ought to be managed. Coleman and Larocque, in their study of Canadian school districts, reported that 'careful monitoring of school performance [was] central to accountability, and a distinguishing characteristic of unusually effective school districts' (1990: 95). But they also argued that for performance monitoring to become an accepted district practice, 'leaders must create and sustain some commitment to monitoring from educators, and particularly from school principals'. In many contexts creating this commitment has proved difficult. Based on a study of aspects of the American experience, for example, a group of HMI commented that: 'the approach, in principle, is to monitor the schools, present them with the performance data and then leave it to the principals, together with parents and general administrative guidance from the district, to take the school forward' (HMI 1991: 22). They go on to note, however, that teachers' reactions '. . .were mixed. Most accepted and worked in the system without complaint . . . [but] saw themselves as having something to lose and expressed a good deal of cynicism about the value of reporting and the time and effort that were involved.'

Few LEAs in the UK would appear to have achieved the levels of commitment that are necessary. Whilst there are signs that British schools may be moving in similar directions to some of the North American ones, the differences between the two systems are more striking. Performance indicators are usually something done to schools, rather than for or with them.

There is a case to be made for schools themselves taking the initiative in developing measures. In his engagingly titled book *Thriving on Chaos*, Peters suggests that 'measuring what's important' should be a 'guiding premise' for any organization's development (Peters 1987). There is some difference between his recommendations and those which have typically been implemented in educational organizations. In his view 'every manager should track no more than three to five variables which capture the essence of the business' (Peters 1987: 482). To date, however, most educational institutions have found themselves in this position by default rather than design.

Building on such approaches in the context of education Beare and colleagues (1989) argue that performance indicators are essential if individual institutions are to answer questions about their relative 'excellence' and, simultaneously, to establish directions for their future development. But they also acknowledge that 'in education the primary criteria are more difficult to calculate than they are in a business firm and that, consequently, secondary criteria must be established relating to: process, patterns, output, organizational structures, and input'. Very little advice has been forthcoming, however, about how a school might set about establishing such measures, other than merely accepting those which others have made available. Hargreaves and Hopkins' (1991) account of how schools might set about establishing what they call 'success criteria', as part of their process of development planning, is a notable exception. And, in practice, Peters' advice about drastically limiting the numbers of measures seems to get ignored. In short, it is an exceptionally well-organized school that can move quickly towards the kind of coherence of purpose and practice that systems of performance indicators imply. In such situations performance indicators can easily come to be seen as unwelcome harbingers of changing regimes of accountability rather than as potential contributors to schools' development.

Stumbling blocks and challenges

It is already evident from our discussion that several of the steps that need to be taken are posing considerable problems. Whatever their promise, the introduction of performance indicators into British schools must rank amongst the most difficult in recent years. Several challenges need to be faced.

The first is the need to be clear what kinds of measures might actually count as performance indicators (and, by extension, which might not) and to concentrate effort on some of the most important ones. Performance indicators should be first and foremost about schools' performance (see Chapter 1, Table 1.2 and Gray and Jesson 1991). Failure to be explicit in this respect can rapidly lead to conceptually sloppy collections of broad evaluative and descriptive statements, which do little to guide the policy and planning processes of an institution.

Scheerens (1990) has argued that performance indicators should allow value judgements to be made about key aspects of the functioning of educational systems in some quantifiable form; they should speak, in brief, to issues of quality. Many of the measures which have been put forward to date as possible performance indicators fail on one of these two counts: they are either not obviously about the schools' contribution to pupils' development or they do not lend themselves readily to assessment. Measures which are of a sufficiently high quality to do justice to schools' efforts usually require time to develop; what is available off-the-shelf is rarely immediately suitable. As Murnane (1987) has shown, in a comparison of indicators available to economists and educators, many of these problems are generic to the development of all indicator systems and not just those in education.

Second, there is an urgent need to develop a wider range of measures. There is widespread agreement that exam and test results by themselves are not sufficient to do justice to schools' efforts. With the introduction of testing at all four Key Stages of the National Curriculum, however, schools have been deluged by information pertaining to their pupils' cognitive performances. Some effort will need to be devoted to constructing further measures to place alongside these kinds of outcomes, if broader views about the nature and purposes of education are to be given credence. As we suggested in Chapter 1 there could be as few as three priorities: (1) more sophisticated approaches to the analysis of pupils' academic progress should be complemented by something relating (2) to pupils' satisfaction with their educational experiences and (3) to aspects of pupil–teacher relationships.

The government itself is committed to introducing more information about pupils' attendance at school and their subsequent post-16 destinations. Important as these measures are, however, they still represent a rather limited view of what schools are about. Small numbers of LEAs and their schools are currently engaged in trying to extend the range of possibilities. Such initiatives are at the stage where they still need to be nurtured (for a fuller account see Chapter 2). A fraction of the energy which has been devoted to the analysis of examination results could yield substantial results, especially where attempts are made to combine different kinds of information about pupils' attitudes and responses (Fitz-Gibbon 1992).

The third area requiring development is perhaps the most controversial. Given the complexity and variety of potential educational outcomes, it is unlikely that the quality of schools can ever be adequately described in pupil performance terms alone. Consequently there has been considerable interest amongst inspectors in so-called process indicators, which relate to the ways in which human and other resources in schools are organized and deployed to realize educational aims. Such indicators are seen as important for two main reasons. They may provide some kind of basis for interpreting or explaining the levels of pupil performance revealed by existing indicators. Differences in attainments in different subject areas may, for example, be accounted for by differences in the quality of the teaching/learning resources available. They may also act as a kind of guarantor that wider educational aims, not easily assessed by testing pupils, are likely to be realized. Regular opportunities for pupils to discuss contemporary issues, for example, may lend some support to the view that certain kinds of intellectual independence are being fostered.

By concentrating on pupil outcomes some would argue that the need to explore process indicators is obviated. Schools should be left to their own devices as regards the means by which they achieve their outcomes. Certainly there is a danger that by entering into this field one is inviting the construction of increasingly lengthy lists of factors, which collectively amount to a form of 'good school' blueprint. On the other hand, to ignore such measures completely gives hostage to potentially dull, uninspiring, instrumentally oriented strategies.

A number of researchers and practitioners have argued that research on school effectiveness provides (or could provide) some important pointers; very few, however, have to date attempted anything very systematic by way of identifying what these might be. A notable exception is a review conducted by Oakes (1989), in which three areas are targeted as good candidates for indicator development. She too generates lengthy lists but also argues that a 'barebones' version can be sustained. Its components are as follows:

1 *Access to knowledge:* the extent to which schools provide opportunities for pupils to learn domains of knowledge and skills.
2 *Press for achievement:* the institutional strategies the school exerts in order to motivate and sustain its pupils.
3 *Professional teaching conditions:* the circumstances that can empower teachers and others as they attempt to implement educational programmes.

Oakes claims, on the basis of her reading of the research literature, that the quality of teaching and learning in a school is likely to be a direct function of these three enabling conditions. Each is, of course, composed of a number of individual school features and characteristics. Consequently, when her conceptual framework is laid out it resembles, superficially at least, the less rigorously derived criteria lists developed in many LEAs. Although Oakes does not make this point, her 'conditions' could be operationalized as indicators using the kind of rating techniques we have described earlier.

Some of the challenges we have outlined may be met through the implementation of recent government policy initiatives. For example, the government appears more aware of the limitations of simple 'league table' approaches to school performance and more favourably disposed towards attempts to complement them with 'value-added' interpretations:

> As age groups of pupils move from one key stage of the National Curriculum to the next and beyond, it will be possible to compare the results they achieve and so measure more effectively the value added to pupils' education by individual schools.
>
> (DFE 1992a: 16)

This commitment to added value is further reinforced by the procedures for dealing with schools at risk of failing as outlined in the framework for the new inspection arrangements of schools (DFE 1992a). One of the factors to be considered in designating such schools will be the level of examination results attained in relation to those of comparable schools.

The new inspection arrangements may also play a crucial role in the more general development and use of performance indicators. Registered inspectors will be required to demonstrate, *inter alia*, that their judgements 'are rooted in a substantial evidence base and informed by specified quantitative indicators' (OFSTED 1992a: 2). A basic core of 11 areas, which are termed indicators, is initially envisaged and broadened to include several concerned with financial performance. Whether these go far enough to meet the concerns we have outlined, however, is questionable.

The inspection framework is also potentially noteworthy in another respect. Although not explicitly based on effectiveness research, the framework sets out a structure for schools organized under a limited number of broad factors: quality of teaching, assessment, recording and reporting, quality and range of the curriculum, management and planning, organization and administration, resources and their management, pupils' support and guidance, liaison and community links. Each of these factors forms headings for major sections in the reports that the independent inspection teams write on the schools they inspect. In addition, it is possible that these factors, or ones very much like them, will form the basis for a number of key process indicators. This is because the inspection reports will also be the main source from which judgements about the school system nationally are made.

If national judgements of the kind offered in the past by HMI are to continue, then they will arise from an aggregation of the ratings made by the inspection teams. If such indicators are to achieve public credibility it will be necessary to demonstrate that the assessments on which they are based can be made consistently, both within and across different inspection teams. Whether or not the training programmes for inspectors and the periodic consistency checks carried out by HMI will be able to offer a sustained guarantee in relation to this requirement remains to be seen.

Furthermore, will a reduced force of HMI and a loose network of independent inspection teams have the time and commitment to establish the organizational structures necessary to sustain a nationwide system of performance indicators – particularly in a future where the role and influence of LEAs may be dramatically reduced?

The development of performance indicators beyond their current relatively limited level of use is therefore at the present time a moot point.

5

DEVELOPING VALUE-ADDED APPROACHES TO SCHOOL EVALUATION: THE EXPERIENCES OF THREE LEAs

Introduction

Sir Ron Dearing's report, *The National Curriculum and its Assessment* (Dearing 1993), put the development of value-added approaches firmly on the educational agenda. In his review Dearing warned of the potential dangers of ignoring value-added perspectives and of relying solely on 'raw' results. In some schools there might be 'unwarranted complacency', in others 'despair'. A 'straightforward approach to value-added which is supplemented by a second measure giving corrections for the main features extraneous to school could . . . make a valuable contribution to appraising performance and to improving accountability'. In his recommendations he therefore called for research to be commissioned 'into operational approaches to a measure of value-added' (Dearing 1993: 77–8). This is a sizeable but not insurmountable challenge.

A number of local education authorities have been in a position to respond to Sir Ron's recommendations for some time and it is to some of their experiences that the rest of this chapter is addressed.

A great deal can be learnt from their efforts. Whilst more research is, of course, always desirable we have reached the stage where this can (and should) be done on systems which are already up and running.

The value-added framework

The strategies being used to establish value-added approaches are based on techniques used, more or less routinely, in studies of school effectiveness (see reviews in, for example, Riddell and Brown 1991; Reynolds and Cuttance 1992; Scheerens 1992). Virtually all the approaches currently being contemplated in the UK have been used by researchers somewhere in the world. There are several important messages from this body of research:

1 The prior attainments of schools' intakes invariably make a difference to how well their pupils subsequently perform.
2 Differences remain between the performances of pupils in different schools, even when differences in schools' intakes have been taken into account. If these differences can be shown to be attributable to factors under the schools' control, then we may begin to talk of differences in schools' 'effectiveness'.
3 Although differences between schools emerge in such analyses, some care needs to be exercised in talking about the size of the differences. A few schools may be performing well above expectation and a few well below. The great majority will, however, be performing pretty much as expected, given knowledge of their intakes. Furthermore, the patterns vary from LEA to LEA; there may be quite large differences between schools in one area and rather small ones in a neighbouring one. Consequently, it makes little sense to group schools in finely ordered rankings; broad-brush statements about effectiveness (such as 'well above' expectation, 'well below' it and 'as expected') are more appropriate.

The basic tenet of the value-added approach is that like should be compared with like. If there are two pupils who are identical in every respect how much difference does it make to their educational progress if they attend different schools? Obviously pupils' progress is not always smooth and regular. The basic question, over the course of their school careers, is whether they make roughly the level of progress that would have been predicted from knowledge of their earlier performance at or around the time of entry to the school.

The bare rudiments of the value-added approach are laid out in Figure 5.1a. This relates information about pupils' performance at or near the point of entry to secondary school to their subsequent examination performance. Each dot on the graph represents the results for one pupil, the exact location on the graph being determined by the pupil's score at entry on the horizontal axis and their subsequent exam score on the vertical axis. The thick slanting line represents the line of 'best fit' between the two items of information about the pupil. It tells one what the typical exam score for a pupil with a given entry score was. Pupils with a given entry score who perform at levels above those predicted (i.e. their dots are above the slanting line) have made more progress than would have been predicted from knowledge of their score at entry. They have, in other words, had more 'value-added' than for the typical pupil; conversely, pupils whose crosses fall below the line have had less 'value-added'.

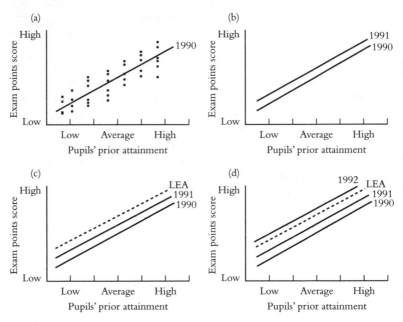

Figure 5.1   The value-added framework.

The strength of the value-added approach for a single school cannot, however, emerge from a single year's data. The exercise should be repeated for a second year on the same basis as the first; and subsequent years after that. This position is presented in Figure 5.1b, where the line for 1991 is shown as well as that for 1990. In this particular school the typical pupil in 1991 has performed better than the typical pupil in 1990 – at every level. The school's overall performance has improved; it has added more value than in the previous year.

It is worth noting at this stage an important feature of the way the overall line can be moved up or down. The position of the line changes as a result of the school's effects on its pupils. There is no necessary reason why a school which recruits more high-attaining pupils in 1991 will necessarily change the position of the line. For the line to change the school must 'add more' than it did with its (similar) high-attaining pupils in the previous year. Conversely, if a school found itself with more lower-attaining pupils the line would not necessarily go down if it continued to work with them as effectively as with (similar) lower-attaining pupils in the previous year; only if it 'added more' than in the previous year would the line go up. This can be verified by adding results for such groups of pupils to Figure 5.1a. Unless most of the extra dots fall above the line, the position of the line will not be affected.

This particular school is improving its performance over time. However, it cannot make a sensible assessment of its overall performance unless it has information about how pupils like its own have performed in other schools. It is at this point that information about the 'LEA line' is required (Figure 5.1c). Although this school has been improving, its typical pupils lag behind those in the 'typical' school in the LEA at every point. It is, in brief, somewhat less effective with the same kinds of pupils than other schools in the authority.

Responsibility for creating the 'LEA line' should lie with the LEA or, perhaps, a group of schools within it. To create the framework described in Figure 5.1c a common piece of information about pupils' prior attainments or backgrounds is required. Figure 5.1d describes a situation in which the school in question has not only continued to improve its performance over time (its 1992 line lies above those for 1991 and 1990) but has also climbed above the LEA line. It is now more effective with pupils at every level of prior performance than the 'typical school' in the LEA.

Before going on to consider the experiences of the three LEAs it is worth rehearsing the basic requirements for building a value-added approach. These are:

1 Data on individual pupils rather than data aggregated to the level of the school; a measure of outcome for each pupil (such as exam results), which reflects all levels of pupil performance (such as a points score) rather than just the higher levels (such as five or more higher grade passes).
2 A measure of each pupil's attainment (preferably one that is finely differentiated rather than one which groups pupils into just three or four broad bands) plus one or two other items of information about pupils' backgrounds (such as gender).
3 In the absence of a measure of each pupil's prior attainment, several items of information about each pupil's background; these really need to include a measure of social advantage as well as the measures of social disadvantage which are typically available.
4 Analysis of the data using the statistical technique known as multi-level modelling.

A fuller description of these basic requirements is offered in Chapter 6, along with a discussion of some of the key features of multi-level statistical approaches.

The development of a value-added approach in Shropshire

Shropshire LEA has been in the fortunate position of having nearly all the various pieces of the jigsaw in operation already. Consequently it has been able to make rapid progress.

A number of elements in Shropshire's experience may be identified. Interest in obtaining a sophisticated picture of schools' exam performance was already in place and it was relatively easy to collect information about the exam results of individual pupils. Crucially, from the point of view of building a value-added system, testing of pupils on a standardized National Foundation for Educational Research (NFER) test at the time of transfer to secondary school already occurred and such information was gathered at the centre. Consequently it was a relatively straightforward matter to match up the two key items of information.

At the same time a number of other factors contributed to the rapid developments. Given the widely varying types of school in the authority (including a selective school) and the extent of social differentiation between different areas of the authority, there was a collective perception that crude comparisons would be inappropriate. This sense had been reinforced in recent years by the tradition in the advisory service of reviewing aspects of schools' exam performances in a regular way.

Finally, there was a commitment on the part of both LEA officers and headteachers to make headway. A senior member of the advisory service was determined, on the one hand, that Shropshire should use (and if necessary pioneer) the most appropriate strategies available, even if they involved some initially more arcane aspects of statistical development. On the other hand there was a willingness on the part of a significant number of Shropshire headteachers to 'allow' the authority to develop something on a pilot basis, provided it did not involve them in a great deal of extra work or damage their schools (see Hedger and Raleigh 1992).

In the event the LEA arranged for the collection of a database on 20 per cent of its pupils for the first-year pilot. An Exam Points Score was generated for each pupil, matched with a prior attainment score and information about gender. Subsequently a multi-level analysis was performed.

Great care was taken to explain to the headteachers how the analysis was progressing. A workshop was attended by most headteachers in the authority. The construction of the 'LEA line' was explained and heads were provided with the information about their own schools and encouraged to make use of it.

The exercise was repeated in the second and third years for all the pupils in the LEA and a little bit more information about individual pupils was also collected, including free school meals. Data collection has been extended to a fourth and now a fifth year. The additional variables enabled more of the variation between schools to be explained (but not a great deal more). Research to date indicates that schools vary in their levels of effectiveness from year to year. Some improve, some deteriorate, some fluctuate and some remain the same. Whatever the case in a particular school it clearly does not make sense to rely on data from just one year.

The analyses have been made available within the Shropshire system for some time now, although they have not yet entered the public domain. The LEA has made a point of ensuring that a good deal of well-presented information is available to the press and public but has not, as yet, felt it necessary to mount a public challenge to any inappropriate assessments of its schools. Privately there has been a lot of discussion. Most importantly, individual headteachers have begun to develop improvement strategies based upon careful analysis of the information now available to them.

Contextualizing results in Nottinghamshire

Nottinghamshire LEA, like Shropshire, has a range of schools serving very different communities. It too wanted to press ahead in developing a framework for interpreting schools' performance. It differed, however, in two important respects when contemplating how best to set up such a system. First, it lacked a common measure of pupils' prior attainment at the point of transfer to secondary school. Second, it needed to rely on schools to provide most of the information it might require.

Given the development of national testing in England over the next few years the LEA was not keen to ask schools to take on additional activities of this nature. A decision was therefore made to adopt a contextualizing approach in which schools' results were interpreted in the context of their pupils' backgrounds. This approach has been the dominant one in the North American research on school effectiveness, was the approach recommended in the report of the England and Wales Task Group on Assessment and Testing back in 1988 (DES 1988b) and has been widely used in research studies in the UK. There was, in short, a good deal of relevant experience on which to draw.

After some discussion with its headteachers the LEA opted for a two-side questionnaire to be completed by schools on a 20 per cent sample of their pupils. Detailed information on the exam results of each pupil was collected along with further items on pupils' backgrounds. These included: gender, family size, ethnic group, eligibility for free school meals and the incidence of what was termed a 'significant life event' as well as a number of other items which were suggested by headteachers.

There was some resistance to collecting information on 'social class' the first time the survey was conducted. Agreement was only given by headteachers to attempt to supply this information for the second survey, after they had been convinced that it would assist the process of contextualization. They needed some convincing. The LEA did, after all, have some information already about the areas in which schools were located (albeit based on the 1981 Census but this was soon to be updated by the 1991 version); none was sure, however, how well this described the pupils attending a particular school.

The LEA could also collect information on individual pupils about eligibility or take up of free school meals fairly easily. Whilst this latter information was useful, it was also recognized that two schools with similar proportions of pupils on free meals could have pupils of very different backgrounds not on them. In one case the remainder might be almost eligible; in another case they might be spread across the whole range of social backgrounds. The research showing that social advantage gave better predictions of subsequent exam performance was also influential. The need for several measures of social background and circumstances to be collected was consequently recognized, although there was some uneasiness remaining about matters of interpretation.

The results were again analysed using a multi-level model and a series of feedback events for headteachers was arranged. Head-teachers expressed a good deal of interest in seeing their own results alongside those of 'schools like theirs'. A number of strategies for creating groups of schools were therefore constructed using a mixture of objective and more subjective evidence to supplement the findings of the survey. Work is continuing in this area. The survey was repeated for a third year on a 20 per cent sample and the LEA and its heads subsequently decided to increase this to 100 per cent for subsequent years.

The LEA made the overall conclusions of the survey public whilst being very guarded about the 'results' of individual schools (a 20 per cent sample would not allow it to make any very reliable statements about individual schools anyway). It produced a series of well-presented leaflets for parents explaining that schools have different kinds of intakes and should consequently not all be expected to produce the same sorts of results. It also indicated publicly, if in a low-key way, that most of its schools were performing at the levels to be expected from knowledge of their intakes, whilst providing heads and governors with further information through which to explore whether their own school was, in fact, performing as might be expected.

Building awareness in Leicestershire

Leicestershire LEA embarked in 1992 on the task of building value-added strategies into its authority-wide approach. It too has a variety of schools straddling an ethnically mixed city, small towns and rural areas. It also has a tradition of supporting its schools in undertaking their own evaluations.

The small working party of headteachers and LEA officers charged with developing an authority-wide approach faced a number of strategic decisions. It eventually opted to pilot work simultaneously at three levels of the system: the upper secondary school with an emphasis on A levels, the secondary school involving GCSE results and the primary school with Key Stage 1 results from national testing. In all three cases it concentrated its initial efforts on creating the 'LEA line' (see Figure 5.1c). This decision led to different strategies at different levels.

At A level a full value-added approach was possible. Information was available for each individual pupil not only on their A level performance but also on their GCSE results, which could serve as a measure of prior attainment. It was a fairly easy matter for a dataset to be constructed on virtually all the pupils in the authority's schools. As a result the LEA was able to move quickly to a multi-level analysis on some 2500 pupils, one of the first occasions on which this had been done with this age group on a complete population of pupils.

The LEA also fed back results to headteachers and published the 'LEA line' in its annual report to parents and governors on exam and test results in Leicestershire schools. As a result of this development it was able to raise issues about the difficulties of interpreting 'raw' results, demonstrate some of the potential of value-added approaches, whilst leaving individual schools to make up their own minds about what to stress in their own presentations.

With respect to results in public examinations at 16-plus and performance on tests at 7-plus the working party decided to limit itself for the first year to collecting enough information to construct an 'LEA line'. It asked schools for background information (including social class and ethnicity) on a sample of their pupils which was just sufficient to set the overall line, again leaving it up to individual schools to decide whether to construct a fuller picture from data in their own records.

Issues and challenges

Each of the three LEAs described here has made different decisions about what to do next. Their choices have been structured, in large part, by what was already available and how far they felt their schools could be encouraged to go in providing further data. In the process they have had to make judgements about various key issues which are outlined below.

The most important issue to be addressed relates to the overall purposes of introducing value-added approaches (Willms 1992). Is the main purpose to hold schools directly accountable for their performance? Is it to identify schools that are markedly under-performing and may even be 'at risk'? Is it to help schools justify their existing levels of performance? Or is it to help them to understand more about their own performance and how to improve it? If it is to be about several of these, are they all equally compatible? It is easy to become embattled about such issues where schools are uncertain of the overall purposes and too little time is given over to clarifying perceptions.

British researchers of school effectiveness have been at the forefront of international developments and there is much to be learnt that is of direct relevance to practice (for an early selection see Raudenbush and Willms 1991). British statisticians have also played a pioneering role in developing sophisticated statistical methods that have immediate application to value-added issues. In such circumstances it is easy to forget that schools and parents may need help in thinking in value-added terms. How familiar are they with the simple approaches described here upon which the more complex strategies are premised? Current developments amongst policymakers may not yet be matched by comparable changes in the ways headteachers and their staffs are conceptualizing the issues. It is difficult to become enthusiastic about the most sophisticated statistical procedures if one's colleagues are still talking exclusively in terms of the 'standards' pupils have reached rather than giving equal weight to the 'progress' they have made. The demand for better approaches will be fuelled, in part, by teachers making more routine use of the basic framework.

The creation of high-quality frameworks for assessing the 'value added' takes time. The LEAs described here have had to make different decisions about the speed of their developments. It takes four or five years for pupils to pass through the separate phases of primary and secondary schooling. Consequently it is not easy to move from a situation where little or nothing is in place to a full-blown system in a very short period of time. The time-frames are longer unless, like Shropshire, key pieces of the jigsaw are already in place. One of the big problems to be faced is whether to facilitate a patchwork of developments across LEAs or work to the lowest common local or national denominator. The former has the advantage of allowing experience about 'best practice' to accumulate more rapidly but needs to be planned with moves towards any wider 'systems' in mind.

Whilst interest in value-added approaches is currently high, as evidenced, for example, by the response to the National Commission on Education's proposals (McPherson 1992), it is easy to get trapped in unproductive discussions. All parties need time to learn more about what is involved. In all three LEAs a piloting phase proved invaluable. Indeed, a pilot, using a sample of pupils, is probably the best initial step to take, even when data on all pupils is potentially available. Everyone involved needs to maximize their opportunities for learning what might come out of the strategies they have agreed to develop. On the LEA's side this may mean focusing on getting the questions and possible interpretations into the arena for discussion rather than investing time in making a 95 per cent accurate database 99 per cent accurate. On the schools' side this may mean having the opportunity to learn how the system is likely to work without immediately having to act defensively. A light sample will provide valuable information that can be shared without putting schools in the position of feeling that their performance is on the line. They can, for example, rationalize any possibly unfavourable outcomes by suggesting that a different 'light' sample of pupils would have produced different results. It may only be worthwhile taking the next steps when a majority of schools intimate that they fully understand what is involved and are committed to living with at least some of the consequences.

The actual nature of the information to be collected is, of course, crucial and each of the three LEAs spent a good deal of time debating what was available. Where they were able to make rapid progress this was usually because some of the information was already, so to speak, in the cupboard. Each, however, had to come to terms with the fact that they would have to go to schools to supplement their extant databases. Schools, for their part, were surprised by some of the LEAs' requests. They felt they already provided a good deal of information to the centre and needed convincing that it could not be bent to other purposes. Time and again value-added working parties have found that information collected for one purpose has not lent itself immediately to others.

There are several reasons for this. Probably the major stumbling block has proved to be the need for data on individual pupils. Administrative systems tend to collect information in the form that is most convenient for their immediate purposes; relevant data, such as the numbers on free school meals or the numbers being statemented are usually aggregated to the level of the school before being passed on to the centre. It is rare for this sort of information to be passed on on an individual basis although electronic systems of data-gathering will make this easier in the future.

The essential requirements are for measures of each individual pupil at two time-points (at or around entry, for example, and in subsequent examinations). The most suitable form for the outcome measure remains a matter for some debate. A finely differentiated scale (which takes account of all levels of pupil performance) rather than a stepped or grouped scale (no passes, 1–4 passes, 5 or more passes) is preferable. The use of such measures has, so far, not produced much critical debate. Comments have been confined to such observations as the fact that middling points scores may be achieved in a variety of different ways through different combinations of numbers and grades of passes. The effects of using different scoring systems can, of course, be explored in this connection. A similar set of issues emerge when attempting to predict performance at A level or Highers from summary scores of 16-plus data.

Doubts have also been expressed about the extent to which a single measure of pupils' prior attainment, supplemented by other background information, can fully take account of the differences in intakes to different schools. It seems improbable that it would take account of all the differences but likely that it takes account of most of them. The total proportion of the variation explained in schools' results in the case of Shropshire's data is close to the upper limits reported from research studies around the world. Unfortunately research (and especially British research) is rather sparse on this issue – more evidence is required.

There is, of course, still a vigorous debate about the nature and suitability of standardized tests which do vary in the jobs they are designed to do and the extent to which they meet their declared objectives. It would be tempting to think that, at some point, Key Stage 2 tests might act as suitable substitutes. But, from the perspective of the mid-1990s it is not yet clear whether such tests will be up to the task. Where LEAs have programmes of standardized testing in place it would seem unwise, as yet, to plan to replace them with these newer ones; the jury is still out.

Most of the international studies of school effectiveness, and almost all the North American ones, have relied on information on pupils' socio-economic backgrounds to take account of differences between schools' intakes; only a handful have used information about pupils' prior attainments. In so far as the findings of the former studies have been accepted largely uncritically (and frequently confirmed other findings) current controversies surrounding the use of socio-economic data to contextualize schools' performances are surprising. Unfortunately we are short of studies where prior attainment and socio-economic data have been simultaneously collected; one has usually been collected to the exclusion of the other (but see Willms 1986). The fact that the two approaches appear to yield similar but not identical findings provides some comfort but also counsels caution about 'over-interpreting' the data when only socio-economic information is available.

What the Nottinghamshire study confirmed was the importance of supplementing information about social disadvantage (as captured, for example, by free school meals) with evidence about social backgrounds reflecting social advantage. The proportion of pupils coming from 'professional' homes proved to be an especially important predictor of subsequent performance. A minority of schools are uncomfortable with discussions based on social background and need to be convinced that this is a route worth pursuing. A pilot study, in these and similar circumstances, may help to change minds.

A decade ago it was possible to use statistical methods for school effectiveness studies which were part of the armoury of any statistician, natural or social scientist. During the mid-1980s academic opinion began to shift as new statistical techniques were pioneered. It was still possible in the late 1980s to argue that the new techniques were inaccessible to the ordinary researcher. By the early 1990s, however, the practical problems of employing what has come to be known as multi-level modelling had been largely cracked. Whilst the group of researchers who can use the techniques is still relatively small, there are now probably just about enough of them around to undertake and facilitate the appropriate statistical analyses (for a fuller account of multi-level modelling see Paterson and Goldstein 1991; Goldstein *et al.* 1993).

A number of researchers have claimed to show that certain types of individual pupil (boys, the more advantaged, etc.) may make greater progress in some schools than others. (Nuttall *et al.* 1989). What may be educationally effective for one young person may not be so effective for another. We need to know more about these differences. Multi-level modelling allows differences in effectiveness to be explored as a matter of routine. It is premature to conclude that effective schools are equally effective for all their pupils although some research points in this direction (see Chapter 6 and Jesson and Gray 1991 for a fuller discussion of these debates).

Much of the recent stimulus to consider the potential of value-added approaches has stemmed from the publication of schools' results in local newspapers rearranged into so-called 'league tables'. Clearly the results from value-added analyses could also be published. Whilst they would not lend themselves to finely ranked league tables they could, in certain circumstances, sustain broad evaluative judgements. However, the headteachers in the three LEAs described here called for caution in moving in such directions. They felt some breathing space was needed to allow an opportunity for staff and governors to familiarize themselves with the implications of the overall approach and the particular conclusions to be drawn with respect to their own schools. But many were subsequently prepared to contemplate moves to introduce the broad conclusions from value-added approaches into the public domain.

The introduction of value-added approaches into the educational system requires sustained support. Individual schools can make some progress on their own. Much of the impetus for developments in the three LEAs, however, came from those whose responsibility it was to secure some overview across schools. People in LEA

and other central positions have usually been better placed to generate and maintain the administrative arrangements that are required.
Their most important role, however, was to communicate a clear
sense of why going down the value-added route might be important
and what advantages might come out of it.

Beyond academic progress

Most of the research to date on value-added approaches has concentrated on aspects of academic progress. Whilst examination results
and similar measures are undoubtedly important there are clearly
other outcomes which need to be considered alongside them. A
broader view of education is required. Schools and LEAs have
already explored a number of these in a preliminary way (see Gray
and Jesson 1991). Amongst issues which would merit further attention are:

- pupils' attitudes towards education and their interest in continuing beyond the compulsory stages;
- aspects of pupils' achievements which do not lend themselves to
  assessment through public examinations;
- general levels of pupil satisfaction with their educational
  experiences.

Many educators are also interested in considering school ethos and
other aspects of the environments within which learning takes place
(see Scottish Office Education Department 1992).

As long as like is being compared with like the general principles
of the value-added approach may still apply. Researchers of school
effectiveness have found differences between schools on a variety of
outcomes and dimensions in addition to academic progress. Of
course, not all these things can be analysed in ways that are statistically sophisticated. In the next few years it seems probable that
LEAs and schools will increasingly turn their attention to ways of
broadening the educational outcomes which they evaluate from a
value-added perspective.

Working for improvement

Knowing that a school is/is not 'adding value' is, of course, just a starting point for further work. The challenge for the individual school is to understand and grasp the levers of change. To do so requires insights into the causes of the school's effectiveness and analyses of how improvements in performance might be brought about. There is likely to be an element of trial and error.

Observation suggests that schools have frequently started by reflecting on the results of individual pupils. This has sometimes taken them a little way forward but not always. Individuals differ and there are usually 'good reasons' why their performances can be explained away. The challenge has been to find common elements that apply across their individual experiences.

Such questioning has resulted in particular groups of pupils (lower-attaining males, for example) or particular subject departments being identified as priorities for action. Some schools have used the evidence to challenge themselves about their own expectations. Others have tried to find factors that could be generalized across more than one department. Some have experimented with changing exam boards and exam syllabuses whilst still others have entered pupils (usually the more able) for more subjects in the hope that they will pick up something more on the way.

Most of these are short-term tactics which are designed to get the school 'moving'. In the medium-term, however, they have found that more fundamental reviews of strategy are required which demand that they grapple with the ways in which the school is organized, its culture and ethos and the ways in which it develops methods of teaching and learning.

The next steps

Schools deserve the best evaluation of their performances we are currently capable of delivering. By the end of this century virtually everyone is agreed that it will be possible for all schools to participate in a value-added 'system'. If this is to happen, however, certain practical steps need to be taken now.

First, it needs to be recognized at national level that a number of LEAs are already well on the way to developing coherent 'value-added' strategies. Furthermore, the number of LEAs in such a position is growing rapidly. The challenge is to build on these developments rather than redirect them. The surest route to a national picture will be to colour in the national map an LEA at a time, identifying the very best practice and then emulating it.

Second, several LEAs have clearly pioneered the kinds of information that are required for value-added analyses to be undertaken. To take this step has, invariably, required them to collect additional data on individual pupils regarding their prior attainments and socio-economic circumstances, sometimes in the face of scepticism and even opposition. Future national efforts need to be consolidated around the lessons that can be culled from their experiences. Schools will collaborate in providing these kinds of data when they are party to the purposes to which they might subsequently be put.

Third, LEAs and their schools need to be encouraged to establish the broad frameworks they will eventually employ for value-added analyses. It is a common experience amongst working parties of LEA officers and headteachers with whom we have worked that they have lamented the failure of their predecessors to set up the requisite frameworks 5 years ago!

Fourth, with the advent of national assessments of pupils and schools, many LEAs have already begun to build structures for handling the resultant data more effectively. A considerable burden can be lifted from schools by careful advance planning of data requirements.

Fifth, and perhaps most importantly, a concerted effort needs to be made by all those involved in the educational system to think 'value-added' in advance of the full framework coming into existence. A firm commitment to analysing the strengths and weaknesses of individual schools from a value-added perspective offers one of the best prospects for improving schools and raising standards currently available to us. It is no surprise that Sir Ron Dearing's review should have been so firmly committed to further developments in this area.

6

ESTIMATING DIFFERENCES IN THE EXAMINATION PERFORMANCES OF SECONDARY SCHOOLS IN SIX LEAs: A MULTI-LEVEL APPROACH TO SCHOOL EFFECTIVENESS

Introduction

Interest in research on school effectiveness amongst policy-makers and practitioners can rarely have been higher. The reasons are not difficult to establish. The research has both substantive and methodological contributions to make to the identification of 'good practice' and to the development of frameworks for school evaluation. But, ironically, at a time when interest is so prominent, there has been a danger that methodological (and notably statistical) advances would remove the opportunities for the practical application of the approaches adopted by school effectiveness researchers. This chapter, building on our previous discussion, is designed, in part, to reduce the danger of such a gap developing still further. It demonstrates how LEAs might make use of the most-up-to-date and sophisticated techniques to explore an issue which has become increasingly central to school evaluation over the past decade, namely the interpretation of schools' examination results. At the same time it aims to make a substantive contribution to research on the extent of differences between schools in their effectiveness.

The factors which have contributed to the development of interest in school effectiveness research are not difficult to identify. At the beginning of the decade, for example, the 1980 Education Act required secondary schools to publish their examination results amongst other items of information; there were understandable worries about the extent to which some schools (and especially those serving socially disadvantaged catchment areas) would be unfairly treated in any ensuing comparisons of their performance.

During the mid-1980s there was extended controversy about the effects of comprehensive reorganization on pupils' performance; again concern that like was not being compared with like was central to the debate (see Gray and Jesson 1989 for a review). There has also been considerable interest in the effectiveness of individual LEAs and the appropriateness of the underlying statistically based models of evaluation that have been employed to establish their performance; in the process some of the limitations of existing databases and statistical procedures have been exposed (see, for example, Gray and Jesson 1987; Woodhouse and Goldstein 1988).

The last few years have seen interest in comparing schools' results increase still further, partly as a result of the new roles for local education authorities prescribed in the 1988 Education Reform Act. The Task Group on Assessment and Testing, however, stepped back from recommending the full-blown 'contextualization' of schools' performance in relation to the publication of pupils' results on the new national attainment tests (see Cuttance and Goldstein 1988; DES 1988b). In a subsequent policy statement from the DES (1989b), some modest interest in 'value-added' approaches was hinted at but no whole-hearted endorsement, in practice, emerged. It is clear that there was still considerable unease about the application of the techniques of school effectiveness research to the everyday tasks of performance evaluation and review. Only in the early 1990s has the government attempted to grasp the value-added nettle, most notably within the Dearing Report (1993). It is doubtful, of course, whether their decision to publish all schools' examination results in November 1992 left them much choice.

There have been a number of British studies of school effectiveness since Rutter's research into 12 Inner London secondary schools in the mid-to-late 1970s (Rutter *et al.* 1979). It is now generally recognized that the number of schools sampled in Rutter's study was on the low side for satisfactory estimates of differences in schools' effectiveness to be established. None the less, a decade later, there have still only been a handful of studies with sample sizes that have been larger. Amongst the studies which offer such estimates of schools' effects we would mention: the ILEA's Junior School Project which looked at some 50 primary schools (Mortimore *et al.* 1988); the studies of Scottish secondary schools conducted by members of the Centre for Educational Sociology at Edinburgh University (see Gray *et al.* 1983; Willms 1986; Cuttance 1988); the study of 18 racially mixed comprehensives conducted by the Policy Studies Institute and Lancaster University (Smith and Tomlinson 1989); and a recent analysis of examination results over a period of 3 years in large numbers of secondary schools in the Inner London Education Authority (Nuttall *et al.* 1989). To these we would add our own earlier and continuing work (see Chapter 1), conducted as part of the Contexts Project on school effectiveness and the interpretation of examination results (Gray *et al.* 1986).

In addition to sharing overlapping substantive concerns each of these studies has incorporated (to a greater or lesser extent) the use of the most advanced statistical techniques currently available, known as multi-level modelling (also known as Hierarchical Linear Modelling, see Raudenbush and Bryk 1986; and Variance Components analysis, see Longford 1986). The statistical problems posed by the underlying structure of educational systems (notably the clustering of pupils into schools and, crucially, the importance of collecting data on individual pupils), were first laid out in an accessible form for educational researchers during the early 1980s (see, for example, Goldstein 1984). Two or three years later, however, they were still largely unknown when Aitkin and Longford (1986) published their seminal paper, using a dataset we had provided on a single LEA as part of the Contexts Project. Since then the accessibility of the techniques has improved considerably (see Goldstein 1987 for a semi-introductory account) but much remains to be explored and understood about these new approaches and their implications. Crucially, each of the studies mentioned above has produced somewhat differing estimates of schools' effectiveness because each has, in practice, conceptualized the problems some-what differently and pursued them using data collected from differ-ent localities incorporating different variables. An extended review of some of these issues, as well as some more general issues raised by studies of school and teacher effectiveness, has been offered by Preece (1989).

There has been some confusion about the extent to which these various studies have produced similar or conflicting results. The enduring questions of school effectiveness research remain the same, however. They are:

1 What information on pupils' backgrounds or prior attainments is required for appropriate comparisons to be undertaken?
2 What is the extent of differences in pupils' performance that may be attributable to differences in the effectiveness of the schools they have attended? What, in other words, are the overall conse-quences for pupils' progress of attending a more as opposed to less effective school?
3 Are schools differentially effective? Do they, in short, have more impact on the outcomes of some groups of pupils (the lower-attaining, ethnic minorities, males or females for example) than others?

The present analysis has something to add to existing research on all three of these issues. But such questions are, of course, precon-ditions for answering what is probably the most important question of all:

4 What factors (and especially factors under schools' own control) can be identified which contribute to schools' effectiveness?

Sources of data

The present study uses data from six different LEAs serving metro-politan, urban and rural communities in England. In four of these LEAs we have been able to obtain two (and in one case three) independent samples of pupils' performance. Eleven distinct data-sets were therefore available for subsequent analysis.

Under the terms of our agreement with participating LEAs we are not in a position to reveal the names of the authorities or their schools. The LEAs whose data we report in this study were situated in geographically distinct parts of the country; whilst they were not chosen to be 'representative' of anything other than themselves, it may nevertheless be observed that they serve a range of different types of communities. LEAs 1, 2 and 4 are situated in the North of England and serve metropolitan boroughs containing numbers of 'inner city' schools; they include significant areas of industrial decline. LEAs 3 and 6 serve urban and county populations in the south of England. LEA 5 comprises data from pupils attending schools in a Midland metropolitan borough; again some areas in this authority possessed 'inner city' characteristics.

Different strategies were employed to gather the data from each LEA. The (rounded) number of schools in each LEA and the average number of pupils per school for which we obtained data are shown in Table 6.1. In all we had data on some 14,000 individual pupils in some 290 schools (some of these schools were, of course, to be found in each of the datasets covering a particular LEA; taking these into account, the data covered, in all, some 150 entirely different institutions). This table also reports the measures of pupil characteristics available in each dataset.

For each pupil the examination outcome is a scaled measure of their fifth form examination performance created by assigning a score to each level of pass obtained in GCSE/GCE or CSE examinations. We refer to this measure as their 'exam points score'. In addition, we had a number of items of information on pupils' characteristics available to us. These included:

1 Measures of pupils' background characteristics in datasets 1A, 1B, 1C, 2A, 2B, 3A, 3B and 4. In all cases these included parental social class, housing tenure (except for 1C and 4) and the number of siblings in the family.
2 Measures of pupils' prior attainment at the point of transfer to secondary school in datasets 5, 6A and 6B.
3 Information on pupils' gender in all 11 datasets.

The data available, therefore, provide a selection of the kinds of variables that might be obtained within an LEA that was prepared to invest some effort in data collection. They represent the minimum that an LEA might try to assemble; clearly information on further variables would be valuable if the resources committed to data collection enabled them to be collected. The variables described here have the distinct merit, in the present case, of being fairly readily available for the purpose of the analysis.

Table 6.1 Summary of the information on pupil characteristics available for each LEA and in each dataset in addition to examination results[*]

LEA data-set	Number of schools	Average number of pupils per school	Prior attain-ment	Social class[†]	Gender	Housing tenure[‡]	Number of siblings
				Variables available			
1A	40§	11	No	Yes	Yes	Yes	Yes
1B	40	12	No	Yes	Yes	Yes	Yes
1C	40	26	No	Yes	Yes	No	Yes
2A	30	11	No	Yes	Yes	Yes	Yes
2B	30	10	No	Yes	Yes	Yes	Yes
3A	10	38	No	Yes	Yes	Yes	Yes
3B	10	44	No	Yes	Yes	Yes	Yes
4	20	35	No	Yes	Yes	No	Yes
5	20	54	Yes¶	No	Yes	No	No
6A	30	181	Yes¶	No	Yes	No	No
6B	20	177	Yes	No	Yes	No	No

[*] For each LEA information about each pupil's examination results, subject by subject, was available. These were summed into an overall exam score using the following scoring system: grade A, 7; grade B, 6; grade C or CSE grade 1, 5; grade D or 2, 4; grade E or 3, 3; grade 4, 2; grade 5, 1; failed or unclassified 0.
[†] In datasets 1A, 1B, 2A, 2B, 3A and 3B social class was based on a measure of father's occupation coded into the Cambridge system; in datasets 1C and 4, father's occupation was coded using the OPCS system.
[‡] Housing tenure was coded into those in owner-occupied property, rented and others.
§ In order to preserve the confidentiality of the data on each LEA these figures have been rounded to the nearest ten in this column.
¶ In LEA 5 this was a measure of verbal reasoning at age 11; in LEA 6 this was a measure of reading attainment at the point of transfer.

The distribution of exam results across pupils and schools

How far did pupils' fifth-year (Year 11) exam results differ across schools and LEAs? Figure 6.1 shows the distribution of pupil level achievement in each of the 11 LEA datasets. We have used 'box' and 'whisker' plots to focus attention primarily on the interquartile ranges of pupils' scores (which are contained within the 'boxes'). The length of each box corresponds to the range of examination

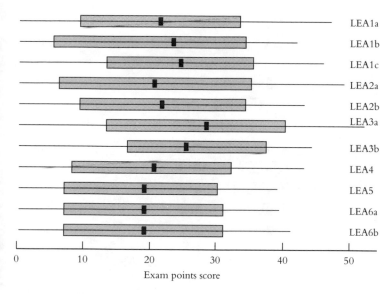

Figure 6.1   Distribution of individual pupils' achievements in six LEAs.

score differences between pupils at the upper and lower quartiles. The interquartile range gives a fairly robust indication of the range of variation in each LEA and is indicated by the shaded areas in Figure 6.1. In all 11 datasets these differences between individual pupils were fairly consistent at around 25 examination score points. Of course, the 'average' level of performance differed somewhat between datasets and also between different LEAs; these differences reflected both the variation of pupils within the samples drawn from a given LEA and also between LEAs serving populations with different social characteristics.

The 'whiskers' of the plots (the lines stretching either side of the boxes) in Figure 6.1 represent the full range of variation between pupils in each dataset. A score of zero was assigned to those who: left school before examinations were taken, who did not take examinations, who took examinations but achieved no credit for these attempts or who simply did not report on their achievement. All six LEAs had some pupils with the lowest scores, although the precise percentages varied. The 'highest' scores were also subject to (sometimes considerable) variation. In LEA 3A, for example, the highest examination score was above 50 points whereas in LEA 5 it was below 40.

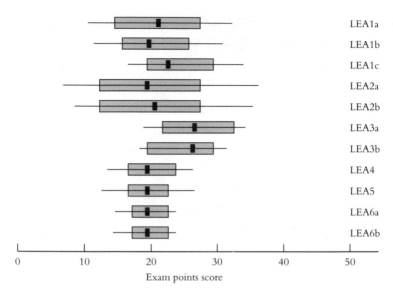

Figure 6.2 Distribution of mean school achievement in six LEAs.

The pupils whose performance we report in Figure 6.1 were grouped by schools and the mean (or average) examination score for each school was also calculated. The resulting distribution of 'school mean' scores is displayed in Figure 6.2.

By contrast with Figure 6.1 we note that the interquartile range of 'school' performance was substantially less than that for pupil performance. Although this was an 'expected' result, it operated in different ways for different LEAs. We observe that whilst the inter-quartile ranges were relatively consistent within LEAs they differed between LEAs (see shaded areas of Figure 6.2). For example, in LEA 6 this range was only about five examination score points whereas in LEA 3 it was 15.

Such differences are not trivial; however, we can draw no conclusions about school performance from them in isolation, as they may arise from a variety of different sources including: differences in pupils' prior attainment, in schools' effectiveness, in LEAs' policies for allocation of pupils to schools, or as a result of other informal 'selection' processes or, indeed, combinations of all or some of these factors.

The first stage of our analysis was to identify the variance lying between schools before any account was taken of differences in

Table 6.2 Results of the model-fitting (Model 1)

LEA dataset	Unadjusted school variance (%)	Fixed effects (%)	(Random) school effects (%)
1A	15.2	20.4	6.4
1B	10.8	11.4	5.2
1C	12.0	12.8	7.9
2A	30.8	12.6	25.0
2B	28.9	11.8	23.7
3A	5.4	14.3	3.7
3B	6.6	10.8	3.5
4	6.2	13.5	3.9
5	7.1	54.5	1.5
6A	3.5	56.3	5.0
6B	3.7	58.1	4.0

Model 1 Fixed effects: pupil level variables, from those available, found to contribute significantly to the prediction of examination scores are included in the model. Random effects: school level (intercepts) and pupil-level residuals are estimated.
Column 2 Variance attributed to (random) school effects prior to controlling for pupil-level characteristics (expressed as a percentage of the overall variance).
Column 3 Variance explained by fixed part of the model (expressed as a percentage of the overall variance).
Column 4 Variance attributed to (random) school effects (expressed as a percentage of the residual variance).

pupils' characteristics. This is basically just another way of exploring the extent of differences already presented in Figure 6.2. The results of this 'null' model (when no account is taken of differences in pupils' individual background or prior attainment characteristics) are presented in column 2 of Table 6.2. They confirm the picture already revealed in Figure 6.2. The range of 'unadjusted' school differences was very marked ranging from a low value of just over 3 per cent in LEA 6 to just over 30 per cent in LEA 2.

Of course, none of the analyses to this point have taken any account of differences in the intakes to the schools in the six LEAs on the various measures we collected. Suffice it to say, at this stage, that these were also large and related, prima facie, to the schools' exam results. There was a general tendency in all six LEAs for the schools with more socially advantaged or higher attaining intakes to obtain the higher fifth-year results (tables not shown).

The main findings

We shall not dwell here on the statistical aspects of our methodology as these have already been explained elsewhere and by others in greater detail (see, for example, Aitkin and Longford 1986). The results we report here, none the less, represent substantial additional evidence about the extent to which schools within particular LEAs differed in their effectiveness. In discussing our findings, therefore, we address four distinct issues raised by the analyses, namely:

1 Estimates of the relative size of the variance attributable to schools after appropriate controls have been applied for differences in pupils' characteristics.
2 The consequent differences in expected examination scores obtained by pupils in different schools.
3 The nature of 'contextual effects' and the role of pupil-level measures aggregated to the level of the school.
4 Whether the schools were differentially effective, that is whether some schools 'did better' with more able pupils at the expense of less able and vice versa.

We then go on to consider the explanatory power (both substantive and statistical) of the procedures we have employed before addressing some of the practical issues arising for LEAs and others who might wish to use the framework and procedures we have outlined.

The variance in pupil performance potentially attributable to schools

All the multi-level analyses reported here were conducted using a statistical package development by researchers at the London Institute of Education (see Rasbash *et al.* 1989). The extensive data sources which we have used gave consistently 'low' estimates of the extent to which schools contributed differentially to pupils' performance. In nine out of the eleven datasets the variance attributed to schools was estimated to be 8 per cent or less (see Table 6.2, column 4); in six of the datasets the estimate was 5 per cent or less. These findings are broadly consistent with Aitkin and Longford's (1986) seminal study which reported that 'only around 2 per cent of the variation in outcomes was assigned to the schools'.

Aitkin and Longford's estimates have not passed without comment. Kilgore and Pendleton (1986), for example, claimed that this particular finding was 'not of special empirical importance, nor consistent with findings based on broader samples'. The present study, however, presents further evidence which casts doubt on the claims made by Kilgore and Pendleton. The results described here, representing extensive analysis of academic performance at age 16, come down clearly in favour of the lower levels reported earlier by Aitkin and Longford.

An important part of Kilgore and Pendleton's argument was based on the view that, because Aitkin and Longford's data were restricted to a single LEA, the 'low' level of variation associated with schools was 'a consequence of the relative homogeneity of policies and practices within that LEA rather than [a general indication of] the relative importance of schools and pupil background'.

On closer examination, however, it appears that some other recent British studies of school effectiveness have reported similarly 'low' proportions of variance associated with schools. In the Scottish studies, for example, Willms estimated a figure of no more than 10 per cent across the broad range of Scottish school types (Willms 1987). From the tables in Nuttall's study of Inner London secondary schools it can be established that the equivalent figure was around 8 per cent (Nuttall *et al.* 1989) whilst in Smith and Tomlinson's (1989) study of racially mixed schools the figures were also around these levels.

Each of these estimates is, of course, a little higher than the levels we report. These earlier studies have, however, employed different databases and definitions and, possibly, different estimation procedures. The particular significance of the work we report here is that the 11 datasets we analysed had a largely common structure of variables and were all processed in much the same way. In at least three of them we also possessed better 'explanatory' variables, an issue we address in greater detail in a later section.

It may, of course, still be the case that the schools in each of our LEAs were relatively homogeneous in (terms of) policies and practices but, as we are dealing with very diverse authorities, the nature of those policies is likely to have been different. Yet, despite this, the 'low' level of between-school variation is a common finding. Our evidence suggests that rather than being a special feature of a single authority, the extent of school variation within an authority was, by and large, fairly 'low'. Our estimates cannot therefore be arbitrarily dismissed as 'not of special empirical importance'.

The unusual and exceptional case was LEA 2. This provides an interesting contrast to the other LEAs analysed. It may therefore provide some insight into the conditions under which any LEA might have larger than average differences between its schools.

In Table 6.2 the unadjusted between-school variances for LEA 2 were the highest recorded amongst the 11 datasets, whilst the proportions of overall variance 'explained' by pupil-level characteristics through the modelling were amongst the lowest. This particular local authority had, at the time its pupils transferred to secondary schools, retained informal selection in some areas and with respect to some schools. Another form of 'selection' was also involved in recruitment to the relatively large voluntary sector. Both conditions seem likely to have increased the differences between schools. Added to this there were very marked social differences between some of the areas administered by the LEA and each area was served by relatively small schools. In sum, we have three sets of conditions which distinguish this authority from the others in our analyses.

As the controls for pupil background in LEA 2 were relatively 'weak' it is likely that, in combination with the differentiating process described above, such conditions resulted in larger proportions of variance being attributed to 'school differences' than elsewhere.

The first, and most important, conclusion, then, to emerge from our analyses across a number of different LEAs was to confirm previous estimates of relatively low levels of between-school variance.

Differences between similar pupils in different schools

Studies of school effectiveness are primarily concerned with establishing the effects schools have in improving (or diminishing) pupils' performance. We therefore translated the somewhat arcane concept of 'between-school variation' into an expected examination points advantage (or disadvantage) for pupils attending different schools.

For this purpose we used estimates based on the interquartile range of school effectiveness scores. In general, we have found that these provide more 'robust' estimates of the differences between schools than those provided by comparisons between schools at one end of the range as opposed to the other (Gray 1989). They may also represent more realistic 'targets' for policy-makers to keep in mind when discussing the impact of such differences on pupils' life-chances.

If LEA 2 is excluded, for the reasons already identified above, the results were remarkably consistent across the different LEAs (Table 6.3). In all nine of the datasets, relating to five distinct LEAs, the advantage for a pupil attending a school at the upper, rather than the lower, quartile of effectiveness was four examination points or somewhat less. The final column of Table 6.3 expresses those differences as a percentage of a standard deviation of an individual's score on the outcome measure; in each case it was a quarter of a standard deviation or less. This was a consistent finding across all our datasets in each LEA, and hence gives us some considerable confidence about its general order of magnitude. However, it should be noted that the results provided for particular schools are subject to errors of estimation which depend, in turn, on sample sizes within individual schools and the power of the model at the level of individual pupils.

Differences of this size are not, of course, trivial. Schools 'do make a difference'. On the other hand they suggest that pupils' performance depends much less on between-school differences than some earlier (notably American) studies have implied (Gray 1989). Putting the matter into the context of GCSE examinations, pupils attending more effective schools could be expected to obtain grade enhancements from say D to B in two subjects, or an enhancement of one grade (from D to C) in four subjects compared with their counterparts in less effective schools. In a much earlier article one of us referred to differences of this size as providing pupils with a 'competitive edge' (Gray 1981a).

The range of differences in school effectiveness between the most and least effective schools was, of course, much wider; furthermore this range differed much more between LEAs (Table 6.3 and Figure 6.3). We would, however, advise caution in accepting one year's results on their own as providing good estimates of the differences between schools at the extreme ends of the range because, as Goldstein (1987) has demonstrated, schools may vary almost as much between years as between themselves. The extremes of the range are, of course, the most likely to be affected. As we have

Table 6.3 Average increments/decrements to pupils' exam scores for schools of differing effectiveness (Model 1)

LEA dataset	Effectiveness of school attended					Range	Inter quartile range*	% of pupil SD†
	Most effective	Upper quartile	Median	Lower quartile	Least effective			
1A	+5	+2	0	-2	-5	10	4	25
1B	+5	+1	0	-1	-5	10	2	13
1C	+9	+2	0	-2	-7	16	4	25
2A	+16	+4	+2	-5	-11	27	9	57
2B	+15	+4	+1	-6	-10	25	10	63
3A	+5	+2	0	-2	-4	9	4	25
3B	+3	+1	1	-1	-4	7	2	13
4	+6	+1	-1	-2	-3	9	3	19
5	+2	+1	0	-1	-1	3	2	13
6A	+4	+2	0	-2	-6	10	4	25
6B	+3	+1	0	-1	-5	8	2	13

School effects were consistent across all groups.

* This column reports the range between the upper and lower quartiles reported in the third and fifth columns. Thus a pupil who attended a school in LEA 1A that just fell into the upper quartile of effectiveness would have scored, on average, four exam points more than a pupil who attended a school in the same LEA that just fell into the lower quartile of effectiveness.

† This column expresses the interquartile range of school effects listed in the previous column as a percentage of an individual standard deviation on the exam points measure. From information available to us from the Youth Cohort Study we have established that this latter variable had a mean of approximately 21 points and a standard deviation (SD) of 16 points.

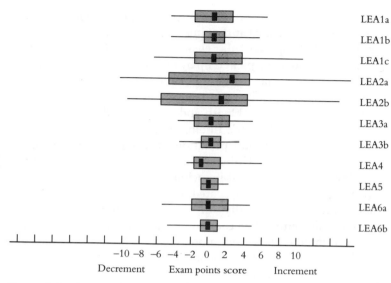

Figure 6.3 Average increments/decrements to pupils' exam scores grouped by school attended for model 1 in six LEAs.

stressed in previous chapters 'one year's results on their own are not, it would appear, a very good guide to a school's performance over time' (Gray 1989). The general thrust of this conclusion has been confirmed in an analysis of Scottish data which looked at changes in schools' performances over a 4-year gap (Willms and Raudenbush 1989).

The role of 'contextual' variables at the level of the school

A number of studies, from Coleman *et al.*'s (1966) major equality of educational opportunity (EEO) survey of equal opportunities in American schools onwards, have remarked on the potential importance of 'contextual' variables at the level of the school. Amongst the British studies Rutter *et al.* (1979), for example, reported that when pupils of apparently similar prior attainments at the point of entry attended secondary schools with differing proportions of more able pupils, those attending the schools with higher percentages of more able pupils did better in public examinations and a number of other aspects. Rutter interpreted this as evidence of the collective effects of group processes on individuals' performances. These findings were, however, criticized at the time on the grounds that they might merely be picking up particular elements of individuals' prior attainments that had not been picked up by the (relatively crude) measures of schools' intakes that had been employed; more finely differentiated measures of prior attainment might have yielded different, and less striking, results (Heath and Clifford 1981).

The debate about Rutter's findings had been paralleled in earlier controversies over the interpretation of 'compositional' effects in Coleman's EEO study. Coleman had found that, when the background characteristics (notably socio-economic and ethnic status) of individual pupils were aggregated to the level of the school, individual pupils from socially 'disadvantaged' home backgrounds appeared to do better when they attended more socially 'advantaged' (i.e. more middle class and more white) schools. Coleman also argued that these effects were evidence of the potential influence of group processes on individuals' achievements. In reanalyses of his evidence, however, a plausible case was put for suggesting that the differences that had emerged were again better explained as unmeasured aspects of pupils' backgrounds. If two children came from similar black working class backgrounds, for example, but one was sent by their parents to a racially mixed school and the other was sent to a largely black one, then the assumption that they were 'similar in all relevant respects' simply did not hold water (see, for example, Jencks *et al.* 1972; Smith 1972).

In a more recent study of Scottish secondary schools, McPherson and Willms (1986) have provided more up-to-date evidence of 'compositional' or 'contextual' effects, although their interpretation of what the effects represent differs from Coleman's. In particular they emphasize the historical traditions and status that socially advantaged schools have been seen to command over decades of Scottish educational history. These are themes which Willms explores elsewhere in a more extended and detailed discussion of what he terms the 'balance' thesis (see Willms 1985).

The substantive interpretation of data aggregated to the level of the school has been reinforced by the often quite substantial improvements to the 'fit' of regression-based statistical models which the introduction of such variables has brought about. In Rutter's study, for example, the school-level variables added almost as much to 'variance explained' as the initial variables on individual pupils had accounted for. In other studies their contribution has also been far from negligible.

The practice has been questioned on statistical grounds because it confounds two distinct 'levels' of units (pupils and schools). In a multi-level model it is possible to incorporate such a structure explicitly into the modelling process and it is this approach which we pursue here. Our datasets contained two types of explanatory data at pupil level: social background measures and measures of prior attainment. Where the former were available (see Table 6.1) we constructed an aggregated school-level variable representing the 'average social class composition' of the school; in the latter cases this variable represented the 'average prior attainment' of pupils entering the school.

When we incorporated these aggregated variables into the modelling process the effects were both dramatic and somewhat confusing (Table 6.4). The effect in the datasets for LEAs 1A and 4 inclusive was to reduce the estimated proportion of between-school variance by at least 25 per cent and in many cases by substantially more. But, by way of contrast, in the datasets for LEAs 5, 6A and 6B there were almost no detectable effects at all.

At first glance, therefore, the different datasets have produced completely contradictory results. 'Compositional' or 'contextual' variables seem to be both massively important and trivial in their effects, depending on which LEA one is exploring.

For reasons which we rehearse in greater detail in a later section we have both substantive and statistical grounds for believing that the estimates emerging from the datasets on LEAs 5, 6A and 6B may be more appropriate. In our view the evidence for strong 'compositional' or 'contextual' effects is relatively weak.

The evidence for differential effectiveness

Multi-level modelling procedures open up the possibility of asking whether schools are 'differentially effective'. Do some schools, in other words, do better in assisting particular types of pupils (the above average, for example), to achieve examination success than they do with others, and vice versa? And, if they do, is this success apparently achieved at the expense of other types of pupils?

The approach adopted by researchers prior to the recent development of multi-level models has generally assumed that schools' effectiveness could be captured by a single figure and that this figure

Table 6.4   Results of the model-fitting (Model 2)

LEA dataset	Unadjusted school variance (%)	Fixed effects (%)	(Random) school effects (%)
1A	15.2	23.0	3.3
1B	10.8	13.6	3.5
1C	12.0	15.5	5.2
2A	30.8	22.8	15.6
2B	28.9	27.3	6.5
3A	5.4	15.3	2.7
3B	6.6	13.9	0.0
4	6.2	14.3	3.0
5	7.1	54.6	1.6
6A	3.5	56.3	5.0
6B	3.7	58.1	3.6

Model 2 Fixed effects: as for Model 1 but with the entry of a composite variable. This provided a measure of school mean socio-economic background or a school mean on the available measure of prior attainment. Random effects: as for Model 1.
Column 2 Variance attributed to (random) school effects prior to controlling for pupil-level characteristics (expressed as a percentage of the overall variance).
Column 3 Variance explained by fixed part of the model (expressed as a percentage of the overall variance).
Column 4 Variance attributed to (random) school effects (expressed as a percentage of the residual variance).

applied equally to all pupils, whatever their background characteristics. Since multi-level models have become available a great deal of emphasis has been placed on the possibility of relaxing this assumption and exploring the consequences for pupils of different characteristics within the same school. Both the Inner London study (Nuttall *et al.* 1989) and Smith and Tomlinson (1989) report evidence of different effects for different pupils. In the former study the effects were most variable amongst the group of pupils whose prior attainment was highest (the Band 1 pupils). In some schools this group of pupils did quite a lot better than in others. Amongst the group of pupils whose prior attainment was lowest (the Band 3 pupils) the effects were more homogeneous. In the latter study there was also some evidence of differential effectiveness amongst pupils of both above average and below average prior attainment; although the effects were statistically significant, however, they were also relatively small.

Table 6.5 Evidence of differential slopes and the major characteristics of each dataset

LEA dataset	Number of schools	Average number of pupils per school	Prior attainment	Social class	Evidence of differential slopes
1A	40	11	No	Yes	No
1B	40	12	No	Yes	No
1C	40	26	No	Yes	No
2A	30	11	No	Yes	No
2B	30	10	No	Yes	No
3A	10	38	No	Yes	No
3B	10	44	No	Yes	No
4	20	35	No	Yes	No
5	20	54	Yes	No	No
6A	30	181	Yes	No	Yes*
6B	20	177	Yes	No	Yes†

* This result was statistically significant (2.05 × se).

† This result falls on the conventional boundary of statistical significance (1.87 × se).

In one sense our own results were very straightforward: we found little substantive evidence for 'differential slopes' in any of the datasets we analysed (Table 6.5). What is more surprising is the similarity of our findings across datasets of very different characteristics. We found this to be the case for those with large numbers of pupils in a relatively large number of schools and with prior attainment as an explanatory measure. We also found similar results with small numbers of pupils in a smaller set of schools again using prior attainment. But even in those datasets where we had relatively large, as well as relatively small, numbers of schools, where we were using pupil background characteristics as explanatory measures, the overall findings were the same; there was little evidence of 'differential slopes'.

In only one case, LEA 6, was there marginal statistical evidence in favour of the 'differential slopes' hypothesis. Even here, however, when we sought a substantive interpretation of the finding we found it made practically no difference to the assessment of schools' effects on pupils' performance; the lines crossed a bit but not very much. Figure 6.4 shows that in LEA 6A the difference of four examination score points between schools at the upper and lower quartiles of effectiveness, which we earlier established for pupils at the median level of prior attainment, was maintained for pupils of both 'lower' and 'higher' intake characteristics. For clarity the graph has been confined to those pupils whose scores fall in the middle 50 per cent (from 85 to 105) in the LEA. The score obtained by a median pupil is represented by 95. In this instance, where we had data on over 4000 pupils (i.e. virtually all of them) in a relatively large number of schools within the LEA, it might be assumed that we were looking at the upper level of precision as far as estimates for a given LEA are concerned. We have subsequently returned to Nuttall *et al.*'s (1989) study to show why their analysis may have overstated the extent of differential effectiveness (Jesson and Gray 1991).

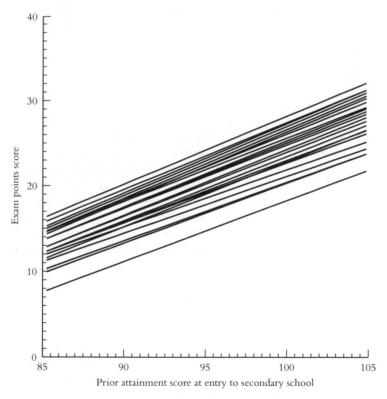

Figure 6.4　Plot of the slopes in LEA 6A showing the extent of differential effectiveness between schools.

In brief, whilst the capacity of multi-level modelling procedures to test routinely for the existence of differential slopes is an essential feature of any attempt to analyse schools' effectiveness, it should not be assumed, equally routinely, that differential effectiveness is prevalent. Most of the schools in our study seem to have had similar effects on most of their pupils.

Explanatory power: substantive and statistical issues

Our analyses confirm many of the findings of earlier studies. None the less, there have clearly been some differences, both in terms of results and their interpretation. It is worthwhile exploring some of the reasons why these may have occurred. The answers are probably both substantive and statistical.

School effectiveness studies are premised on a key assumption, namely that major differences in the intakes to different schools have been taken into account in the analysis. Although we have rarely seen it articulated in the precise way we outline below, researchers mostly agree about the relative importance and desirability of different kinds of 'explanatory' variables.

Assuming that they could arrange for the collection of the variables they wanted, rather than merely make the best use of those available, their rough order of hierarchy might go as follows:

1 At the top would be finely differentiated measures of prior attainment (say at age 11) of the same measures that were subsequently to be employed as outcome measures (say at age 16). If, for example, attainment in mathematics at 16 is of interest then the best 'intake' measure is a score on a test in mathematics at age 11. In practice, researchers frequently have to settle for approximations such as a summary score of examination results at 16 and a summary score of attainment at 11 on a (related) cognitive test (or tests). To date, very few studies indeed have had satisfactory measures of this kind available to them.

2 Next in line would come grouped measures of prior attainment for individual pupils. In the Inner London Education Authority, for example, pupils were assigned to one of three groups, based on cognitive tests, at the point of transfer to secondary schools. A complication, in this particular case, is that the three groups

were not equal in size: 25 per cent were allocated to Band 1, 50 per cent to Band 2 and the remaining 25 per cent to Band 3, which means that the score eventually attributed to individual pupils is only a rough approximation of the actual score(s) that particular pupil achieved. This was a factor to be taken into account in Rutter's earlier study (see Gray 1981b) and may well be important in interpreting the results from the ILEA study (see Nuttall *et al.* 1989).

3 Whilst there would probably be fairly general agreement about 1 and 2 above, there is not quite the same consensus amongst researchers about the next-most-desirable strategies to adopt. One frequently adopted approach is to collect information on pupils' social backgrounds. Most, but not all, of the Scottish studies have used these kinds of measures and they have the advantage that they are independent of the effects of teaching provided by schools. Parental background may affect the kind of school a pupil attends but the school's effects are unlikely to influence the parents' background.

The main problem with social background measures is that they are not usually very finely differentiated. Two pupils who are both recorded in the data as 'middle class' may, none the less, differ in various other important respects. One, for example, may have parents who take deliberate steps to get them into a particular kind of school with a strong orientation towards maximizing exam achievement; another may not. The overwhelming desirability of employing prior attainment measures whenever possible, in preference to social background measures, is underlined by one of the Scottish datasets where both kinds of measures were available (see Willms and Raudenbush 1989). The former variables dominated the modelling exercise.

Another strategy quite frequently adopted by researchers is to administer a so-called 'test of ability' at or near the time when the outcome measures themselves are being collected (see, for example, Blakey and Heath 1988). This approach, in contrast to measures of social background, has the disadvantage that it cannot be assumed to be independent of the schools' influence; the school which boosts pupils' exam achievements may also be boosting their performance on the tests of attainment or ability as well. It is unlikely that the school can influence the one and not the other, whatever the proponents of so-called 'ability' measures maintain.

4 Measures of the pupils' social or cognitive characteristics aggregated to the level of the school lag some way behind the above measures in terms of their desirability. An LEA might, for example, have calculated the percentage of pupils on free school meals or know what proportion of pupils entered a school with 'below average' reading scores, as a result of some screening exercise. Obviously, such measures are the more worthwhile, the more they relate to the particular pupils whose outcome measures have been the focus of interest. Often the main function of the existence of such data is to signal the possibility of establishing individual-level records without actually providing them at the time of analysis as noted in Chapter 5. A variety of such measures may be found in an earlier review by Gray (1981a).

5 Finally, there are measures of the characteristics of the neighbourhoods in which particular schools are located, drawn from the Census and similar surveys. Measures of this kind have often been assembled by LEAs because they can be obtained without making demands on schools; they are the kinds of measures that the Task Group on Assessment and Testing (DES 1988b) recommended LEAs create to aid the interpretation of results from national attainment testing. However, these are generally the least useful for studying particular schools as they rarely relate to the actual pupils to be found in each school. Pupils attend schools outside their neighbourhoods; schools in particular areas draw pupils from (much) further afield; some pupils do not attend state schools at all; and the nature of whole areas can change between one census and the next.

In the present study we possessed information of types (1) and (3) above. As a direct consequence we were able to reconstruct our data in the form of (2) as well. In general, we found that our data behaved much as would have been predicted from knowledge of previous studies. The simple correlations between individual pupils' social background characteristics and their fifth-year examination results were around 0.35 (ranging from around 0.3 to around 0.4) and for measures of prior attainment and examination results the correlation was around 0.7. These estimates are well within the range of earlier studies.

If the reasoning outlined in points (1) to (3) above is accepted, however, then there are good reasons for placing greater emphasis on the results emerging from the datasets for LEAs 5, and 6A and 6B; in each case a finely differentiated measure of prior attainment was available (see Tables 6.1 and 6.2). There was a fair measure of consistency in the ways the data in these three datasets behaved but they were also the datasets that most strongly challenged some of the findings of earlier research. Amongst other things they yielded:

- estimates of the variation between schools that were at the lower end;
- weak (or non-existent) evidence for 'compositional' or 'contextual' effects;
- little evidence of differential effectiveness across schools for sub-groups of pupils.

The substantive discussion outlined above indicates that, depending on the types of controls for intake that are employed, very different answers about the relative importance of between-school differences can be obtained. This view is reinforced by the statistical evidence. As the third column in Table 6.2 demonstrates, the amount of overall variation between pupils in results that can be 'explained' by social background factors varied between about 10 and 20 per cent; the equivalent figures for models incorporating measures of prior attainment, in contrast, 'explained' getting on for 60 per cent. The proportion of variance in the outcome measure which remains 'unexplained' is then apportioned (in the two-level model) to variance which lies 'between schools'. It is this latter estimate which has been presented in column 4 of Table 6.2, where the 'between-schools' variance ranges from about 1 to 5 per cent in the models incorporating prior attainment measures, and from about 4 to 25 per cent in those including just social background measures.

Focusing on the 'between-schools' variance can be useful in so far as it has concentrated attention directly on the potential effects of schools on pupils' performance. However, there has been a tendency, in some recent multi-level analyses, to ignore to some extent the underlying 'goodness of fit' of the fixed part of the model, and this can be misleading. As our discussion has already shown, the underlying explanatory power of the variables that are used to control for differences in schools' intakes can be crucial to the kinds of conclusions that are drawn. In brief, estimates of schools' effects need to be seen in the context of the total variance in the outcome measures as well.

Implications for policy and practice

A number of lessons may be drawn from the research reported here, both for the development of policy and for the implementation of practice.

The first, and most important, relates to the creation of strategies for maintaining records on individual pupils. Without such procedures any attempts to foster more appropriate frameworks for the evaluation of school performance will founder.

The second concerns the data that are gathered to describe (and model) schools' intakes. The analyses reported here underline the value of obtaining data on the prior attainments of individual pupils; data on their social backgrounds can provide an important supplement, when prior attainment data are already available, but are unlikely to prove an adequate substitute.

The development of national attainment testing will potentially aid both these concerns, provided that LEAs take steps now to build suitable frameworks for the collection of the resultant data and their subsequent interpretation.

Third, we believe LEAs will need to give some attention to the ways in which they analyse and report their schools' results. The focus should be on the 'progress' made and the schools' contribution to that progress. In particular, it will be necessary for them to test whether schools are differentially effective with pupils of different prior attainments. Only by providing firmly based and realistic estimates of the extent of prevailing differences in schools' effectiveness (as well as their effects on particular subgroups of pupils) will they be able to counter the more extreme (and often 'raw') results that are frequently injected into public debates by the media and others. If schools are to be protected from inappropriate comparisons, then their LEAs need to be able not only to assert that 'schools make a difference' but to indicate by how much.

In our interactions with policy-makers and practitioners over the years we have frequently heard it asserted that sophisticated analyses of schools' performance are beyond the means and capabilities of most LEAs and their schools, even if they wanted to undertake them. We would merely remind them that this discussion stands as testimony to the possibilities.

PART 3

*THE CONTRIBUTION
OF SCHOOL INSPECTION
TO SCHOOL
IMPROVEMENT*

7

INSPECTION AND SCHOOL IMPROVEMENT: RHETORIC AND EXPERIENCE FROM THE BRIDGE

Introduction

We have entered a period in which inspection of schools' activities is to occur on a hitherto unknown scale. Every school in the country is to be inspected once every 4 years. The resulting 'evidence', it is maintained, will simultaneously inform parental choice, hold schools accountable and provide an agenda for school improvement.

It is to the third of these concerns that this third section of the book is particularly addressed. How, if at all, will this unprecedented flood of evaluative activities impact upon schools' development? To understand something of its potential we must look both at its antecedents and at more recent events.

The HMI experience

At the centre of any account of the impact of inspection must be some assessment of the role of Her Majesty's Inspectorate (HMI). That HMI have been influential is undoubtedly the case. Indeed, historians may one day note that they were so influential on the national stage that they were disbanded. We know something about their involvement in government policy-making (see, for example, Lawton and Gordon 1987). Their various annual and national reports have also clearly attracted attention. Occasionally there have been *causes célèbres* regarding individual schools which have brought their activities to public notice. And, once in a while, individual headteachers have expressed somewhat sceptical views after inspections of their own schools (see, for example, Barnes 1983). Unfortunately, however, we lack a good account of HMI's mundane, everyday interactions with particular schools. It is in this latter respect that they are most likely to have 'improved' the performance of individual institutions.

Writing about the activities of HMI at the end of the 1970s, former HMSCI Sheila Browne noted that just under half HMI's total time was spent in institutions. They divided their time roughly equally between two activities. Half was employed 'talking briefly with teachers and senior staff about the work that had been seen and recording this in the appropriate institutional file. Anything of particular strength, novelty or weakness was explored with a view to generalisation, development or remedy.' For the other half 'reporting was more formal and the outcome more identifiable and perhaps more durable, although not necessarily more useful' (Browne 1979: 41).

Writing about the potential of inspection Browne commented:

> ... intimate acquaintance with institutions and teachers has never been more than relative. *However frequent their visits, HMI have always had to remember that their selective observation can never match the collective knowledge of the head and teachers*; it is they, after all, who day by day with their pupils are and make a school or college. Even the so-called full inspection, developed particularly for use in secondary grammar schools and still used with suitable variations in a wide variety of special cases today, is 'full' only in the sense that the school is considered as a whole and a broadly-based team of inspectors together sample all that is there to be seen at the time. A full inspection provides a detailed action snapshot which should give a fair indication of future performance and promise. *The discussion surrounding the setting up of the cameras and the resulting picture may well be conducive to improvement. But it has to be recognised that circumstances*

change and latent resources may lie unrevealed. A full inspec-
tion report is never the last word.

(Browne 1979: 37, our emphases)

The focus of Browne's account (written in an era when reports were not available to the public) was on the accountability of HMI so it is not very surprising that improvement *per se* fails to feature prominently. The reports are intended, she argues, to 'serve the interests not only of the Secretary of State but of the teachers in the institutions, the governing body, the administrators in the local education authority or other providing body, and elected members of education committees. Skilled readers . . . learn to take what they require from an individual document' (Browne 1979: 42).

An alternative approach: inspectors based in schools

During the mid-1980s the ILEA set up the IBIS (Inspectors Based in Schools) project (Hargreaves 1990). The IBIS teams tried to take a systematic view of how school improvement might be fostered, and this was deliberately reflected in the procedures they adopted. They usually worked in schools that were recognized to be in need of 'improvement'. Their experiences provide an alternative perspective on how 'inspection' activities might be organized. They also challenge some prevailing assumptions about the most appropriate sequencing of the 'stages' in an inspection.

A fuller account of the IBIS approach has been provided by one of the IBIS inspectors (Jenkins 1987). The first phase (pre-entry) was very similar to that of HMI, involving the collection of a good deal of information from school and extra-school sources. The second phase seems to have been more concerned, however, to share the agenda with schools to 'allow staff to feel fully prepared and to reduce anxiety'.

During the third and fourth phases, after a set period of data-gathering and diagnosis, the team would withdraw from the school to 'write their initial findings, which were presented as a series of discussion documents . . . the whole-school report focused on whole-school issues such as aims, ethos, school policies, management and administration, curriculum and assessment. Examples of good practice and areas of concern were indicated.' At this stage the documents were kept confidential and not presented formally to governors; the main emphasis was on 'building agreement amongst the staff about priorities for school-focused INSET' (Jenkins 1987: 4). At the same time the whole-school report was complemented by specialist reports which also had the status of discussion documents. These too were used by individual inspectors to 'highlight good practice and identify specific areas of concern from which to negotiate priorities for action and strategies for change' (Jenkins 1987: 4).

The fifth phase was a developmental one of variable length, 'depending on the needs of the school'; it offered the inspectors the opportunity 'to be involved in an intensive period of school-focused and school-based INSET brought about by their evaluation of the school'. INSET was designed to promote a wide variety of activities including: team building, role clarification and self-evaluation, collaboration on the preparation of syllabuses, schemes of work and teaching materials, devising assessment strategies, organizing visits to centres of good practice, providing exemplar materials and exhibitions, raising awareness of institutional factors affecting equal opportunities and the curriculum in general, 'team teaching and the analysis of the decision-making and consultation systems' (Jenkins 1987: 5). Throughout this phase regular meetings were held amongst the IBIS team to enable them to develop 'an organic model which assists in identifying the barriers to whole-school change'.

The sixth phase involved evaluation and comment by the school staff on their interactions with the IBIS team and marked the end of the team's formal involvement in the school.

It was only after the team's withdrawal from the school that the final, formal report was produced. This included: the initial whole-school discussion document, summaries of the specialist reports, details of the developmental phase, work-in-progress in the school, indications of future developments and an evaluation of the IBIS team's involvement. The overall report was based on both staff and IBIS perceptions and it was this final report which was formally presented to the school's governors.

Moves towards monitoring and evaluation as a strategy

The demise of the ILEA in the late 1980s meant that the consequences of the IBIS approach for school improvement could never be fully established. Other LEAs, however, in the years following the Education Reform Act (1988) were increasingly involved in the development of systematic approaches to the monitoring and evaluation of their schools.

Early in 1992 we surveyed all LEAs in England and Wales to determine the pattern and prevalence of these approaches for the previous school year (Wilcox *et al.* 1993). We found that in the 2 years or so following the 1988 Act there had been a significant increase in the amount of school evaluation undertaken by the majority of LEAs. This increase was almost entirely due to the adoption of one or other forms of inspection. Although the proportion of schools undergoing a full inspection in 1990–1 was small, nevertheless just over one-fifth of LEAs carried out some form of substantial inspection in at least one-fifth of both their primary and secondary schools.

Further analysis of the results of our survey indicated that LEAs tended to favour the involvement of school staff in the various aspects of the inspection process. As Table 7.1 shows, just over a quarter of LEAs claimed that their schools had 'considerable' involvement in determining what was to be inspected. A similar proportion involved schools in the collection of data, although this was almost certainly mainly the bringing together of school documentation and statistics. In a minority of LEAs school staff also participated in: determining how to inspect, analysing inspection data, and deciding the content and recommendations of inspection reports. Overall then the picture was one in which the line between those carrying out inspections and those experiencing them was somewhat blurred.

The involvement of school staff in the inspection process is also mirrored by the involvement of inspectors in the aftermath of inspections. Maychell and Keys (1993) found that the majority of LEAs (64 of the 80 in their study) followed up inspections with advice, and almost as many (62) said they normally held discussions with the head/staff to review progress on implementing the inspection's recommendations.

At the very least, the tacit assumption behind such involvement is that inspections should lead to school improvement. Perhaps surprisingly, little or no research has been done to test this assumption. The introduction of radically new arrangements for the inspection of schools arising from the Education (Schools) Act (1992) had the effect *inter alia* of raising the volume of school inspections

Table 7.1   Involvement by LEA of school staff in inspection activities

Aspect of inspection	Degree of involvement			
	None/ minimal	*Some*	*Considerable*	*Not answered*
What to be inspected	28	41	27	4
How to be inspected	54	34	7	5
Collecting data	19	53	24	4
Analysing data	75	13	4	8
Content and recommendations of report	52	32	11	5

Questionnaire to all English and Welsh LEAs (*n* = 100).

considerably. From Autumn 1993 all schools were to be inspected once every 4 years. In place of the former practice of 'inspection in all its forms', a standardized full inspection model has been developed by the new Office for Standards in Education (OFSTED). A major aim of the new arrangements is proclaimed to be the improvement of schools (OFSTED 1993a). The issue, therefore, of whether inspections do have such an effect is one of considerable significance.

We have had the opportunity of addressing this issue in our ESRC-funded project 'Programmes For Assessing the Quality of Schooling' (PAQS). This enabled us to examine different LEA approaches to the evaluation of schools through surveys, studies of individual inspections and interviews with LEA chief inspectors. We were also, incidentally, able to study the last phases of the so-called former inspection 'monopoly', at least as conducted by LEA inspectorates, as they moved into the new market of independent inspection teams. In what follows we review some of the evidence drawn from our chief inspector interviews in order to explore some of the conditions associated with improvement through school inspection.

Interest in monitoring and evaluating schools' performances at local level is by no means confined to this country but has begun to assume greater significance worldwide. In their pioneering study of Canadian school districts Coleman and Larocque (1990) identified a number of features of the more successful ones. Amongst the strategies officers adopted to raise performance were: efforts to generate a productive ethos, the negotiation of a 'master contract' which determined what schools were to be about and the offering of 'leadership' on instructional issues. Activities connected with monitoring and evaluation also featured prominently in the accounts. The impact of these was mediated, however, by a parallel concern to generate professional commitments to change and adaptation and the 'co-production of learning'. In brief, the more successful school districts took responsibility not merely for judging performance but for enhancing it.

Inspection and improvement – the views of chief inspectors

As part of the PAQS study we identified a panel of 22 chief inspectors from a stratified random sample (approximately one in five) of all LEAs in England and Wales. The chief inspectors were interviewed individually on three separate occasions over a 2-year period from January 1992. Semi-structured interviews were carried out, each lasting up to an hour, and were tape-recorded. The interviews explored a series of interlocking themes concerned with the development, the rationale, and the approach to inspection in their LEA. Amongst the themes addressed in the first and second interviews was the relationship between inspection and school improvement.

During the first interview the inspectors were asked to identify the aspects of inspection which they associated with the subsequent improvement of schools. All of the aspects identified were found to be capable of grouping under one or more of six broad factors. These are summarized in Table 7.2, both as the number of individual aspects suggested and the number of inspectors suggesting them. As can be seen the factors given decrease in frequency in the following order: (1) features of the inspection/review process; (2) partnership and collaboration; (3) support and follow-up; (4) characteristics of school staff; (5) characteristics of inspectors; and (6) context.

In the second interview we attempted to obtain a more specific focus on the improvement issue by asking our sample of chief inspectors and advisers to describe to us two recent inspections or reviews. Between them they described experiences relating to 44 schools. In choosing the examples we asked them first to describe an occasion

Table 7.2 Factors associated with school improvement as identified by chief inspectors

Nature of factor	No. of chief inspectors	No. of separate aspects
Aspects of the inspection/review process	20	56
Partnership/collaboration	15	28
Support and follow-up	9	18
Characteristics of school staff	7	9
Characteristics of inspectors	5	8
Context	2	2

Interviews with chief inspectors and advisers ($n = 22$).

on which the inspection or review of a school had not gone well and 'had probably not contributed to school improvement'; then we asked them to describe one where things had gone better and where the inspection or review process 'had probably contributed to school improvement'. It should be stressed, of course, that we were in the hands of our panel members as regards the selection of 'cases' for discussion. Consequently the account of key factors that we were able to derive from them, whilst being located in detailed evidence about specific schools, was based solely on their side of the story. In more recent work we have looked at some of the claims in greater detail and from other perspectives (see Chapter 10). The analyses reported here should, therefore, be regarded as tentative at this stage.

All of the aspects identified in the inspectors' accounts could be grouped under one or more of the same six factors which emerged from the first set of interviews. In this case, however, it was possible to analyse separately those factors inhibiting and supporting the impact of inspection and review activities on school improvement as viewed by those who have had overall responsibility for their organization (Table 7.3).

Factors inhibiting the improvement process

The panel members' accounts of factors inhibiting the improvement process fell mainly into three areas. These were to do with: (1) characteristics of the school staff; (2) characteristics of the inspectors; and (3) the inspection/review process itself.

Table 7.3 Factors identified by chief inspectors as inhibiting or facilitating improvement based on specific inspections of schools

Nature of factor	Inhibiting improvement	Facilitating improvement
Aspects of the inspection/review process	6	7
Partnership/collaboration	2	8
Support and follow-up	1	11
Characteristics of school staff	10	5
Characteristics of inspectors	7	2
Context	3	1

Interviews with chief inspectors and advisers ($n = 20$).

Two notes of caution are necessary in reviewing the data. First, given that the method of questioning was open-ended, one cannot infer too readily that because something was not mentioned it did not occur. In the analyses that follow, reference is confined to the broad proportions of inspectors in the panel study where a factor emerged from the accounts offered. Second, no inferences at all are possible from these data about the general incidence of inspections going well or badly, either within particular LEAs or across them.

In the accounts offered by chief inspectors, the attitudes and responses of headteachers and other senior management staff were central to the process. Just under half the panel members made comments in this area.

Not surprisingly, there were reports of headteachers being 'defensive' and 'feeling threatened'. In one LEA, a headteacher perceived as sexist, faced with a wholly female inspection team, fought them 'tooth and nail'. In another, the view from the panel member was that the headteacher 'lived by the seat of his pants'. It was clear in many of the LEAs that a measure of commitment was required for the process to work and that this could be jeopardized by an 'unenthusiastic' or 'uncommitted' head or deputy. An 'obdurate' or 'evasive' head could frustrate the process whilst inspectors were collecting evidence in the school or by 'not playing the game'.

Later on in the cycle, when it came to taking the report to the governing body and acting on the recommendations, a head might be 'unenthusiastic', 'obstructive' or 'possibly subversive', attempting in one way or another to 'discredit the report'. What was at issue was the school's 'openness to criticism and ability to move forward'.

It is easy enough to blame schools when things go wrong. Around a third of the panel, however, blamed the members of their own inspectorates. There were doubts about: the 'confidence and competence' of particular advisers; they simply lacked 'expertise' or they were too new in their posts to have had time to get to know the context of the school they were inspecting. In another case insufficient guidance had been given by the inspectorate's management about how to proceed.

Relationships between inspectors and between inspectors and schools also featured prominently. Problems had arisen, in one case, before an inspection had begun because the inspectors had not put in enough time to ensure that they 'shared common standards'. During one inspection there had been a 'lack of communication between the two (main) inspectors involved'. In another LEA the 'tone of some advisers' had left something to be desired, whilst in yet another there had simply been 'a breakdown in the relationship between the headteacher and the adviser'.

Just over a quarter of the panel members also mentioned factors to do with the inspection/review process itself. Again these can be regarded as matters which were essentially under their own control. In one case there was a lack of clarity about the procedures with respect to reporting to governors. There were several comments about the process being under pressure of time. One described the review as 'rushed'; another talked of 'over-optimism about what could be tackled' in the time available; whilst another referred to an 'inadequate debriefing of the headteacher' at the end of the process. There were also difficulties at the stage of writing-up. One LEA had simply found the final report 'difficult to write' and, in another, these difficulties had led to a 'long delay in publishing'.

A number of other factors were identified as inhibiting the impact of the process by a minority of LEAs. Three LEAs, for example, mentioned factors to do with the context within which the inspection/review had taken place. One remarked on the 'absence of an evaluation culture in the school and community'; another on the school's absence of 'previous experience of inspections'; and a third on the 'influence a negative review had (previously) had on a sister school'.

Factors facilitating the improvement process

The factors identified as facilitating improvement fell into four areas: (1) partnership and collaboration; (2) the inspection/review process itself; (3) support and follow-up; and (4) the characteristics of school staff.

Over a third of the panel members mentioned the efforts their LEAs had made to build a sense of partnership and collaboration for the inspection process. Joint planning had been undertaken with the schools a number of months previously so there was 'a lot of common ground to start with'. There had been 'clear negotiations' and 'consultations' about what was to take place and the construction of a 'joint brief for inspection'.

Considerable attention had been paid to developing mutual trust and respect between the school adviser(s) and the school staff. Major emphasis was given to 'support as opposed to accountability' in order to 'prepare a school to look at a focus causing concern' or to help a staff to 'accept the credibility of the findings'. 'Honesty and openness' were perceived as central ingredients in this process. LEA teams had had to work hard to get themselves perceived as 'supportive and helpful'. The nurturing of 'staff involvement' was seen as a guiding principle in these activities. Pervading all these responses was a sense that the most appropriate relationships and skills are those of the consultant rather than the outsider.

About a third of the panel commented on aspects of the inspection/ review process. 'Pre-planning', 'precise contracting' and a 'clear framework of procedures' were seen as important means through which the commitment to improvement could begin to be generated.

There were comparatively few comments about the mechanisms of the data collection phase. One LEA mentioned that the inspectors needed to be 'rigorous in collecting the evidence and sticking to their guns'. Another emphasized the importance of 'focusing on pupil achievement'; what mattered was 'what pupils had learned rather than what teachers had done'. The same LEA also talked of the efforts it had made to ensure that there was a 'strong protocol [amongst its inspectors] to see the totality of teaching events'.

Several comments were also made about the reporting-back stage. Particular attention was given at the 'drafting stage to the major issues for oral feedback'. There was concern to write the final report so that the 'school could go forward whilst, at the same time, indicating that progress had been made from a low baseline' and to 'nurture the green shoots in a school at risk whilst still being honest'. In these comments there was a recognition that this was a crucial stage of the proceedings where a school's capacity for improvement could be developed or inhibited.

About half the panel drew attention to aspects of support and follow-up in the post-inspection phase. Particular emphasis was laid on formal and targeted provision of in-service activities and the making available of advisory teacher support. The importance of informal but intensive work with headteachers by inspectors and advisers was mentioned; this work was usually undertaken by the school adviser. One LEA reported having developed a system of 'minders', which involved a heavier inspector presence after an inspection had shown a school to be in particular difficulty.

Follow-up also took place in a number of other ways. There was formal monitoring of progress after inspection, including the setting of targets. 'Without follow-up the review would have had little impact.' Schools were encouraged to include recommendations in their action plans; and sometimes they were given extra resources to encourage such developments. A few LEAs also reported having procedures for longer-term follow-up as much as 12 months later.

Discussion

What status and significance can be ascribed to the six factors which have tentatively emerged from the above account? Do they, for example, represent possible components of a model of 'improvement through inspection'? In seeking answers to this question it may be helpful to assess the factors against considerations arising from three perspectives: a logical analysis of the inspection–improvement process; the requirements of the new inspection arrangements; and key findings from research on school effectiveness.

The status of the evidence as the basis for action

If inspection is to lead to improvement then there would seem to be several necessary conditions to meet. First, the outcomes of the inspection report would need to be accepted by most (or many of) the school staff. An inspection report typically sets out the strengths and weaknesses of a school. In other words it represents an account of the effectiveness of a school – an account, moreover, which implicitly claims to be 'true'. Where such an account corresponds to the general view of school staff, and particularly of senior staff, there may be few difficulties. If, however, inspectors and staff differ significantly in their views of the school it is likely that attention will be focused on the inspection process. Staff will need to be convinced that the methods used to collect and interpret information about the school were the 'right' ones. In conventional research terms, they will need to be persuaded of the validity and reliability of the methods employed. Although we see some references to the inspection *process* in our chief inspectors' accounts, these tend to emphasize the importance of clarity and precision of procedures generally and the logistical requirements of the feedback and reporting process.

The inspection handbook (OFSTED 1993b) sets out in detail the nature of the evaluation criteria inspectors are to take account of and the kinds of evidence they are to collect. It is assumed that the requirements of reliability and validity will be met by ensuring that inspectors' judgements 'are consistent with the evaluation criteria . . . and that they accurately reflect the standards which are actually achieved' (OFSTED 1993b: 6). The handbook assumes tacitly that this is an unproblematic business. This is unlikely to be the case, as the criteria proposed are in the nature of very general statements, which are far from being transparently unambiguous. Nowhere in the handbook is there any indication of how the substantial amount of evidence obtained by multiple collectors is actually analysed and transformed into specific judgements which guarantee reliability and validity. It would seem that inspectors are to continue to neglect a dilemma which lies at the centre of the inspection process – the failure to address the complexity and challenge represented by the data analysis task (see Wilcox 1992). This is, however, an issue which the recipients of inspection – the teachers – are likely to take very seriously indeed, particularly as schools now have access to the inspection handbook.

Establishing some conditions for implementation

Acceptance of the report by staff will not in itself guarantee that changes will occur to improve the school. A second condition to be met, therefore, is that the findings or recommendations of the report will need to be translated into a strategy for effective implementation. Schools are likely to differ in their collective ability to carry out this important task and some assistance may therefore be required. The views of our panel suggest that the provision of support and development is, indeed, associated with successful post-inspection outcomes. Another requirement is the willingness of staff to engage in change – a characteristic which was identified in our study and one particularly associated with headteachers.

In the OFSTED era, advice and follow-up to an inspection report are likely to be less easy for an LEA to provide than formerly. There are several reasons for this. As a consequence of financial stringency some LEAs have had to face reductions in their inspect-orate and advisory services, and may therefore be unable to deploy suitable staff for this purpose. Even where this is not the case, the delegation of funding under Local Management of Schools (LMS) means that LEAs are increasingly dependent on the schools to buy back such services. In addition, although the governing bodies of schools are required to draw up an action plan following an inspec-tion, they are under no obligation to seek assistance with this, or with its subsequent implementation, from the LEA or indeed anyone else. If, moreover, particular inspectors do provide support and follow-up then they are likely to be precluded from bidding for future inspection contracts for these selfsame schools. This is because inspection teams have to demonstrate their independence by remain-ing free of any close connection with schools they seek to inspect. Prior involvement in advising would be regarded as jeopardizing the inspectors' independence.

The general assumption is that by properly implementing an appropriate action plan a school is thereby improved. In so far as the weaknesses identified by the inspection were subsequently remedied then improvement can be said to have occurred. This will be the case, however, only if the 'correct' weaknesses were identified in the first place. How are we to tell? The construction of an inspection report is based on a generally implicit notion of what constitutes a 'good' school. The inspection handbook reflects such a notion in terms of two main aspects. First, there is the way the school is con-ceptualized as an entity. The handbook sees the school in terms of a performance model in which the key categories are 'standards and quality', 'efficiency', 'pupils' personal development and behaviour', and 'subjects of the curriculum'. Each of these categories is further subdivided. Second, there are the criteria, already referred to, which effectively define the categories and subcategories. Many of the main criteria are outlined further in terms of contrasting vignettes repre-senting a 'good' example and an 'unsatisfactory' one. The inspection model is also quasi-causal in that a key element (and a key section of the subsequent report) identifies a series of factors which are considered to contribute to the inspection findings.

The search for the characteristics of 'good' (or more commonly termed 'effective') schools has been a major research concern in recent years (see Reynolds and Cuttance 1992). One of the common findings of this research has been the emphasis given to leadership and, in particular, the role of the headteacher; this is something to which several of our panel members would also attest. The relationship between school inspection, school effectiveness and school improvement is worthy of further exploration. How far inspection approaches have been influenced by research is a moot point. Certainly one chief inspector claimed that the LEA's own inspection criteria had, in fact, been based on the findings of school effectiveness research.

The acid test of a school's improvement is, of course, that the learning experience of pupils is enhanced and their achievements increased. Convincing demonstration of the latter is likely to prove difficult. One of our inspectors claimed that the examination results of a particular department had improved dramatically from a 30 to a 40 per cent A–C GCSE pass rate to one of 60 per cent following an inspection and follow-up – the intake not being different from previous years. The evidence in this case did not, however, stretch to the whole school; many others interviewed felt unable to offer such specific evidence.

The emphasis given by our inspectors to collaboration and partnership becomes perhaps a less appropriate potential condition in future inspections. The inspection model now excludes the involvement of school staff in any of the inspection activities listed in Table 7.1. The distinction between the inspector and the inspected will be sharply maintained.

A potential benefit of the OFSTED system is that all inspectors will have been trained by HMI in the procedures for organizing and carrying out inspections. As a result, some of the problems associated with the factor 'characteristics of inspectors' concerned with competence, confidence and communication are likely to be minimized. The inclusion in the Handbook of a 'code of conduct for inspectors' may also help to reduce the personal frictions which can sometimes arise between inspectors and teachers.

Looking to the future

Our study of the views of chief inspectors throws some light on the crucial issue of inspection and school improvement. Some further points of reservation, however, need to be made. We are not suggesting that the factors which were identified are necessarily the most important ones, or even that they are discrete entities. Almost certainly they are not. For example, the factor concerned with the inspection process itself is undoubtedly capable of more detailed analysis than we have given to it. The perspective provided here is essentially one-sided, with chief inspectors reflecting, at a distance, on inspections in which they may not have been fully involved themselves. It is a perspective 'from the bridge' so to speak by those influential in determining the inspection approaches in LEAs and is therefore important for that reason alone. But how do schools and teachers react to inspections? And do inspections actually achieve what their proponents claim? They have emerged as a central vehicle for facilitating (and enforcing) school improvement in recent years. But is this confidence in their efforts really justified? It is to such issues that we turn in Chapters 8 and 10.

8

REACTIONS TO INSPECTION: A STUDY OF THREE VARIANTS

Introduction

Despite the heightened interest in inspection in recent years it has remained a relatively under-researched area of educational activity. The little research there is has generally been concerned with three aspects of inspection. First, several surveys of local education authorities (LEAs) have been carried out (Nebesnuick 1991; Maychell and Keys 1993; Wilcox *et al.* 1993) which have shown something of the range of inspection approaches adopted and their prevalence in practice. Second, some attempts have been made to examine the nature of inspectors' judgements. Gray and Hannon (see Chapter 3) looked at the extent to which Her Majesty's Inspectorate (HMI) contextualized the references made in its reports to the examination results of individual schools. Elliott and Ebbutt (1986), also using HMI reports, were concerned with the criteria employed in inspections. This focus of enquiry has been extended more recently by Nixon and Rudduck (1993) to LEA inspectors. They have explored, through interviews, the implicit and explicit criteria involved in making judgements on schools. Third, there has been the occasional study of an individual inspection. For

example, Barnes (1983, 1984) has described, from his perspective
as a secondary headteacher, the experience of having undergone an
HMI 'full inspection'. Miles (1982), a teacher in a secondary school
which also underwent such an inspection, was able to interview
a sample of the staff about their reactions to the process. He noted
that the inspection generally reinforced confidence in existing practices although there was disappointment that few new insights were
produced.

This chapter is concerned with the last of these three areas. We
believe that a wider range of studies by external researchers is
needed in order to understand better how different kinds of inspection may affect individual schools and teachers. An important part
of our research project is a study of over 20 inspections of both
primary and secondary schools across some half-dozen LEAs. The
LEAs were chosen originally to explore the effects of different
approaches to the inspection and evaluation of schools. The passing
of the 1992 Education (Schools) Act, requiring a radical replacement of existing inspection agencies by new 'independent' teams, in
the early months of the project's life had an inevitable effect on our
LEAs and their approaches to inspection. If the LEAs were to compete successfully for inspection contracts under the new arrangements of the Office for Standards in Education (OFSTED), they
needed to adjust their existing arrangements to conform to the 'full
inspection' model which would become the norm. An unanticipated
aspect of the project has therefore been the opportunity to observe
that adjustment taking place.

Three cases of inspection

We have selected for consideration a primary school inspection
from each of three LEAs. The inspections took place over the period
May 1992 to January 1993. Each inspection reflected a different
approach. Although one of the three was designated a 'self-
evaluation' we use the generic term 'inspection' throughout both for
ease of reference and because, as we shall see later, there was a
tendency for the teachers to perceive it as a kind of inspection. We
have chosen primary inspections to examine here because most of
what is known of inspection has related to secondary schools, and
because primary schools, being less complex organizations, may

show some of the effects of inspection more clearly than secondary schools.

The three inspections have been specifically selected because they reflect variation in several potentially significant ways:

- the degree of negotiation allowed to the school in determining the aspects to be evaluated;
- the extent of comprehensiveness of coverage;
- and conformity to the model of the new inspection arrangements.

Collecting the data

Individual, semi-structured interviews were conducted for each inspection with samples of teachers and inspectors. The samples included the headteacher, the deputy headteacher and the inspection team leader. The same questions were asked of all interviewees. The aim, in essence, was to elicit individual reactions to the inspection process and its findings. Interviews usually took about 45 minutes, were tape recorded for subsequent analysis, and were carried out after the draft inspection report had been prepared and/or findings fed back to the school staff. This timing of the interviews was chosen to ensure that the teachers would all know of the general findings of the inspection. In practice this meant that interviews took place from 3 weeks to 2 months or so after the event, depending on the inspection and the ease of negotiating access and arranging interviews.

In addition, during the interviews, estimates were obtained of the time spent preparing for the inspection (attending pre-inspection meetings, studying school documentation, etc.) and contributing to the production of the draft report. These estimates, in the case of the inspectors, were extrapolated to the whole team and expressed in terms of 'inspector days'. These were then added to the number of inspector days spent in school to give a total for the inspection process as a whole.

Interviews were supplemented, where possible, by opportunities to observe the planning and the conduct of pre- and post-inspection activities.

In what follows we are not claiming that the reactions reported to us are inevitable consequences of particular forms of inspection.

Neither are we attempting a complete account of these forms. Our aim is to identify a range of issues and concerns which arise when schools undergo inspection and to see to what extent these are common to the different forms.

Inspection A

Inspection A was of a junior school situated in an inner city area of very substantial social disadvantage. The school underwent a 'self-evaluation' which was validated externally. Such evaluations, as envisaged by the LEA, involve the staff of a school planning and carrying out an evaluation using a checklist of LEA criteria. The same staff subsequently write an evaluation report in consultation with their colleagues. The school inspector carries out a sample evaluation in order to validate the school's report.

In this particular case the topic chosen by the school for evaluation was language – with reading as the specific focus. The evaluation took place over 2 days and was carried out by the school's language coordinator, the school inspector and the headteacher. It was therefore an example of an 'inspection' where there was: a very considerable degree of negotiation about the aspects to be evaluated; partial coverage, albeit focusing on an area of central importance to any primary school; lack of conformity, in any key respects, to the new arrangements.

Teachers were observed (by the inspector and coordinator visiting classrooms together, and also by the head), children's work was examined, and relevant school and teacher documents scrutinized. In addition, all teachers completed a questionnaire on the topic of reading constructed by the coordinator.

A meeting of the team involved in the evaluation activities was held in the afternoon of the second day to agree the provisional findings of the inspection. The discussion was led by the inspector and organized under the main headings of the LEA's inspection scheme – 'intentions', 'delivery', 'achievements' and 'context'. The last consisted of statistical data on the school and was provided by the head, who also added a detailed commentary. A draft report was prepared by the coordinator from notes of the meeting provided by the inspector. The final report (approximately ten pages long) included details of the inspector's validation and a proposed action plan.

In validating the evaluation report, the inspector recorded: 'The school had made careful arrangements for the conduct of the evaluation. The evidence produced by the school was of good quality. Sensible conclusions were drawn from the evidence. The proposals for development are relevant to the school's needs.'

The action plan committed the school to considering, amongst other things: the future of the existing language scheme; developing further long-term planning within the subject and across the curriculum; and enhancing liaison between the language, infant, and special educational needs coordinators.

Inspection B

Inspection B involved an infant–junior school situated in a mixed residential area. About a quarter of the pupils were from (mainly Asian) ethnic minority groups. The inspection took place over 2 days and involved a team of four inspectors.

The foci for the inspection were agreed between the headteacher and the inspectors. These were: English, mathematics, science, technology and four whole-school issues (special educational needs, equal opportunities, assessment and recording, social and cultural development). Although a 'part inspection', it covered several major aspects of the curriculum and organization of the school.

Inspection methods included classroom observation, examination of pupils' work and informal discussion with teachers and pupils. The inspection team also decided to use for the first time some aspects of the Framework of the new inspection arrangements (OFSTED, 1992b), including the classroom observation procedure.

The 13-page inspection report followed in some respects the format required by the new Framework. For example, the categories of 'standards of achievement', 'quality of teaching', and 'quality of learning' were used to organize the comments made under each of the curriculum subject headings. However, the LEA convention was retained of allowing the head the opportunity of appending comments on the inspection to the final page of the report.

The report praised the good relationships in the school and the behaviour of pupils. Standards of achievement were considered satisfactory. In all subjects achievement was considered to be higher in those attainment targets concerned with knowledge than those with process. Pupils worked hard and made progress although some under-achievement was noted especially for able pupils. There was also some imbalance in the time spent on each of the National Curriculum subjects. The tight space in the school could also have been used better.

Although no explicit action plan was required the inspectors envisaged that the school would draw on its entitlement of advisory teacher and in-service support to help in addressing the issues raised in the report. The staff anticipated that action would be taken, especially in mathematics and science. The head intended to take a personal lead in mathematics by following, at the suggestion of the inspector, an in-service course in the subject. In the event this responsibility was taken on by a teacher.

Inspection C

Inspection C was of an infant–junior school situated in an urban locality of considerable social disadvantage.

The school was examined as a 'full inspection' over a 4-day period by a team of four LEA inspectors. A fifth day was spent in formulating conclusions and feeding them back to the head and deputy. The inspectors had decided to follow much of the new inspection Framework, three of the team having recently attended the national training programme. This was, then, an inspection with: non-negotiable foci; comprehensive coverage and close conformity to the new Framework.

The methods used in the inspection included classroom observation, examination of pupils' work and school and teacher documentation, as well as formal interviews with head and staff.

A 29-page report was produced in accordance with the format laid down in the new Framework, although in greater detail than will be expected with the new inspection arrangements for primary schools.

The report praised the high value placed on the spiritual, social and moral development of the pupils and the consequent good relationships which existed within the school. Despite this, however, the inspection team reported that, overall, the school was characterized by widespread under-achievement and poor curriculum, staff and resource management. The school was considered to be failing to give its pupils an acceptable standard of education and was therefore 'at risk'.

The inspectors had suggested that an action plan be devised and indicated that advice would be available from the school inspector and others. The head was committed to taking urgent action on the issues identified by the report and intended to ask the governors to request a further inspection in a year's time.

Reactions to the inspection findings

An inspection report implicitly claims to describe a school as it really is. For many teachers the school represents perhaps the most intimate focus of their professional identity and esteem. An inspection report of a school and its findings will, therefore, be of central importance and interest to the teachers concerned. The production of a credible account of a school is also a test of the professional expertise of the inspectors. Both groups – teachers and inspectors – therefore have a strong professional and personal investment in the outcomes of an inspection. We turn now to the reactions of teachers and inspectors to the findings of the inspection in which they were involved.

Inspection A: 'acceptance and no surprises'

Inspection A was generally felt by the teachers to have confirmed the way they were working and the developments that were already being considered – there were, as far as they were concerned, no new insights. The head was also in agreement with this view but pleased that certain issues of concern (e.g. pace of learning) had been identified. The coordinator, however, thought that the inspection had not been necessary given the school's existing review system, which it appeared to duplicate. The coordinator also expressed uncertainty as to whether it was language or reading which had been examined. This point was further elaborated by the inspector:

> One difficulty is that it is fairly easy to look at the use of reading – not as easy to look at the direct teaching of reading. We oscillated unsatisfactorily between looking at language generally and at reading in particular. I wasn't sure how far the

head had emphasised 'reading in the context of language'. It was an unresolved dilemma. In the end we might have done a better job looking solely at reading. There was a 'fuzziness' there.

However, the inspector was in no doubt as to the value of the inspection. It gave the inspector a much better opportunity to observe classrooms than would otherwise have been the case and, thereby, a better basis for discussing the development of the school with the head.

Inspection B: 'acceptance with some reservations'

In inspection B the head and staff also considered that the inspection had largely confirmed what they already knew. However, there were some surprises, at least for the head. The provision of equal opportunities had been assessed as better than expected, whilst the inspectors were more critical of the display of pupils' work than had been anticipated. Some findings were disputed. For example, the head was not convinced of the need for a special policy on equal opportunities, as this was not considered a priority.

The head's overriding criticism was that the report did not give sufficient recognition of the fact that some of the issues had already been identified by the staff and some changes had recently been made. After taking up the post the head had organized an audit of the school. This led, for the first time, to the formulation of a school development plan – the report gave no credit for this. In addition, the head felt that some judgements would not have been made had the inspectors looked more thoroughly at the planning materials available to them. Several staff suggested that the report implied that if something was not seen, then it was not happening.

The inspectors had learned a great deal about the school, the head, the staff and the curriculum. They did, however, express some reservations about the overall picture. They had failed to get a clear understanding of the use, location and management of resources. There was doubt as to whether the whole picture on continuity and progression had been obtained by looking at separate subjects.

Both inspectors and school staff were in agreement that the inspection had been valuable in reviewing the present position of the school and indicating its way forward. The inspectors expected the report to provide support for the head's ideas. According to the deputy an incidental benefit of the inspection had been to encourage staff cooperation.

Inspection C: 'disagreement and trauma'

In inspection C the head and staff accepted that some of the criticisms made were justified. Nevertheless, overall, the report was considered 'unfair', 'negative' and 'destructive'. Both the head and deputy found it difficult to accept that 'good relationships' in a school could coexist with unsatisfactory management and standards of teaching.

The deputy disagreed with the contention of low educational standards, saying that there had been no complaints from the secondary schools to which they sent their pupils. Furthermore, the school had always received trainee teachers from the local university – this was thought to be surprising if the standards were as stated.

A particular concern about the neglect of context surfaced several times in the comments of the head and deputy. 'Context' here refers to the conditions, both in the school and beyond, within which the school's work was conducted.

> Things are taken out of context and the context not reported – things are not in place because . . . and the 'because' is not mentioned.
>
> (head)

> The context/background was noted briefly but not taken into account. Most children are from Council homes, many are extra-district – many moved to the school by parents who weren't satisfied. The school draws on one of the poorest areas in [name of LEA].
>
> (deputy)

The head's concern with context was in part to stress factors which helped to explain some of the shortcomings. For example, the head had been aware that there was no PE policy but, in this case, this was because the PE inspector had written to all schools indicating that they should not formulate a policy because he would do so. The English policy statement was not up to date because of the secondment of the school's English coordinator. The head's problems with financial planning were the result of not having had, until after the inspection, a secretary competent in the relevant computer skills. Although the report alluded to these points they were probably not seen by the head as being expressed in ways which suggested justifiable extenuating circumstances.

The head wondered whether the school's Standard Assessment Task (SAT) scores – which were well below the LEA averages – had coloured the inspectors' perceptions of pupil under-achievement. The head stressed that the school had many behaviour and learning problems, the implication being that more account should have been taken of these in judging the school's performance. Moreover, the head had reservations about SATs generally, believing that some schools had 'cheated' in reporting their results. Doubts about the level of pupil under-achievement claimed on the basis of these results were, in the headteacher's view, supported by the fact that scores for the SAT cohort on National Foundation for Educational Research (NFER) tests were 3 to 4 points above the national average although other interpretations of the evidence are, of course, possible depending on which test or tests one regards as the most reliable.[1]

The inspectors' view of the school was initially presented to the head and deputy head at the oral feedback stage on the Friday of the inspection week. The head described the experience as feeling 'like being in the dock', 'brutal', and the 'worst that could be remembered'. The inspectors' comments also had a profound effect on other staff. One commented 'if this report is true then I should never have been in the job'. Two teachers expressed concern about the possibility of word getting around and affecting career prospects. A particular anxiety for teachers was not knowing whose teaching in particular was considered poor.

The effect of the inspection and its findings was also felt within the inspection team. The team leader referred to the emotional strain building up during the inspection as it became apparent what would have to be said. The team was unprepared for 'the enormity of what was wrong with the school' and the impact on the school staff. Two staff had cried at the feedback session.

In the headteacher's view the experience of the inspection had been 'totally demoralizing'. 'We actually had a totally happy staff who worked as a team; all of this has been pulled from under you and has got to be restored.' The inspection team leader hoped that the head would take the issues on board and that, as a result, the school would benefit. Much depended on how the school inspector managed to break down any barriers: 'It all depends on personalities.'

Reactions to the inspection process

Reactions to the findings of an inspection may sometimes reflect concern about aspects of the process of inspection, the way the inspection was conducted and carried out. An example of this is the perceived neglect of 'context' referred to above. Other concerns were also expressed in comments made specifically about the processes.

Many of these comments were about the issue of time. The 2 days of inspection A were considered by the teachers to be insufficient to obtain 'a true picture'. With so much to look at in the time available it was difficult to do justice to the full range of evidence. For example, the coordinator commented that the data from the teacher questionnaire on reading had been 'flicked through' and put aside. Teachers in inspection B also considered that 2 days was too short a time for an inspection. The inspection team also found the time insufficient too for reflecting on the outcomes of the first day and refocusing for the next. Although the duration of the longer inspection C (5 days) was not mentioned directly, the teachers shared a common concern with those in the other two inspections about the general lack of time to carry out essential requirements. These included opportunities for the teachers to explain the context of lessons observed and to receive feedback on them from the inspectors involved. In inspection C the lack of opportunity to do this may have contributed to the inspectors being perceived in a generally negative light.

> The inspectors were there, very secretive, concentrating on their business, not able to communicate with them . . . no one put you at ease – they concentrated on the fixed criteria they had to look for.
>
> (teacher)

The inspectors were aware of the problem and attributed it, in part, to the experience of working to the new Framework. The Framework was certainly more detailed and rigorous than the inspectors' former 'review' approach but was considered to leave little space for giving feedback to teachers during the inspection. The team leader commented:

> My first reaction on coming away from the inspection was 'I don't want to be an inspector'. Everything previously learned went out of the window and ways of dealing with staff had to take second place.

Even in inspection B where the inspectors were generally seen in a favourable light – 'polite, considerate and unobtrusive, model guests' – the head nevertheless commented that in adopting the new approach they were 'less personal, more threatening'.

Lack of time was also experienced when looking at children's work (inspections A and B). Time may pose a particular challenge in a full inspection. The team leader in C commented that even with four inspectors it was difficult to cover all areas in the time available. Moreover, some things may not be 'on' during the inspection.

Inspection versus self-evaluation

As already noted, inspection A was a form of self-evaluation or, as both the inspector and school staff were involved, a 'joint inspection'. The classroom teachers tended to be in favour of this approach, emphasizing the teacher involvement associated with it and the value of having the impartiality of an external person (the inspector) to provide the balance.

> With an inspector we would have got to where we are with the action plan but would not have had every teacher involved in reading the report, writing notes and knowing exactly what the action plan involves.
>
> (teacher)

The headteacher was also supportive of the approach:

> Inspection is done to you, evaluation is done with you. Evaluation is a rigorous process, it does examine critically and supportively. [It's not] an easy option, not a cosy tête-à-tête.

The deputy, however, saw it more as 'inspection with a friendly face' and thought that the alternative of a 2-day inspection would give a similar although 'tougher picture'. There had been some 'smoothing off of the rough bits in the final report'.

The coordinator, who played a major role in the exercise, had several reservations.

> I would have been happier having two external people. This model felt much safer and lulled one into a false security. I felt this was an inspection – inspection on the cheap. I don't feel in control of the report. I do all the collection and [the inspector] says what to include. It is all quite prescriptive and might as well be an inspection.

The inspector was satisfied with the general approach but more concerned with issues inherent in any evaluation, such as the problems of observing learning outcomes and ensuring the typicality of the judgements made.

The other two cases (inspections B and C) were more typical inspections and although there was some preference for a self-evaluation alternative amongst the heads and staff this was neither strongly expressed nor characteristic of all. Even for inspection C, which produced the most negative of the three inspection reports, the need for some kind of external evaluation was recognized, although carried out over a longer period of time and 'without the pressure and in a user-friendly way'. The inspectors generally were favourable to inspection and had reservations about self-evaluation.

> Inspection is one of the quickest and most thorough ways of doing it [i.e. evaluating a school].
>
> (inspector for C)
>
> Self-evaluation is a possibility if the school had reflected and been open but I don't think [name of school] could do it.
>
> (inspector for B)

Resourcing the inspections

As indicated earlier, it was possible to compute the number of inspector days devoted to each inspection. This is a measure of the amount of inspector resource deployed. In the case of inspection A, the 'inspectors' were considered to be the school inspector, the language coordinator and the headteacher.

The total number of inspector days for each inspection was: A = 14; B = 27; C = 33. In all three the total was substantially greater than that for the inspection period alone. This was because of the considerable time demands of the pre- and post-inspection activities of preparation and report writing respectively.

Although the head and language coordinator in A were both involved as members of the inspection team, other teachers reported that they too took additional time in preparing their lessons during the inspection period. One teacher estimated spending 15 hours in this way, including word-processing the lesson plan for the benefit of the inspectors. Other teachers reported differing amounts of preparation time from half an hour to 3 to 4 hours. Heads in B and C were involved in pre-inspection meetings and compiling/collating school documents for the inspection team (1.0 and 0.75 days, respectively). Deputy heads too were similarly engaged (1.5 and 0.5 days).

Inspections may also involve additional human resources. The provision of 4 days of supply cover was required in A to release the language coordinator, both before and during the inspection. The cost of this was borne by the school. Moreover, some of the teachers felt that a cost to the children was also involved because the co-ordinator's own class had been affected through cover by a supply teacher. In inspection B the head was able to cover classes when teachers were interviewed by inspectors. Also in B, the non-teaching assistant, children's mothers, and even children themselves were useful in getting the school 'ready for inspection'.

Implications for the future of inspection

Since these schools were studied the OFSTED Framework has become the dominant inspection approach. Few LEAs or schools have the resources available to consider alternative 'inspection' activities alongside them. The three cases are, none the less, instructive for the range of issues they reveal about the problems and possibilities of inspection-based approaches to school improvement.

Process

Our findings provide a salutary reminder that the human resource involved in the whole process of inspection can be considerable – even when the additional time required of school staff is ignored. Estimates of the actual time involved in the various stages of the inspection process are essential if inspection bids are to be costed realistically in the new competitive climate.

If it is assumed that it is effective to inspect a large number of issues in a short amount of time, then the two part-inspections (A and B) were relatively less 'cost-effective' in terms of their coverage than the full inspection C. But this assumption may not be justified. Part inspections could have the advantage of providing for a limited number of areas covered; better quality judgements; more detailed judgements; or a more manageable action agenda for the school. On the other hand, it may be less easy to identify a school in difficulties through an inspection where the coverage is less than comprehensive. In practice, the balance of advantage between a full and part inspection is likely to be influenced by the quality of a particular school and its staff.

Time is always likely to be a problem, especially during an inspection. The amount of time available to inspectors in a school can affect at least two aspects of the inspection process – the social courtesies required and the credibility of the methods involved. By social courtesies we mean not only the friendly demeanour which teachers expect inspectors to display but also the opportunity of allowing teachers to explain what they are doing, and to receive feedback on how they are doing. Meeting this need is difficult, however, given the relatively short period of time that inspectors are in school and the sheer range of activities which it is felt must be seen and reported on.

Of course, more than just social niceties are involved here. Teachers would probably argue that if credible judgements are to be made by observing individual lessons, then it is essential that judgements are contextualized. In other words a particular lesson needs to be understood in terms of the general scheme of which it is a part. This may be done by talking with the teacher and/or, as in inspection A, having access to the lesson plan and the teaching forecast.

The credibility of an inspection will depend in part on the extent to which the evidence available will have been given proper consideration. This will be so irrespective of whether evidence is derived from lesson observations, the scrutiny of pupils' work or interviews. It may be difficult to achieve this in practice given the expectation that inspectors will have analysed the evidence in sufficient detail to provide a presentation of the findings immediately following the inspection period. There may be a case, therefore, for extending the period of a full inspection beyond the almost universal time norm of 5 days.

Context

Context is an issue encountered at the 'macro' level of the school as well as at the 'micro' level of the individual lesson. All three head-teachers were concerned to contextualize the accounts of their schools provided by the inspection process. In inspection A the head provided a commentary to explicate the statistical data on the school required by the LEA's scheme. The report of inspection C contained a detailed statistical section as set out in the new inspection Framework. Despite this, however, the head felt that the account did not sufficiently reflect the particular difficulties under which the school was labouring. In the case of inspection B the head was concerned with another aspect of context – the need to provide adequate recognition of what the school had already achieved in the period before the inspection.

The concern to contextualize the achievements of a school is analogous to that of interpreting pupils' examination results or test scores in terms of their prior attainments. In other words, it is another manifestation of the concern for 'value-added'. The Framework gives some recognition of this issue by the requirement for an introductory section in the inspection report setting out a range of school data and indicators. The implicit assumption would seem to be that, with a knowledge of this largely statistical background, the reader of a report will be able to set subsequent judgements into context. This is probably an unrealistic expectation. Appropriate contextualizing of judgements within the main text of a report is essential and is, surely, the responsibility of the inspectors. Although an appreciation of this point is implicit in the new inspection handbook there has, until recently, been little indication of how it might be done in practice.

Learning and development

Inspections can be regarded as potential learning experiences for those involved. In each of the three inspections the inspectors clearly learned a great deal about the school – indeed the inspection reports were, in a sense, a formal record of their collective learning. The heads and staff in inspections A and B apparently learned little that was new. Much was as expected and the report provided confirmation of what was already known. Given the considerable human resource involved in the enterprise it may be asked whether such an outcome is good enough. To put the question bluntly, should not the expenditure of 20 inspector days or thereabouts come up with some unexpected results even in schools which may be generally satisfactory? However, perhaps even where there are 'no surprises', expenditure on inspection may be justified in terms of other potential outcomes such as enhanced staff cooperation, public recognition that the school is basically on the 'right track' and boosts for staff morale. Of course, a major justification of inspection in the government's terms is that it should also provide useful information for parents in their choice of schools.

The situation is different in an inspection like that of C. Here a great deal is potentially learned by teachers about their school, albeit of an apparently very disturbing nature. The learning is potential in the sense that staff have first to be persuaded that the findings are 'true', then internalize them and finally accept a share in collective responsibility for doing something about them. Given the trauma experienced by staff in such a situation it is crucially important that the 'record of evidence' on which the findings are based is impeccable and above reproach. This rather extreme case highlights the importance of the interpersonal dimension in all inspections. It is not a question of simply maintaining the social niceties previously referred to but one of maintaining proper respect for the integrity and worth of individuals whose sense of professional self-esteem can be severely bruised by an inspection. It is noteworthy that the new 'Code of Conduct for Inspectors' refers in several of its eight principles to attributes such as 'courtesy and fairness', 'sensitivity', 'respect' and specifically to 'sensitivity to the impact of judgements on others' (OFSTED 1993b).

Concluding comments

We have considered here some of the issues arising from three primary school inspections. Extending the size of the sample could well reveal other important concerns. Moreover, a consideration of secondary school inspections would show whether the concerns which have been identified are specific to primary inspections, or apply more generally. Some differences might be expected to arise from secondary inspections as a result of the greater size and complexity of the schools. Furthermore, the generally larger size of secondary inspection teams means that most, if not all, curriculum areas can be the responsibility of a specialist inspector. In the smaller primary teams each inspector has to be familiar with more than one curriculum area. Another possible difference arises from the requirement that all inspection teams in the future are required to include one 'lay inspector'. In a primary team of four or so inspectors a lay inspector has potentially a greater range of responsibilities than would be the case in a larger secondary team of perhaps around a dozen. Some of these issues we intend to explore later.

In recent years inspection has moved in from the educational margins to a prominent centre-stage position for both policy-makers and practitioners. If the teachers and inspectors interviewed here are at all typical of their colleagues throughout the country then it would seem that inspection or, at the very least, some form of evaluation with an external component is generally supported. Although LEAs were pursuing different approaches to the evaluation of schools following the Education Reform Act, they are now required – if they wish to participate in the new arrangements – to adopt the new inspection model. Whether or not this attempt to standardize the inspection process will lead to a better understanding of individual schools and, crucially, how they might be improved, remains an open question.

Note

1 It can be argued, of course, that these results do actually support the contention of under-achievement, even though this was not the headteacher's view.

9

THE METHODOLOGIES OF SCHOOL INSPECTION: ISSUES AND DILEMMAS

By way of justification

Methodological issues in the conduct of inspections have been largely ignored. In this chapter we seek to redress this imbalance and to explore some of the assumptions and procedures that they typically employ.

We have detected a certain resistance to such discussions amongst some inspectors in the past. Indeed, we have had some difficulty in identifying any substantial discussion of the issues in the extant literature. HMI, for example, have argued that they are not like researchers and cannot be expected to adhere to the same methodological canons. We are inclined to agree. From our perspective, however, the methodological integrity of a set of procedures cannot merely be asserted. All human enquiries, of which inspection is an important example, are likely to be strengthened by addressing their methodologies, explicit and implicit. Our observations are offered, therefore, in the belief that inspections are as good as their methodological foundations and that it behoves those who would inspect to be aware of some of their potential limitations.

The inspection of a school typically results in the production of a report. This report is a special kind of account or description; one which sets out the strengths and weaknesses of the school. The assumption here is that inspection should lead to improvement. Behind this, however, there lies a more fundamental, albeit implicit, assumption that the account of the school represented by the report is accepted as being 'true'. What guarantees that this is indeed the case? On what do the truth claims of inspection rest?

In essence inspection involves the collection, analysis and interpretation of evidence and data of various kinds by inspectors individually and collectively. Acceptance of the subsequent findings of the inspection will therefore depend in part on the confidence which people, especially teachers, have in the process. This in turn implies having confidence in the methods and procedures employed and those who carry them out.

These are the issues we address in this chapter. By way of illustration we first draw on some empirical data from four inspections carried out in a single LEA.

A study of four inspections

The LEA concerned is one of a half-dozen or so in which we have worked in the course of a major study of school inspection.[1] Table 9.1 summarizes some of the main features of the four inspections.

The inspections were of two primary schools (A, B) and two secondaries (C, D). Two (B and D) were 'full' inspections, which covered all aspects of the schools' activities and organization and closely followed the requirements of the OFSTED (1992b) Inspection Handbook. The other two inspections (A and C) dealt only with some aspects of the curriculum and its organization and are termed 'part' inspections. In both cases the aspects or foci inspected were negotiated with the school. The two part-inspections took place over 2 days, the full inspections took 5 days. About twice as many inspectors were involved in the full inspections as in the part.

Our approach has been to carry out individual interviews with the teachers and inspectors involved in each inspection.[2] The interviews provided an opportunity *inter alia* for teachers and inspectors to comment on the methods employed in the specific inspection in which they were involved. This was made possible by posing the

Table 9.1 Details of four inspections

	School A	School B	School C	School D
Type of school	Junior Infant	Junior Infant	13–18 Secondary	11–16 Secondary
Type of inspection	Part inspection, OFSTED style, negotiated foci	Full inspection, OFSTED style	Part inspection, negotiated foci	Full inspection, OFSTED style
Duration of inspection	2 days	5 days	2 days	5 days
Number of inspectors	4	Core team of 4 plus 4 others	5	Core team of 5 plus 8 others

The four inspections were conducted within one LEA during a 1-year period.

question: 'Do you have any comments to make on the adequacy of the methods which were used in the inspection?' In addition, some interviewees made comments relating to methods in responding to other questions. It is the data from these two sources that we discuss below.

Teacher and inspector comments on inspection methods

The vast majority of comments were either about specific methods, most notably about classroom observation, or about what may be regarded as more general methodological issues. Table 9.2 summarizes the main points.

The figures in the table represent the different types of comment given, which have been classified under each of the categories listed in the left-hand column. The vast majority of these figures refer to comments which expressed some concern about aspects of the inspection process. The figures in brackets relate to comments which actually commended some aspect of inspection.

Table 9.2   Comments made by individual inspectors and teachers on their experiences of particular inspections

Nature of comment	School A		School B		School C		School D	
	T	I	T	I	T	I	T	I
Accuracy and representativeness	6	2	5	3	8	3 (1)	3	6
Classroom observation	7	5 (1)	10	1	3	1	(1)	–
Context	4	–	2	–	2 (1)	– (1)	2	–
Interviews	1	–	2	–	–	2	4	1
Documents	–	1 (1)	1	1	–	–	–	–
Number interviewed	5	3	5	2	7	5	5	3

During their interviews respondents were asked: 'Do you have any comments to make on the adequacy of the methods which were used in the inspection?' Most comments made were of a negative kind. The incidence of positive comments is indicated by the bracketing of the relevant figure. The table is based on the responses of 22 teachers (T) and 13 inspectors (I).

Accuracy/representativeness

This category was numerically the largest, constituting over 40 per cent of the total number of responses. It reflected a concern that inspection can lead to an incomplete or even incorrect description of aspects of the school. It is a concern which was reflected amongst both teachers and inspectors, to some degree or other, in all four inspections. A common expression of this was the feeling that the duration of the inspection was too short:

> The amount of time was insufficient, you need at least a week to give a picture of a school.
>
> (headteacher, School A)

> Two days is not long enough for reflecting on the day and refocusing for the next day.
>
> (inspector, School A)

The time was also seen as insufficient even for the longer 5-day full inspection:

> Under the new pattern [OFSTED] time will be squeezed and gaps will be shown up – the problem was to fit everything into a crowded week.
>
> (inspector, School D)

Another concern was the suspicion that if something was not seen then it was not happening:

> Some comments were out of line with what was actually happening, for example – not getting children to talk. In fact this *is* done but not in *every* lesson.
>
> (teacher, School C)

> There is a problem of not seeing something and then saying it doesn't happen.
>
> (inspector, School B)

A further problem referred to by inspectors in three of the inspections was that of obtaining the views of individual inspectors on some common aspect of a school and then collating these to give a consensus view. This was particularly commented on by three inspectors in school D:

> On pupils' behaviour people were just making comments but we couldn't summate these systematically. For example, we couldn't say how often 'minor disruptions' occurred.
>
> (inspector, School D)

Other concerns which were felt to detract from obtaining an accurate picture of the school included: the atypicality of what was seen, reliance on what was considered to be anecdotal evidence and inspecting areas in which the inspector was not a specialist.

Classroom observation

Nearly all of the comments about classroom observation (of which there were a substantial number) came from inspections A, B and C. Some teachers reported being under-visited in their classrooms whilst others may have been over-visited:

> What the inspectors did in my classroom was fair but I didn't seem to get as many visits as other staff. One supply teacher got more visits than the established staff.
>
> (teacher, School B)

Observation of individual lessons or subject areas could be perceived as inadequate:

> In the limited time available inspectors only saw one RE lesson.
>
> (teacher, School C)

> Only visited one member of staff for 10–15 minutes.
>
> (another teacher, School C)

Too much time in the classroom, however, could be at the expense of other things:

> We spent too long in classrooms and failed to get a clearer understanding of how resources were used, where they were and how they were managed.
>
> (inspector, School A)

Teachers and inspectors tended to differ about the desirability of giving prior notice of classroom visits:

> One fault was that the inspectors didn't come to classes sometimes when they said they would.
>
> (teacher, School A)

> More flexibility was needed about what classes to observe and when; the timetable was limiting if you were not seeing what you were looking for.
>
> (inspector, School A)

Many comments about inspections A and B drew attention to the lack of time and opportunity which teachers had to discuss with inspectors the lessons in which they were observed. This was a difficulty also appreciated by the inspectors. Provision of feedback on lessons was one issue:

> Didn't have time to talk to inspectors afterwards; inspectors didn't have time to feed back their observations.
>
> (teacher, School A)

Another was the need to explain the background to a lesson:

Would like more time to explain to the inspector what was happening in the classroom.

> (another teacher, School A)

Although the latter requirement may be obviated in part by the practice of submitting lesson plans in advance this can lead to further difficulties:

Teaching had to be mapped out and rigidly kept. Had to slow down the work on cress seeds so as to do it on time.

> (teacher, School B)

Understanding the context

'Context' represents a concern of teachers, and especially headteachers, that an inspection should explicitly recognize the particular circumstances and background of the school.

They could have trusted the coordinators to say what had happened over the year. The past was irrelevant, they were only concerned with the present.

> (headteacher, School B)

The report does not recognize what was *already* identified by the headteacher and staff and the changes recently made ... In future if reports go public then there should be some recognition of previous history to explain why.

> (headteacher, School A)

At a more 'micro' level the use of contextual information may be exploited with effect:

Was reassured on how good the department's exam results were. The inspector provided an excellent analysis which took into account socio-economic background of pupils, qualifications of staff, etc.

> (head of department, School C)

Conducting interviews

Talks or formal interviews with teachers were carried out in all four inspections and also, with the exception of C, with pupils. The few comments from inspectors were concerned with the need to develop a more focused, standardized approach to questioning. There was some indication amongst the teachers in school B of a misunderstanding of the purpose of interviews:

> The inspectors asked questions about schemes of work, children's work, etc. as though they hadn't seen these details. They said they were being devil's advocates. Were they quizzing members of staff against each other?

Queries were raised about the value ascribed to the views of individuals.

> I am concerned when pupils are questioned and the value put on their replies, also the choice of which pupils are questioned. One question asked of an infant in my class was: 'Is this all the Maths equipment you have got?' Is this question relevant to the age of the child?
>
> (deputy, School A)

A comparable concern was also expressed in inspection D, although in this case in the context of teacher interviews:

> The opinion of someone not backed by evidence is not itself evidence. For example, the coordinators said that the senior management team had asked for things to be done by them every week. However, only one example of this could be given when the coordinators were asked by myself.
>
> (headteacher, School D)

Making sense of documents

Very few spontaneous comments were made about the use of documents, either by teachers or inspectors. All four inspections made use of various school documents. For inspection A there was an indication of somewhat differing views about the effectiveness of their use:

> On the team day we got inside the documents and were able, with the four of us round the table, to lift out the pre-inspection issues.
>
> (inspector, School A)

> Time spent talking is not so productive as it should be . . . there was a lot of material to get through, not the best way to do it.

Would have been better if each person had looked through the material. How do you come to a common view on the documents?

(team leader, School A)

The other type of document examined, at least in the case of inspections A, B and D, was a sample of pupils' work. Only two comments were made on this aspect, both in school B. The deputy would have liked to have had more direct feedback from the inspectors on the quality of the work. The inspection team leader also expressed some concern.

How do colleagues view the availability of children's work? Colleagues tackled this differently, some were less sure; difficult for curriculum areas with which they were not familiar.

(team leader, School B)

Reflections on data

The purpose of explicating the data summarized in Table 9.2 is not to attempt an 'evaluation' of the four inspections; after all only a relatively small amount of the total data available has been considered. Rather, our concern has been to present some of the issues which an inspection team is likely to encounter as it goes about its business in schools.

The snapshot

The major concern, particularly for heads and teachers, is that the picture which the inspection produces of the school should be 'accurate', 'fair' and 'representative'. A frequently used metaphor is that of the 'snapshot'. Teachers often say that an inspection is a snapshot of a school over a day or more, perhaps even a week, and so cannot be a 'true picture'. This will undoubtedly be the case if the picture is solely built up from what is observed to be taking place during the period of the inspection. Inevitably there will be some things not going on during that period which nevertheless do take place at other times. Equally there may be some things taking place which the inspectors may just fail to see because, even with a large team, they cannot be everywhere all the time. Lessons and other school activities can only be sampled. In the case of classroom lessons, for example, the recommended sample ranges from 7 to over 20 per cent of the lessons (OFSTED 1993b: 3, 11). Consequently inspectors do need to be particularly careful to avoid saying that something (whether an aspect of teaching, curriculum content or whatever) is not taking place solely on the basis of what is actually observed. In the longer term it may be appropriate for inspection teams to experiment with patterns of visits that are more closely matched to the rhythms of the school year.

Although the bulk of inspectors' time is spent in classrooms (a minimum of 60 per cent is recommended; OFSTED 1993b: 3, 11) their other activities include interviewing and scrutinizing documents. Much of the information obtained from these two sources will relate to situations and events which occurred before the inspection period. In other words they will relate to the past – a past which is not precisely defined but which, in most cases, corresponds to the current year in which the inspection takes place and may even go back beyond that (e.g. details of the previous years' examination results). So an inspection is not really a snapshot at all, with all the clarity and instantaneity this implies but rather a somewhat blurred image or set of images. In brief, it is a description of the condition of a school from an indeterminate point in the recent past to the time when the inspection took place.

The production of such a description implicitly assumes that the characteristics of a school are reasonably stable over time. Clearly if they were not, and changed significantly from one moment to another, then description would be difficult, if not impossible. This notion of stability is assumed to carry over into the future, at least for that period between the end of the inspection and the appearance of the report. An inspection, however, always marks a potential point of discontinuity at which the school may move, by following up the report's recommendations, from one state to another.

The notion of a pre-inspection past is also reflected in concern that the account of a school should be adequately contextualized, not only by its location and clientele but also in terms of its immediate history. The nature of this history helps to account in part for the current situation and description of a school. If explicit recognition is not given in the report to significant developments which occurred before the inspection, then teachers are apt to regard the description of the school as unsatisfactory. Perhaps a helpful analogy may be made here with the assessment of a person.

Although such an assessment will describe the individual's current abilities and skills it will also draw on significant happenings in the past as, for example, represented in a curriculum vitae.

Although a concern for what has gone on before an inspection can no doubt sometimes be an attempt by teachers to find excuses, nevertheless it is difficult not to see merit in the view that to 'know' a school requires some understanding of its background.

Inspection methods

Most of the comments made about the methods of inspection were concerned with classroom observation. This is perhaps not surprising as it is usually the main method adopted and the one which most closely and obviously addresses the central act of teaching. Competence in teaching lies at the very heart of the professional 'self'. Being observed teaching is therefore a very significant experience for all teachers. Although inspectors may often repeat the old HMI adage that 'they are looking at the teaching and not the teachers', teachers see it in a somewhat different light. For the individual teachers concerned the inspectors are very much looking at them. As a consequence, most teachers, in our experience, have a real need to receive comments on how their efforts have been perceived. They may also feel that if an inspector is to understand an individual lesson they will need to explain how it is related to previous and subsequent lessons.

Finding time to talk to teachers before and after an observed lesson can be difficult, given the limited time available during the inspection and the multitude of things inspectors are expected to observe. This is likely to be even more a problem with OFSTED inspections, which are much more comprehensive in their coverage than any 'full' inspections have been in the past. However, if opportunities are not provided to talk to teachers they are likely to feel and voice a dissatisfaction with the inspection experience.

Comments on the actual observation process itself tended to be about perceptions of the inadequacies of sampling – sampling of individual teachers, time in individual lessons and the teaching of specific subjects. Whilst these problems may be minimized by working out in advance details of who to see and when (and certainly teachers like to know when to expect a 'visitor') there may be reasons for changing the arrangements as the inspection proceeds. For example, a teacher may be away, a class may be cancelled at the last moment and an inspector will have to decide how best to fill the resulting gap. More importantly, an inspector may want to follow up a promising 'lead' by extending or modifying the sample to include others or seeing again those already encountered.

Although teachers sometimes express an implicit or explicit concern with the criteria which inspectors use in judging teaching this was not markedly apparent in the four inspections described. With the public availability of the OFSTED Handbook teachers can now at least see what the ostensible criteria for judgement are and can assess their validity. Certainly, in our more general discussions with teachers we find that many are quite happy with the criteria, regarding them as professionally acceptable. However, closer scrutiny of such criteria reveals them to be rather general statements. Questions could therefore be raised about the extent to which such statements are consistently interpreted and used by inspectors in making their judgements. The process of moving from criteria to judgements is a complex and poorly understood one (cf. Wilcox 1992: 191–6). Although this does not appear to be a concern of teachers at the present time it is more likely to press with inspectors. At the risk of some simplification it can be said that teachers' concerns are ones of validity whereas those of inspectors are more likely to focus on the issue of reliability.

Very few comments were made spontaneously on the other two main methods employed in inspection – interviewing and the use of documents. There were, however, some hints of possible pitfalls. In interviewing, for example, teachers can be concerned about the value apparently ascribed to the comments of specific individuals. There are, of course, many occasions when it is reasonable to accept such comments, particularly where they refer to personal feelings and reactions. But automatically giving the comments the status of valid descriptions of social reality would not generally be acceptable. For example, one teacher's view of the style of the senior management team would not have the warranty of constituting a valid assessment of that aspect of school life. At the very least it would be necessary to show that the view was shared by other teachers.

The analysis of documents as sources of inspection evidence is perhaps less obviously guided by broadly recognized procedures than is the use of observation or interviews. In the latter cases the format in which evidence is presented for analysis is essentially determined by the inspector in terms of pre-formulated categories, criteria or questions. In using documents the inspector is faced with formats and styles which may vary markedly from author to author. The task of making sense of multiple documents is therefore a challenging one. This problem is well illustrated by the inspection practice of examining a sample of pupils' work drawn from across the ability range. How such evidence is placed in context and judged remains problematic.

Judging standards

There is an expectation that the inspection process will result in summary judgements about the 'standards' that have been reached. Such expectations have been formulated in the various OFSTED Handbooks. None the less, some dilemmas remain and much has been (and is currently) left to the discretion of the individual inspector.

In the case of data relating to examinations and test results the yardsticks for comparison are now reasonably well established. There is increasing recognition that like should be compared with like. However, practice lags behind. The first editions of the OFSTED Handbook confined advice about how schools should be compared to general expressions of principles. Data which would permit useful comparisons to be made were not available, and such data as were related mainly to the national picture. The national average is only suitable for those schools which happen to have intakes that are representative of the national position – the vast majority of schools depart, of course, from this position.

Since then, steps have been taken to assist inspectors by providing evidence on performance levels for schools of different types, where school 'type' is taken to include schools serving different socio-economic communities. How prominent such contextualized data will become in inspectors' reports remains to be seen. An analysis of the judgemental positions revealed in HMI reports a decade ago suggested that attempts to contextualize the data on schools' examination performances were partial and inconsistent (see Chapter 3). Since that time, judgements appear to have become more consistent but not necessarily more appropriate. Some distinct breaks with past practice may be required.

Whilst exam and test data may lend themselves to systematic comparisons between schools, other kinds of data obtained by inspectors are less easily judged in these terms. It is assumed that experienced inspectors carry around with them a 'record' of experience which they can call upon to help them interpret evidence. Historians also lay claim to a similar 'second record' (Hexter 1971). Difficulties may arise, however, when they are required to bring it into play. The appropriate comparison (as with exam and test data) is with similar pupils in similar schools. The ways in which inspections are usually timetabled may make this problematic. The school visited last week is likely to be most prominent in individual and collective memories; however, the school visited last month, or even earlier, may be the most appropriate comparison. The latter 'record' is likely to be more remote than the former. Such considerations have been largely ignored in previous inspection practices. If they have been recognized at all, it has usually been assumed that experienced inspectors could make the necessary adjustments to their perspectives. But, until such issues are addressed more explicitly in inspection timetabling, inspectors may remain vulnerable on this score. Traditionally, HMI relied on the authority accorded them by their experience. Developments in connection with OFSTED have shifted the basis for such claims, however, and the involvement of so-called 'lay members' in the inspection process has accelerated this process still further. Claims to authority now rest as much (if not more) in the methods inspectors use as in their experience.

Inspection as qualitative evaluation

Given the trend in recent years towards increased systematization (culminating now in the apparent detail and precision of the OFSTED approach) it is difficult not to regard inspection as a form of educational evaluation. It is, moreover, a form of evaluation which draws mainly, although not exclusively, on the availability and production of qualitative data. Like the qualitative evaluator or researcher generally, inspectors face the task of making sense of a variety of pieces of evidence from several different sources. In the case of inspectors the 'making sense' is ultimately tested by the ability to produce an account of a school which will be broadly accepted as 'true'.

Looking at inspection as an exercise in qualitative evaluation reveals the formidable nature of the task. The part or full inspection of a school is generally carried out over a period which is seldom more than 5 days. This is a rather short period of time within which to carry out what is required. Moreover, the near universal practice of presenting the main inspection findings orally to the senior staff on the last day of the inspection means that the whole process of collecting, analysing, interpreting and reporting on the major sources of evidence has to be completed within the week. The timescales within which inspectors currently work are dramatically shorter than those of qualitative evaluators generally.

Throughout the week inspectors will be accumulating data related to their own specialist areas as well as to various whole-school and cross-curricular aspects to which others will also contribute. Given this considerable volume of data, and the severe time-constraints under which inspections have to operate, it is very difficult for inspectors to apply systematically the analytical techniques which qualitative researchers and evaluators employ. How, then, are the data treated so as to yield the relatively succinct descriptions and judgements of the final report? Practitioners of inspection have generally been mute on how this substantial data reduction and transformation task is actually accomplished. Inspection, particularly as required by the OFSTED Handbook, uses various forms of data summary including the attempt to objectify judgement through the use of rating scales. Nevertheless, inspectors are still faced ultimately with the task of distilling from a considerable volume of data, in a variety of formats, a relatively few crisp descriptions and judgements. The OFSTED Handbook merely reminds an inspector of 'the issues for consideration when reviewing evidence' in order to make judgements.

The crucial process of 'review' remains undefined. Reviewing evidence presumably involves such operations as: weighing the importance of one thing against another, interpreting apparently contradictory trends, and determining where different forms of data and evidence are sufficiently corroborative. All of these operations are largely private to the individuals concerned. The judgements which are the outcome of these private processes are expected to command the agreement of all members of the inspection team. This is formally accomplished through discussion involving all team members at a meeting held at the end of the inspection, and prior to the presentation of an oral report to the headteacher and other senior staff. It is difficult to see, however, how such collective endorsement can be given to the judgements made by a single inspector about a specific curriculum area which has not been inspected by others. A team might, indeed, reach consensus on judgements concerning those aspects of a school to which all will have contributed. Much will depend on whether there is sufficient time available to allow real or 'unforced' agreement to occur.

The problematic nature of inspection

From what has been said so far it is apparent that the methods and procedures of inspection, regarded as a form of qualitative evaluation, are always potentially problematic. They are always prone to the possibility of being challenged. As a result, the account of a school which inspection provides is always at risk of not being accepted as 'true'. This risk may be minimized by careful attention to sampling, clear definition of criteria, making explicit the operations of data reduction and transformation, and the more rigorous pursuit of unforced agreement. There are, however, limits to what can be achieved, particularly as long as inspection is cast in its present highly time-constrained framework.

Eisner (1991: 86) reminds us that evaluation is a form of criticism and that:

> . . . every act of criticism is a reconstruction. The reconstruction takes the form of an argued narrative, supported by evidence that is never incontestable; there will *always* be alternative interpretations of the 'same' play, as the history of criticism so eloquently attests.

So there will always be alternative interpretations of the 'same' school. Is inspection, therefore, doomed to produce, at best, the agreed views of an inspection team thus leaving the possibility of its acceptance by others (particularly teachers) as uncertain? Perhaps one way out of this apparent impasse is to adopt the kind of pragmatism that Rorty (1991: 38) recommends more generally as a philosophic stance:

> [W]e can always enlarge the scope of 'us' by regarding other people, or cultures, as members of the same community of inquiry as ourselves – by treating them as part of the group among whom unforced agreement is to be sought.

Inspection privileges the voice of the inspectors and, by extension, those they work for and are accountable to. It is they who constitute the Rortyan 'us' in the context of inspection. The 'us' could be extended, however, to include the teachers of the school as the group within which unforced agreement might be sought. That would require going well beyond the present practice of reporting the findings of an inspection to school staff and others where only matters of factual accuracy can be challenged and not the judgements actually made. Such a change, if introduced, would of course result in a form of inspection radically different from the one intended under OFSTED's current requirements.

Notes

1 The LEA was chosen because it is typical of many which, in the aftermath of the Education Reform Act, had moved from a position where inspections were rare occurrences to one in which they were increasingly part of a high profile systematic programme. The inspections took place over the period November 1992 to February 1993. They are not claimed to be representative of all the inspections which occurred over this period. There are two reasons for this. First, they are inspections to which the LEA gave us access consistent with our own availability at a particular time. Second, the inspectors, like those in most other LEAs during this period, were in the process of changing their inspection approaches to meet the requirements of the 1992 Education (Schools) Act. This was necessary if they were to operate under the new inspection arrangements arising from the Act and overseen by the Office for Standards in Education (OFSTED), which began in September 1993.

2 The first set of interviews took place within 3 months of the completion of the inspections, by which time the inspection findings had been disseminated within the schools by oral feedback and/or the circulation of the final report. The aim of the interviews was to elicit teacher and

inspector reactions to the inspection and its outcomes. A second set of interviews (and a third set in the case of the secondary inspections) were carried out later to determine the extent to which the inspection findings had been addressed.

A semi-structured interview schedule composed of a dozen or so broad themes was used. This allowed interviewees to describe their reactions to the inspection in their own words and within their own conceptual framework. Interviews generally lasted for about 45 minutes and were tape-recorded for subsequent analysis and summary. Interviews were carried out with two to five inspectors in each case, always including the team leader. Teacher interviews included, in each case, the headteacher, the deputy headteacher and three to five others covering the range from class teacher to head of department (secondary) or curriculum coordinator (primary).

10

THE INSPECTORS RECOMMENDED... A FOLLOW-UP STUDY IN SIX SECONDARY SCHOOLS

Introduction

The formal outcome of a school inspection is the production of a report. This report is an account of a school's specific strengths and weaknesses based on judgements made by the inspectors. The number of such judgements is often large; they are therefore invariably summarized in the form of main recommendations or, in the parlance of the Office for Standards in Education (OFSTED), 'key issues for action'. As the OFSTED inspection Handbook puts it:

> The report should provide a clear indication of the most important issues that need to be addressed. The specific points for action should be practicable and as few as are consistent with the inspection findings.
>
> (OFSTED 1993b: 2, 16)

Such key issues or recommendations may be regarded as a skeletal plan for school change. How do schools in fact respond to such recommendations and how far, as a result, do schools actually change? These and related questions are important ones to answer, not least because inspection is a relatively expensive and potentially intrusive intervention into the normal functioning of schools. Inspection has also become one of the dominant 'improvement strategies' on the current educational scene.

Over the last 30 or so years the study of educational change has been a major focus of research, both in this country and elsewhere. Such research has, however, neglected the role that inspection might play in the process of change. This is partly because inspection has been absent from the portfolio of monitoring activities in many countries. It is also partly because inspection of schools has not hitherto been envisaged on the scale currently planned in the UK.

Michael Fullan (1982, 1991) has developed one of the most comprehensive accounts to date of the processes of educational change. We draw on his work for two reasons. First, because it is one of the most influential and widely read sources of advice to practitioners about how to bring about educational change, especially in its recent, more popular forms (see Fullan 1992; Fullan and Hargreaves 1992). And second, because we were particularly concerned to see whether, in the absence of strongly formed 'theories' about how inspection works, there were clear parallels with other strategies for inducing change in schools. Is inspection, in comparison with other approaches, a change strategy which is driven by factors connected with compliance or can it generate and draw on a school's commitment? And if compliance is the dominant factor are there limits to what can be secured?

Several other strands in Fullan's work may also be relevant to the task of understanding the implementation of recommendations arising from inspection reports. He emphasizes, for example, that implementation is often a lengthy process taking place over several years. Is this the kind of timescale we should expect for inspections? Furthermore, 'change' appears typically to be a problematic issue with neat, tidy and complete implementation being the exception rather than the rule. Is this likely to be the case as well for the aftermath of inspections? And, running through his accounts at every level, are concerns about the extent to which 'real change' can be mandated from above. Again the implications for inspections are obvious.

Studies of inspection to date have neglected questions about its effects on educational change. Those which have been done have tended to concentrate on such aspects of inspection as the criteria for inspection judgements (see Chapter3; Elliott and Ebbutt 1986; Nixon and Rudduck, 1993) or the reactions of teachers and inspectors to the process of inspection (see Chapter 8; Dean 1994; OFSTED 1994b. There have, to our knowledge, been no major studies to date of the effects of inspection on the subsequent development of schools. Our studies therefore represent an initial foray into new research territory.

But first we need to unpack some assumptions about how inspection is supposed to bring about school improvement as these have affected the evidence we have collected and the interpretations we have made of it.

Unpacking some assumptions about inspection

Implicit in the rationale of inspection is the view that it should lead to improvement. Indeed, this is apparently the central purpose of the new OFSTED agency, captured in its motto 'improvement through inspection' (OFSTED 1993a). To date, however, we have not encountered a sustained account of how the inspection process might actually work out in practice to bring about such improvement. Doubtless part of the reason for this omission is that it is assumed to be 'common sense'. None the less, we believe it is worth while teasing out some of the basic assumptions.

The first is that the inspection process leads to a set of recommendations. The second is that these recommendations describe the main areas requiring improvement. From this the third follows, namely that 'improvement' can be gauged from the extent to which the recommendations are implemented.

In practice, each of these assumptions needs to be tested out against experience. Not all so-called 'recommendations' have clear implications for school improvement; whether 'improvement' would actually result from implementing certain recommendations may be contestable; and gauging whether a recommendation has, in fact, been implemented may be difficult.

There is a further concern, which leads us to modify the third of the above assumptions. Fullan's analysis reminds us that the litmus test for most changes is that they become 'institutionalized', taking on some more permanent form within the organization. If we take this view seriously then our third premise must maintain that improvement results from the extent to which the recommendations of the inspection are implemented *and remain implemented*. Establishing that this has happened within relatively short time-scales is likely to be problematic.

The inspections studied

The study was concerned with the inspection of six secondary schools[1] in five LEAs. In what follows the schools and inspections are identified anonymously as A, B, C, D, E and F. Two of the schools (B and C) were located in the same LEA. The schools ranged in size from under 40 to over 80 full-time equivalent staff and drew on catchment areas from the very disadvantaged to the advantaged. The details are summarized in Table 10.1.

The inspections took place between October 1992 and February 1993 and were carried out by inspectors from the host LEAs.[2] They were, in all cases, 'full' inspections and in effect 'trial runs' of the OFSTED inspection arrangements, which were to be introduced in September 1993. Each inspection resulted in a report which, in all but one case, corresponded closely to the prescribed OFSTED format. The exception was inspection F, where the report could be described as a hybrid of OFSTED and LEA formats.

Our choice of schools to study was largely dictated by the timetable of our research and is best described as an 'opportunity' sample. Given that we had wanted to follow-up the schools about 18 months after they had been inspected, and that we had studied two secondary schools in each LEA from amongst the small number being inspected, there was little discretion about which cases to analyse. Thus we make no claim to representativeness in a statistical sense.

None of the schools, as judged by us from their inspection reports, could be considered to be giving major cause for concern. All had a range of strengths and some weaknesses requiring attention. Equally none of the schools could be regarded as outstanding in the quality of the education they provided. They appeared, in other words, to represent that broad spectrum of quality on which the majority of schools nationally might be expected to be located.

Table 10.1 Characteristics of six secondary school inspections

Characteristics	Inspections					
	A	B	C	D	E	F
School type	11–16	11–16	11–16	11–16	11–18	11–16
Approx. no. of teachers	50	60	80	50	40	40
Catchment area	Disadvantaged	Advantaged	Average	Disadvantaged	Average	Average
LEA	Met. Dist.	Met. Dist.	Met. Dist.	Met. Dist.	County	County
Type of report	OFSTED style	OFSTED style	OFSTED style	OFSTED style	OFSTED style	OFSTED/LEA hybrid

Met. Dist. = Metropolitan District.

The rationale and methods of the research

Our main aim was to determine how and to what extent these secondary schools had implemented the key issues or main recommendations of the inspection reports they had received. We did this by conducting individual, semi-structured interviews in the schools with samples of five or six teachers. These included the headteacher, the deputy headteacher, two or three heads of department and one or two main-scale teachers. However, in school C the headteacher did not agree to the release of staff for the purpose of interviews; it was only possible to interview the headteacher. In each case (apart from A and C) interviews were also carried out with the inspector who had responsibility for liaising with the school after the inspection (the 'school' inspector). In the case of school A the inspection team disbanded immediately after the inspection as a result of a major reorganization of the LEA. Only two inspectors remained for interview, only one of whom had revisited the school but could not really comment on the progress towards implementation. Interviews took place on two occasions: 9–12 months after the inspection and then again some 15–18 months later.[3] In inspection D the liaison role was performed by an officer. Only one interview was carried out in this case as the officer had made no further visits and was therefore unable to report on progress.

The same questions were asked of all interviewees on both occasions, and essentially required a description of the actions which had been taken on each of the recommendations. This was supplemented with a rating for each recommendation on a scale of 'implementation'. Interviewees were also asked to identify any influences which they considered to have been significant in either facilitating or inhibiting the implementation of each recommendation. At the same time, views were sought on whether there had been any other significant outcomes of the inspections (whether beneficial or otherwise) and the nature of any post-inspection support from the LEA.

Interviews lasted approximately 45 minutes and were tape-recorded. The resulting audiotapes were used to supplement brief notes taken during the interview. This process resulted in the production of substantial summaries organized initially in terms of the responses of individual interviewees to each question. A series of categories was then derived inductively by scrutinizing these summaries. The categories provided a basis for analysis and presenting the results in the form of matrices of the kind proposed by Miles and Huberman (1984). Tables 10.2–10.4 are, in turn, derived from these matrices and constitute a final stage of data reduction.

Evidence from the six inspections

Our first concern during the fieldwork was to build up a descriptive account of the action. What happened as a result of the inspections? What recommendations were made? Which of them were subsequently implemented? And what were some of the factors facilitating or inhibiting their implementation?

We turn first to a more detailed account of what was recommended.

The structure and focus of the recommendations

The actual structure of recommendations varied somewhat both within and across the reports. The majority of recommendations took the form of short statements concerned with a single theme. Some statements, however, linked together two or more separate themes. In these cases the statements were divided into parts so that each was regarded as a distinct recommendation. The number of such recommendations ranged from five to ten, with a total of 43 for all the inspections.

We decided to concentrate our attention on what we considered to be the main focus of a recommendation. This was done by assigning each recommendation to one of several different categories. These represented major features of the curriculum, organization and management of schools. In cases where the main focus was not immediately apparent reference to the context of the recommendation in the report usually clarified the situation.

In Table 10.2 the main recommendations of each inspection have been analysed into 14 categories. The most frequently occurring categories were those concerned with: curriculum delivery, assessment, and teaching and learning.

Recommendations relating to 'curriculum delivery' were characteristic of five of the six inspections. For example:

Table 10.2 Types of recommendation in six secondary school inspections

Main focus of recommendation	A	B	C	D	E	F	Total
Assessment (A)	1	2	1	2			6
Curriculum delivery (CDe)	1	2	1	1	1		6
Teaching and learning (TL)	1	1	1	2	1		6
Curriculum monitoring/evaluation (CME)	1		2			1	4
Management/administration (MA)	1	2			1		4
School development plan (SDP)			1		1	1	3
Curriculum documentation (CDo)	1			1		1	3
Curriculum [specific] (CS)	1		2				3
Organization (O)		1				1	2
Environment and accommodation (EA)		2					2
Equal opportunities (EO)			1				1
Pastoral/discipline (PD)						1	1
Special educational needs (SEN)					1		1
Resources (R)	1						1
Total	8	10	9	6	5	5	43

> Develop more consistent progress towards reaching the goals of National Curriculum implementation which the school has set itself.
>
> (School D)

Four of the inspections had recommendations relating to 'assessment'. For example:

> Continue the developments towards pupil self-assessment in relation to developments in teaching and learning styles.
>
> (School C)

Recommendations concerned with 'teaching and learning' were made in five of the inspections. For example:

> Offer a range of opportunities across more departments, particularly through the issue of differentiation to extend the achievements of all pupils to the highest levels they are capable of.
>
> (School B)

The next most frequently occurring recommendations (appearing in three out of the six inspections) were concerned with other aspects of the curriculum or with management and planning. Those in the former category were 'curriculum monitoring/evaluation' and 'curriculum documentation' (concerned with policies, schemes of work, etc.). Examples of each of these types are given below:

> Senior and middle management should be more consistently involved in monitoring various aspects of curriculum planning and implementation.
>
> (School F)

> Develop policies for reading, writing and study skills across the curriculum.
>
> (School A)

A further curriculum-related type was 'curriculum (specific)' – where the emphasis was on particular subjects or aspects of the curriculum:

> Fulfil statutory requirements for Religious Education in Key Stage 4.
>
> (School C)

Recommendations on management and planning related either to general management/administrative procedures or to school development planning as a whole:

> Operate careful monitoring procedures with reference to actual expenditure.
>
> (School B)

> The school's management plan now needs to include: clarification of priorities, with time-lines for specific targets; details of staff with key responsibilities; resource requirements; and success criteria for evaluation.
>
> (School E)

The majority of recommendations (80 per cent) were concerned with assessment, the curriculum, and teaching and learning (the eight types exemplified above). This is perhaps not surprising, as these represent the core concerns of all schools. Nevertheless, some clear differences in the 'recommendation profile' of each inspection could be discerned. Inspection D was somewhat exceptional in that the recommendations were exclusively concerned with the core. In contrast, the other inspections had recommendations related to both the core and some of the other aspects of schools including management/administration, organization, school development planning, special educational needs, equal opportunities, environment/accommodation, pastoral/discipline and resources. Rather greater emphasis was given to these features in inspections B, E and F than in inspections A and C.

The implementation of recommendations

Studies of school improvement have usually relied on participants' accounts to establish the extent to which changes have been implemented. In the absence of any practical alternatives we did the same. When the implementation ratings for each recommendation were examined we found a good degree of consensus amongst teachers and inspectors. For some recommendations, however, rating differences were apparent. There are several possible reasons for such discrepancies. For example, headteachers may have tended to give more favourable ratings than their staff. Teachers may have had a partial view of school-wide implementation and really only known how recommendations affected their class or curriculum area. The school inspectors also often admitted that they had insufficient knowledge of how things had progressed since the inspection. This lack of complete consensus struck us as the way things were 'on the ground'. Several perspectives on implementation can be legitimately held within the same institution. We suspect, as well, that interviewees gave themselves and their institutions the benefit of the doubt when deciding whether implementation of recommendations had actually taken place; our picture may be a little optimistic.

In such circumstances we looked particularly closely for consistency and corroboration amongst the descriptions given by interviewees of the form which implementation had actually taken. As a result we felt more confident about assigning an overall rating on a (slightly modified) implementation scale covering the range: full implementation, substantial implementation, some implementation, limited implementation and no implementation. The results are summarized in Table 10.3 which shows the extent of implementation approximately 12 and 18 months after the inspections. Specific recommendations can be identified by the inspection (A, B, etc.) and by number (1, 2, etc.). Thus the recommendation about assessment made during the inspection of school A (labelled A1) was reported to have been 'fully' implemented. The figures not in brackets refer to the situation at our 12-month follow-up; those in brackets to the position after 18 months.

It may be seen from the bottom row of Table 10.3 that some 12 months after the inspection only 7 of the 43 recommendations could be considered 'fully' implemented. Even when combined with those assessed as 'substantially' implemented the number was only 13, or about 30 per cent of the total number. At the other extreme, ten recommendations (about 25 per cent) remained either 'not implemented' or only implemented to a limited extent. The largest category of recommendations (just under half) were described as having been implemented to 'some' extent.

Six months on, or 18 months after the inspection, some modest improvement in overall implementation was apparent. The number of recommendations at least substantially implemented had risen to 17 (40 per cent) whereas the number that were still virtually unimplemented had only decreased overall by one.

Although there was a general trend for implementation to improve over the 6-month interval there were some reversals in a small number of cases. Three of these were in school A, where recommendations had initially been assessed as fully or substantially implemented and were revised downwards on the second occasion. This may have indicated that implementation had not been maintained in these cases or, more likely, that interviewees were more realistic the second time around in making assessments of recommendations which implied a knowledge of all departments and teachers.

Undoubtedly some recommendations were, by their very nature, easier to implement than others. Those concerned with curriculum delivery (CDe) and teaching and learning (TL), which effectively often require wholesale changes in the behaviours of teachers and pupils, were amongst the most difficult to implement, generally reaching at best partial implementation. An example of such a recommendation was A6, which was concerned with the lack of progress of some pupils (particularly boys) and the need for provision to be more closely matched to the needs of individual pupils. Factors thought to be influencing implementation were: the low level of literacy and oracy of many pupils on entry, the huge range of ability which made the kinds of differentiation advocated by the inspectors difficult to achieve and the lack of motivation to succeed

Table 10.3 Perceived extent of implementation of the various types of recommendations

Recommendation type	Extent of implementation					Totals
	Full	Substantial	Some	Limited	None	
Assessment (A)	A1 (B1a, B1b)	B1a (A1, D2)	B1b, C1, D1, D2 (D1)	(C1)		6
Curriculum delivery (CDe)	A2		B2, D3 (A2, B2, B3, D3, E1)	B3, E1 (C2)	C2	6
Curriculum documentation (CDo)		A3, D4 (D4)	F1 (F1, A3)			3
Curriculum monitoring/ evaluation (CME)	A4, C3 (A4, C3, C4)		C4	F2 (F2)		4
Curriculum [specific] (CS)	(A5)	A5 (C8)	C8	(C5)	C5	3
Organization (O)			B4b (B4b)		F3 (F3)	2
School development plan (SDP)	F4 (F4)	(C6)	C6, E2 (E2)			3
Environment and accommodation (EA)	(B4a)	B4a	B5 (B5)			2

Category						Totals
Equal opportunities (EO)					C7 (C7)	1
Management/ administration (MA)	A8, B6 (A8, B6)			(E3)	B7, E3 (B7)	4
Pastoral/discipline (PD)			F5 (F5)			1
Special educational needs (SEN)				E4 (E4)		1
Teaching and learning (TL)		(B8)	A6, B8, C9, D5, D6, E5 (A6, C9, D5, D6, E5)			6
Resources (R)	A7 (A7)					1
Totals	7 (11)	6 (6)	20 (17)	4 (6)	6 (3)	43

Entries in the cells refer to the recommendations for individual inspections. Thus the first recommendation in school A (A1) was about assessment and was fully implemented; the second (A2) was about curriculum delivery and was also fully implemented; the third (A3) was about curriculum documentation and was substantially implemented; and so on.

Entries enclosed in brackets refer to implementation approx. 12 months after the inspection. Entries not enclosed in brackets refer to implementation approx. 18 months after the inspection. Thus recommendation B1a was judged to have been 'substantially' implemented 12 months later and fully implemented after 18 months.

in school in an area severely affected by unemployment. Although efforts were being made the staff generally felt, as far as the boys were concerned, at a loss to solve what they felt had been recognized as a national problem.

Other recommendations such as A8 (to extend the school day) can, once a school is convinced of their validity, be unambiguously implemented. The recommendations concerned with school development planning (SDP) required either greater conformity to a prescribed format (E2, F4) or for the plan to be reflected in the development plans of individual departments (C6). Once again, if the school can be persuaded that these are desirable features, then they can be relatively readily accomplished.

Those recommendations which were characterized by little or no implementation were often ones which were perceived as presenting particularly difficult problems. For example, meeting the statutory requirements for Key Stage 4 Religious Education (C5) was a problem in school C because of the lack of teacher expertise in, and commitment to, the subject. Also, where a school remains unconvinced of the wisdom of a recommendation it is all too likely to remain unimplemented. In school B, unlike in school A, a recommendation to extend the school day did not meet with any great enthusiasm from either the governors or the staff and the *status quo* prevailed. Occasionally a school will regard a recommendation as desirable but of lower priority than others. Recommendation C7 (to 'complete the formulation and implementation of equal opportunities and multi-cultural policies') fell into this category. The headteacher commented, however, that this would be tackled before the school received a 'real' OFSTED inspection.

Some 18 months after the inspection the extent of implementation was found to vary from inspection to inspection. This can be seen in Table 10.4, which gives the proportion of recommendations which fell into the categories of 'full or substantial implementation' and 'limited or none'. Implementation had apparently been greatest in schools A and B and least in schools E and F, with the other two (C and D) occupying intermediate positions.

Factors influencing implementation

What determined which recommendations were implemented? A summary of the influences reported across all six inspections is

Table 10.4 Overall extent of implementation of recommendations of each inspection

Inspection	Proportion of recommendations which can be categorized as having	
	Full or substantial implementation	*Limited or no implementation*
School A	High proportion	Low proportion
School B	High proportion	Low proportion
School C	Medium proportion	High proportion
School D	Medium proportion	Low proportion
School E	Low proportion	High proportion
School F	Low proportion	High proportion

provided in Table 10.5. The influences (positive and negative separately) are recorded on the two occasions – 12 months and 18 months after the inspections. A wide variety of influences (over 20 in all) were identified. It is immediately apparent from the table that most influences had both positive (facilitating) and negative (inhibiting) effects. Four such influences appear in the top half dozen or so items of both halves of the table. These are: staffing, teachers, headteacher/senior management team (SMT) and funding.

Staffing

Where staffing appeared as a positive influence it tended to be associated with opportunities for: making new appointments, promoting staff, and creating new staffing structures. In school C, for example, the staffing structure was reorganized to include the appointment of two senior teachers as separate curriculum co-ordinators for Key Stages 3 and 4. As the organization took some time to be completed, the consequent lack of an appropriate staffing structure was initially perceived as a negative influence. However, once completed the positive benefits became apparent as the new coordinators were able to carry out the curriculum review and monitoring functions identified in two of the inspection recommendations. This opportunity to restructure had arisen, in fact, from a rather unpromising set of circumstances. It had been necessary to reduce staffing costs as a consequence of the LEA having to cut its education budget. This had prompted the school to review its senior

Table 10.5 Reported influences on implementation of recommendations 12 and 18 months after inspection

Positive influences on implementation after:		Negative influences on implementation after:	
12 months	*18 months*	*12 months*	*18 months*
Often mentioned			
Staffing	Staffing	National Curriculum	National Curriculum
Teachers	Inspection itself	Staffing	Time
		Funding	Funding
		Time	Teachers
			Staffing
			Headteacher/SMT
Sometimes mentioned			
Curriculum development	Headteacher/SMT	Teachers	Pupils
Headteacher/SMT	Organizational groups		Local initiatives
Funding	Curriculum development		
Inspection itself	Other non-local initiatives		
Organizational groups	Inspectors		
School documentation	Teachers		
Time			

staffing structure. By taking advantage of the LEA's voluntary retirement scheme the school had been able both to meet its savings target and to fund the reorganization described above.

Where staffing was cited as a negative influence this generally referred to situations where the existing staffing structure was perceived as having certain weaknesses. For example, in school F a structure based on heads of departments posed problems; small departments had fewer teachers, who also tended to teach in more than one area. Consequently there was less opportunity to share the duties of the department. One head of such a department felt overburdened and, as a result, less able to carry out the kind of curriculum monitoring functions envisaged by the inspectors.

Teachers

The qualities or actions of teachers, collectively or individually, could be influential. In school D a senior teacher was identified as the key influence in carrying through two recommendations concerned with assessment and recording. This teacher was highly regarded by staff as an expert in these areas and had the added advantage of being linked in to work on assessment within the LEA. This example also pointed up the difference between having a policy and actually implementing it. The headteacher commented that the school had had an assessment policy for some time but until recently 'we didn't walk the talk'. The commitment of the senior teacher and others to making the policy a reality was well under way although, in the headteacher's view, 'there were still "dissenters" who were not committed to a shared view'.

In contrast, in school E, progress on implementing one of the recommendations was limited because of the 'lack of push' of the teacher with responsibility in the area concerned.

Headteacher/senior management team

Although not found as an 'often mentioned' positive influence the headteacher and/or the senior management team could exert effects. This was apparent in school A where recommendations to do with concerns in the area of curriculum policies (whole-school and departmental) were implemented on the initiative of senior management. The three deputy heads were actively involved in monitoring developments although, by the time of the second interviews, time pressures were already limiting what they could do.

Developments in school E took a different form. Although the headteacher and senior management team had sought to follow up the inspection, the process was not generally perceived to be tightly managed or monitored. In addition, the headteacher tended to be critical of recent policy (particularly that related to the National Curriculum) and was concerned not to put pressure on staff suffering from 'innovation weariness'. Although not directly blocking the implementation the overall effect was to slow the process down.

Furthermore, as we have already noted in the previous section, headteachers could directly inhibit implementation, particularly where they disagreed with individual recommendations or regarded them as relatively unimportant in their schools' order of priorities.

Funding
The effects of funding, or its lack, were very apparent in school B. There the library was seen as a major way of addressing the recommendation concerned with 'develop[ing] clear strategies for resourcing the learning process'. Although much had been done since the inspection to develop the library as a multi-resource area, lack of funds was seen as the principal constraint. Funding was needed not only for providing further materials but also for appointing someone to manage the developing facility.

On the positive side the provision of funding through the LEA's capital programme (although already in the pipeline before the inspection) had enabled the same school (B) to tackle a further recommendation concerning 'the isolated and dilapidated nature of music, art and home economics accommodation'. The result had been a brand new technology block. This had helped to give impetus to tackling the related recommendation of a 'possible development of a creative arts faculty'. The full realization of this recommendation, however, was thought to require the appointment of a faculty co-ordinator which was not possible within the existing school budget.

The National Curriculum
Top of the list of negative influences was the National Curriculum. Continual change in the National Curriculum was seen as a major inhibitor of curriculum-related recommendations in several of the schools. In most cases schools were awaiting the changes which were to emerge from the Dearing Review (SCAA 1994), which had

begun its deliberations soon after the inspections; they were tending to defer implementation. As one head of department put it, 'you don't spend half your time putting fancy painting on a coffin!'

Non-local initiatives

Other non-local initiatives could have a positive effect. In school C, for example, the government's policy of publishing examination 'league tables' had done much to galvanize action on 'monitor[ing] standards in classrooms . . .' The headteacher had expressed concern about the school's recent decline in examination performance and commented that, in a climate of competition from other schools, staff were aware that their jobs were at stake. As a consequence examination targets had been established for departments and the monitoring of performance made more systematic and explicit. In school F staff were very conscious of the prospect of a 'real' OFSTED inspection within the next few years. This had motivated them to tackle the recommendations and ensure that the school was in good shape well in advance of the next inspection.

Time

Time, or the lack of it, was referred to frequently as a factor militating against carrying out the tasks that would ensure implementation.

Inspectors and the inspection process

Some of the other positive influences on the implementation process merit brief mention. Inspectors were almost invariably cited as facilitating influences. The inspection process itself was also viewed as a catalyst, especially where the proposed changes had been previously mooted.

Curriculum development

Curriculum development activity and the use of organizational groups were particularly evident in school A. These included: the introduction of new policies for curriculum development, the targeting of pupils to raise standards, the development of reading and writing skills and the introduction of new documentation. This comprised a hefty package of within-school innovation achieved through *inter alia* a combination of working parties and staff discussion.

From what has been said it is clear that the pattern of influences varied from inspection to inspection. This is indicated in Table 10.6, which identifies only those items which made up 10 per cent or more of the total positive and negative influences reported in each individual school. The table shows that some factors were perceived as consistent influences on both occasions. For example, curriculum development was seen as a positive influence in School A and the National Curriculum was perceived as a negative influence in School D. Where a factor appears on only one occasion (for example, teachers as a positive influence in School F), its apparent absence on the other occasion generally indicates that, although reported, its frequency fell below the 10 per cent criterion.

Other inspection outcomes

The recommendations of a report are the formal expression of what an inspection team hopes will be the ultimate outcome of the inspection process. Our interviewees also identified other outcomes which for them were significant, despite the fact that these may not have been specifically included in the recommendations or the report generally.

Incidental changes in the running of the school were frequently mentioned. For example, in school E the inspection was thought to have made the senior management team look more critically at its management systems. One result of this had been the introduction of 'Key Stage management' of the curriculum.

Headteachers and their deputies tended to see the recommendations as providing support for their existing ideas and desires for change. It sometimes appeared as though inspection had added an authority and legitimacy to existing and proposed agendas.

Teachers commented on the effect of the inspection having sharpened their thinking on aspects of their work or of the school as a whole. They indicated that the report had provided staff with a much needed 'pat on the back', although one or two talked of disappointment or a drop in morale as a consequence of comments made in the reports.

Table 10.6 Most-frequently reported influences on implementation of recommendations 12 and 18 months after inspection

	Positive influences on implementation after:		Negative influences on implementation after:	
	12 months	*18 months*	*12 months*	*18 months*
School A	Curriculum development Time Staffing	Curriculum development Organizational groups Staffing		
School B	Funding		Funding National Curriculum	
School C	Other non-local initiatives	Staffing Inspectors	Staffing	
School D	Teachers	Teachers Inspectors	Time National Curriculum	National Curriculum
School E	Staffing		Time	Headteacher/SMT Teachers Staffing
School F	Teachers	Other non-local initiatives	Staffing National Curriculum	National Curriculum

LEA post-inspection support

All schools indicated that they had received some post-inspection support from their LEAs, mainly through contact maintained by the 'school' or 'link' inspector. Some other specialist inspectors and advisory teachers were also involved to a limited extent. Access to appropriate in-service education (INSET) was mentioned specifically in schools A and B.

Generally, though, the extent of post-inspection support by the LEAs concerned was modest. This was attributed to the increasing programme of inspections under way in the LEAs, which had the result of leaving the inspectors with little opportunity for follow-up work in the schools. The headteacher of school D particularly singled out the role played by individual specialist inspectors who had been able to work with certain staff on the curriculum-related recommendations. This headteacher was very supportive of the inspectorate and had invested in substantial post-inspection consultancy.

Discussion

We are now able to address the questions referred to in our opening section together with some others raised by our data.

Recommendations and their implementation

The major emphases reflected in these inspections reveal a sample of schools, no doubt like many throughout the country, which were still adjusting to the profound educational changes initiated by government policy in recent years. In essence these changes constituted a significant reconceptualization of the curriculum in terms of a nationally prescribed product to be 'delivered' through the agency of an explicit management system. The system is one in which precise documentation, planning and procedures are seen as central.

The embodiment of this approach is apparent in the current preoccupation with school development plans (SDPs). This notion has been vigorously promoted by the government and LEAs and supported by an influential body of related educational writing (Caldwell and Spinks 1988, 1992; Hargreaves and Hopkins, 1991).

Perhaps more than any other aspect of school organization the possession of an appropriately constructed SDP has come to be seen as the *sine qua non* of the 'good' school.

Our data suggest that the extent to which schools are able to respond effectively to the findings of inspections is likely to be somewhat uncertain. A year after the inspections the pattern of implementation was patchy. Only a third or so of the recommendations could be said to be at least substantially implemented and for just about a quarter there had been little or no implementation at all. It is interesting that these figures are virtually identical to those obtained in a parallel study which we have carried out on primary schools (Gray and Wilcox 1995). After a further 6 months there was some additional, albeit modest, improvement in the level of implementation. It may be that the rate of implementation begins to fall away after a year. If this is so it may take a long time for the process to be completed – if, indeed, that is possible.

At least two factors are likely to threaten this process. First the commitment of staff needs to be maintained and that may not be easy. Second, schools do not exist in an unchanging environment; they are continually subjected to external influences which can disrupt current plans and preoccupations. The headteacher of school F commented, as early as the time of our first interview, that the inspection 'had disappeared into the background against Key Stage 3 English in the summer and the county review of sixth forms'.

Some types of recommendation seem more likely to be implemented than others. There may be several reasons for this variation in implementation. For a small number of recommendations it was clear that the headteacher was unconvinced of either their validity or urgency. In such cases the fact of little or no response is not surprising. In the majority of cases, however, there was little evidence of such overt blocking. Most recommendations were treated seriously and differences were more likely to be the result of some recommendations being intrinsically easier to accomplish than others. Recommendations which implicitly or explicitly require some consequent change in the practice of teachers (often by implication, all teachers) are likely to be among the most difficult to accomplish in the short term. Indeed, some recommendations, such as those involved in changing the pedagogic skills of teachers, represent major change programmes in their own right.

The resources to which a school has access – particularly in terms of the skills of its staff – are likely to be crucial. If these are not appropriate and readily available then successful implementation may be delayed or even not occur at all. The role of the headteacher and senior staff can often be significant as in other examples of school change.

Over and above the specific characteristics of individual recommendations it was apparent that certain other features within schools, such as the nature of staffing structures and arrangements, could also exert an influence on implementation. In addition, the problem of insufficient time was often mentioned by school staff. Some prioritization is therefore a realistic response; consequently action on some recommendations will inevitably take place rather later.

It should not be forgotten that our study essentially provides 'snapshots' at two points in time of what is actually a dynamic and evolving process. The snapshots do, however, reveal a process which is complex and problematic. It would be unwise to suppose that inspection necessarily leads to a 'quick fix' or, for that matter, any 'fix' at all.

Relevance of the Fullan model

Fullan's accounts of the educational change process offer us a framework against which to assess some of the assumptions of the inspection-induced changes described here. The factors he identifies are useful in so far as they provide a fairly comprehensive checklist against which to explore our findings. To what extent can the factors he points to be seen in operation? And which, if any, are missing?

The first set of key factors Fullan identifies relate to the nature of the proposed changes; he terms these the 'characteristics of change'. They include: the perceived 'need' for the changes, their potential 'complexity', their 'clarity' and their 'quality/practicality'.

At a superficial level the 'need' for the changes identified in the various inspections we studied was recognized by most of those we interviewed. There were, however, a few cases where the headteacher in particular disagreed with an individual recommendation. Generally speaking, though, the reports and their recommendations tended to be in line with the need for change as understood by senior staff and expressed, to varying extents, in their own agendas for change. Indeed this is endorsed by the frequent comment we heard in an earlier stage of the study[3] that there had been 'no surprises'.

The clarity of a report's recommendations for a particular school was not always evident. The headteacher of school C thought that the recommendations in their written form were not initially clear but that they became so when the school inspector talked them through with the senior management team. Staff in the other schools also occasionally volunteered the observation that they were not really sure what the inspectors had in mind in proposing a particular recommendation.

There were a few intimations of staff doubts about the 'quality / practicality' of proposed changes which did not take account of what were considered significant external limitations. This was apparent with some of the curriculum-related proposals in the context of the then impending Dearing Review of the National Curriculum (SCAA 1994).

Recognition that recommendations alone may not necessarily constitute a clear programme for change is apparent in the OFSTED requirement that a detailed 'action plan' be produced in which targets and responsibilities are specified (DFE 1993). None of our schools developed a formal action plan of this kind although, in all cases, discussions about the report and its implications had taken place at various staff levels.

Even an action plan, however, may not be enough to generate real commitment unless it can also be expressed as a worthy vision for those involved. Securing this is likely to be a highly creative task. Although, as already noted, there was some indication that head-teachers saw inspection recommendations as a means of furthering their own aspirations for their schools, we found little or no evidence of any overt efforts to ensure wider ownership of the change process. To neglect this aspect is to run the risk of 'implementing the recommendations' being seen simply as a crude exercise of power legitimation on the part of the headteacher; superficial compliance rather than genuine commitment to change is the likely outcome. In the schools we studied we saw little attempt by the headteachers involved to turn inspection recommendations into broader visions and strategies which were owned by the staff. 'Implementation' was apparently seen as a more mundane process.

The second group of factors to which Fullan refers are what he terms 'local characteristics'. These would include factors associated with the headteacher, teaching staff and governing body. Such factors, especially the first two, are discernible in our analysis. Also noteworthy was the extent to which LEA inspectors, despite the difficulties under which they were working, could be influential in promoting and securing change.

A variety of influences are grouped by Fullan under his third heading of 'external factors' operating beyond the school and the LEA. In our study the inspections arose in part from the LEA inspectorates preparing themselves to operate under the new OFSTED arrangements; as a result, the inspections could be said to reflect some kind of mandate from beyond the LEA. This kind of pressure has been strengthened since OFSTED inspections became mandatory in September 1993. Together with the publication of inspection reports this may help ensure that follow-up action is taken seriously by schools. Fullan (1991: 92) maintains that successful innovations include elements of both pressure and support. In the likely absence of other external agencies, whether this is also likely to apply in inspection-induced change will depend on how far the LEAs will be able to take part in any post-inspection follow-up. Recent Education Acts have made it much more difficult for LEAs to be involved in this way.

'Institutionalization' represents a later phase of Fullan's model. Typically, he argues, this can take from 3 to 5 years. When schools and the education system are in a relatively stable state extended timescales of this kind may present few problems. In the current climate, however, schools may experience difficulties in maintaining the momentum to tackle recommendations arising from inspections as new pressures emerge. If implementation is not achieved relatively quickly schools may be tempted to discontinue the effort in order to respond to later demands and pressures on them.

Ultimately, of course, the hope is that implementation and institutionalization lead to improvements in the quality of education on offer and the learning achieved by pupils (Fullan's 'outcome' phase). Our results indicate that the majority of recommendations were not directly concerned with teaching and learning *per se* but with more general processes of curriculum delivery, management and other features of school organization. The assumption here would seem to be that recommendations, if implemented, constitute necessary if not sufficient conditions for changes at the classroom level. Significant changes in pupils' learning are therefore likely to be apparent only at the stage of institutionalization or beyond. Certainly, none of the schools, within the timescales of our study, were able to cite any evidence meeting this acid test of improvement.

Conclusion

Whether or not a school is considered to have been improved by inspection is likely to be informed by the extent to which recommendations following from it are implemented in practice. Making such a judgement is unlikely to be a simple and straightforward process. An examination of the aftermath of an inspection, if it is to be more than just a superficial process, is unlikely to yield neat 'yes, it has improved' or 'no, it has not improved' assessments. Even in the most favourable circumstances the implementation of some recommendations may necessarily require protracted time-scales of eighteen months or more.

The extent of implementation will be determined, at least in part, by the nature of the individual recommendations and the quality of the implementation strategies adopted. The latter, as our study has shown, will be influenced by the qualities and skills of the school staff. There will be some schools, no doubt, which will be able to mobilize successfully the human and other resources necessary to ensure an effective implementation strategy. Others, in our experience, will benefit from support and expertise from beyond the school. In the past this function could reasonably have been expected of the LEA through its inspectorate / advisory service. Because of the effects of government policy many, if not all, LEAs are finding it more and more difficult to sustain such a service and maintain the levels of support which they would like to provide to the generality of schools.

Assessing 'improvement' is more than just an academic exercise. The fate of individual schools may rest upon the resolution of the issue – particularly those which at the time of the inspection are deemed to be 'failing'. In this, as in other aspects of inspection, we need to be continually reminded that judgements must be as secure as possible, both to avoid injustice to individuals and institutions and to promote a sounder basis for initiating improvements.

Notes

1 Programmes to Assess the Quality of Schooling (PAQS) was a 3-year research project funded by the Economic and Social Research Council. The project had three major components: surveys of inspection activity, a panel study consisting of a one-in-five sample of LEA chief inspectors and case studies of individual LEA inspections.
2 In some LEAs inspections have been carried out by staff known as 'advisers' rather than 'inspectors'. However, for the sake of consistency and convenience we use the term 'inspector'.
3 We had in fact interviewed the samples previously, soon after the inspection had been completed. Our aim in the first interviews was to understand how teachers and inspectors had reacted to the inspection *process*.

PART 4

LOOKING TO THE FUTURE

11

THE STATISTICS OF SCHOOL IMPROVEMENT: ESTABLISHING THE AGENDA

Introduction

The concern to link the findings of school effectiveness research to strategies for school improvement has been around for some time. In practice, however, remarkably few studies have attempted to link the two paradigms directly. In this paper we explore some of the conceptual, statistical and methodological steps it would be necessary to take to secure such developments.

There are a number of barriers to integration, many of which have already been outlined elsewhere (Reynolds *et al.* 1993). Amongst those we would draw particular attention to are the different methodological orientations of the two groups, with school effectiveness researchers inclining towards the quantitative and school improvement researchers towards the qualitative. The former group have often been content to describe the differences between schools whilst the latter have been concerned to change them. Most importantly, perhaps, school effectiveness researchers have almost uniformly based their research frameworks on pupil achievement measures of one kind or another, whilst school improvement researchers have focused on various process measures. The seasoned observer will also have noted, on occasion, a certain rivalry between the two approaches.

There have, none the less, been signs of change in recent years. On the school improvement side there has been an increasing willingness to specify in more precise terms what might count as evidence of improvement. The use of 'success criteria' in school development planning is one recent example (Hargreaves and Hopkins 1991). Another is Louis and Miles' (1992) large-scale follow-up of schools which had developed 'Effective School' projects in the USA, although they mostly relied on principals' self-assessments of the progress that had been made. And a third is to be found towards the end of Fullan and Hargreaves' (1992) recent book on school improvement. Within the framework of a series of 'guidelines for action', which are firmly within the improvement tradition, they comment that 'pupil achievement and performance data, widely defined and interpreted, should also be used as a springboard for action, provided that the other guidelines are followed; effective collaborative schools are actively interested in how well they are doing, and seek evaluative data to monitor and improve on progress' (Fullan and Hargreaves 1992: 127).

On the school effectiveness side there is also considerable interest in how the research findings may be translated into educational practice. In part this may be explained by the traditional concern of such researchers to generate research findings that can inform policy development. In part it reflects a good old-fashioned approach to exploring causation – the most powerful form of validation is to identify and generate the levers for change. And, in part, it reflects the difficulties researchers have experienced when they have moved into the action mode. The conflicting pressures on the Halton project provide one such example (Stoll and Fink 1992). The recent attempts to test the so-called 'Effective Schools Model' systematically in the USA provide another. Witte and Walsh (1990) have concluded, for example, that many of the so-called 'effective' factors were heavily confounded with schools' social composition. The generally sceptical overviews of many of the more familiar school effectiveness findings offered by Creemers' (1992) and Scheerens' (1992) reports of Dutch replications offer a third.

As we began work on this chapter a further reason began to strike us as a more formidable obstacle to the integration of the two paradigms. The research design that is required to study school improvement from a school effectiveness perspective is quite difficult and time-consuming to construct and implement. Indeed, as we read the existing literature we began to wonder how much of it was strictly relevant. Much of what we encountered bore out the old adage that the data one has tend to structure the way one sees the problems, and the way one sees the problems tends to structure the data one attempts to collect. It is to the initial problems posed by breaking out of the familiar that the rest of this chapter is addressed.

Framework I: the correlates of effectiveness

The framework typically used in studies of school effectiveness is outlined in Figure 11.1, where the relationship between pupils' characteristics on intake are plotted against their subsequent attainments. Each line represents the results for a separate school. Much North American research is premised on what is essentially a one-off cross-sectional research design in which measure(s) of pupil outcome are regressed against measure(s) of pupils' social backgrounds collected at or around the same time; some British research has employed a similar strategy. Other North American and British research has attempted to construct a longitudinal (or quasi-longitudinal) design in which pupils' outcomes are regressed against measures of prior attainment; in a typical study of a secondary school this is usually taken to be a measure of pupil performance around the point of transfer from primary school. The advantages of employing research designs of this kind, which focus on pupil progress, are becoming increasingly recognized.

The main interest in this kind of research is in the extent to which pupils attending one school make greater progress than those attending others. The 'key statistic' in Figure 11.1 is the vertical distance between the lines for School A and School D, which expresses the extent to which the 'same pupil' attending one school as opposed to the other reaches higher levels of performance. This is often referred to as the 'school effect'. School A is the 'more effective' school and School D the 'less effective' one.

In the 'simple' model this difference is expressed by the distance as estimated for the median pupil. In the 'advanced' model estimates are obtained for other pupils as well (at, for example, the 25th and 75th percentiles) although, for the purposes of explication,

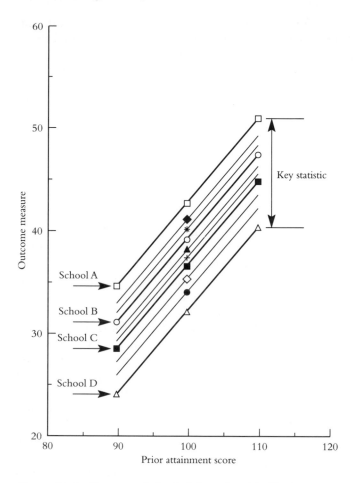

Figure 11.1 Framework for judging schools' effectiveness.

examples of these are not shown in Figure 11.1. Recent developments in multi-level modelling make testing for so-called differential effectiveness almost routine (Goldstein 1987). Although there is
still some debate about the substantive significance of 'differential
slopes' their existence is not in dispute (see Nuttall *et al.* 1989;
Jesson and Gray 1991).

A good deal has become known about the general structure of
school effects since Aitkin and Longford's (1986) pioneering analysis
(see Chapter 6). Estimates of the so-called 'key statistic' have varied

somewhat from LEA to LEA and have been shown to depend, to a certain extent, on the nature of the prior attainment and background factors taken into account.

The next step in a typical school effectiveness study is for the various factors on which data have been collected to be correlated with the differences in overall school effects. Those which turn out to be correlated most strongly are then referred to as the 'key' factors.

More cautious researchers usually like to enter at least two caveats at this juncture. First, that often what has been identified are literally correlates rather than causes of school effectiveness. And second, that the so-called 'key' factors may only explain part of the variance between schools (rather than all of it) and consequently represent, at best, partial causes.

The implications for school improvement

Let us suppose, for a moment, that a particular study has shown that just five factors 'make a difference'. This is, of course, precisely the claim that Edmonds (1979) made in his various manifestos and which other researchers have subsequently sought to replicate. What are the implications of these findings for school improvement?

In Edmonds' account the reason why some schools were more effective than others was because they had: (1) strong administrative leadership; (2) high expectations for students' achievement; (3) an orderly atmosphere conducive to learning; (4) an emphasis on basic-skill acquisition; and (5) frequent monitoring of pupil progress. What other less effective schools needed to do, therefore, was to develop along the lines of these characteristics, if they wanted to improve pupils' performance. As all of these factors could surely be assumed to be present to a greater or lesser extent it was by generating *stronger* leadership, *higher* expectations, a *more* orderly atmosphere, a *greater* emphasis on the basic skills and *more* frequent monitoring that a school would 'make the difference'.

It was a convincing story and it is not difficult to understand why many North American schools bought it, especially those serving socially disadvantaged pupils. It was, however, built on a largely unexplored (and possibly flawed) assumption (albeit a seemingly reasonable one). Had the more effective schools *become* more effective by working on these particular factors or had they already possessed these particular correlates of school effectiveness over lengthy periods of time?

In the early 1980s, Purkey and Smith (1983: 447) identified a number of issues to which we are still seeking solutions. Amongst the questions they asked were: 'Are different strategies required for low-achieving schools to raise their scores than for high-achieving schools that are beginning to decline? Once a school is deemed academically effective, what is needed to maintain its success? And how do different improvement strategies affect sub-populations in a school?'

Such questions are not easy to answer when one has information on only one year of schools' performance. It is to studies that have obtained data on schools' performance over more than one year that we now turn.

Framework II: the search for stability

The stability of schools' effects is an important, if neglected, area of study. To what extent have data on a second or subsequent year's effects confirmed the patterns emerging from a single year? Pursuit of such questions has been largely driven by a concern for replication. It has taken on a particular significance, however, when the research design has revolved around the identification of 'unusually effective' ('outlier') schools (see Levine and Lezotte 1990 for an extensive review of this kind of research). It is a familiar characteristic of 'outliers' that they tend to be unstable. A second year's data reduce the chance element.

Figure 11.2 presents the two patterns most frequently described in the research literature. The school lines in Figure 11.2a portray a position where schools' effects are highly stable – the two lines representing each school lie close to each other. Figure 11.2b portrays a situation where there are quite large changes in schools' effects across 2 years – not all the lines lie particularly close to each other.

Only a handful of studies have looked at issues of stability so there are few guidelines available about how best to interpret the correlations between 2 years' school effects. There is a general tendency, however, to refer to correlations of 0.9 and above as demonstrating

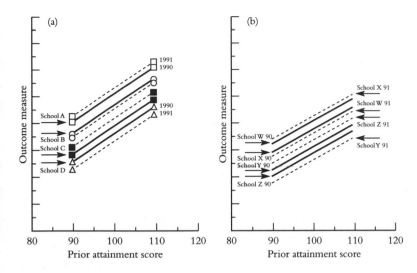

Figure 11.2 Patterns of stability/instability. (a) More stable; (b) less stable.

'high' levels of stability in effectiveness and correlations of 0.5 and below as 'low' levels; correlations falling between these two figures would seem to indicate 'reasonable' levels of stability. We shall follow these interpretations in our own discussion of the evidence which now follows.

Previous research on the stability of school effects

An extensive search of the literature (supplemented by correspondence with various researchers who have already published in this field) has so far revealed around ten studies which are germane to our purposes. From the various ways in which the studies have emerged we would expect, eventually, to discover a few more; we would be surprised, however, if there were many more.

The most salient characteristics of the various studies are summarized in Table 11.1. They vary in terms of the countries from which they emanate, the age-ranges studied, the number of years over which data were analysed, whether the controls for intakes were based on measures of prior attainment or socio-economic status and whether the latest multi-level statistical techniques were employed in the analyses. Several of these factors will almost certainly have influenced the extent to which stability was discovered and reported.

A range of conclusions about levels of stability might be drawn from the results reported in Table 11.1. One particular result is, however, of especial relevance to the present study. All the British studies on the compulsory stages of secondary schooling report 'reasonable' to 'high' levels of stability from year to year.

The implications for school improvement

What are the implications of these stability studies (Framework II) for school improvement? In practice they are not much different from those emerging from Framework I discussed earlier. Most of the studies have been concerned to establish whether the same schools would be identified as effective from an additional year's data – and they have mostly concluded that they would. Their dominant focus has been on replication.

None of the studies has been addressed to the more stringent question of whether the same factors were revealed as correlates of effectiveness as in the previous year. This is not altogether surprising since, in practical terms, it would have meant doubling up on data collection as well.

Researchers reporting lower levels of stability have faced a dilemma. They have appeared to adopt one of two strategies to try to resolve it. One response has been to comment on the difficulties of making substantive interpretations of the results – the research serves as a salutary warning to those who would rush to judgement. The other response has been to argue that there was in fact greater stability around than has been revealed – that the 'true' correlations have, for one technical or statistical reason or another, been underestimated.

Whichever patterns have emerged in the data there appears to have been a strong inclination to push the interpretation towards one or other of the two underlying positions (high or low stability). Only the Louisiana project seems to have been a partial exception to this general tendency (Teddlie and Stringfield 1993). Most researchers in this area would seem to have concurred (wittingly or otherwise) with Scheerens' conclusion that 'effectiveness appears to be a fairly permanent school characteristic' (Scheerens 1992: 71). It follows from this observation (although Scheerens omits to say so) that 'ineffectiveness' must be 'a fairly permanent school characteristic' as well. Scheerens may well have been largely right, as we ourselves shall show. It is a moot point, however, whether the research we have considered so far could have led researchers to alternative conclusions.

The search for stability takes us close to the heart of the debate about the links between research on school effectiveness and research on school improvement. It is a fundamental belief of researchers in the improvement tradition that at least some of the factors contributing to schools' effectiveness are not 'fairly permanent characteristics' and that they can be isolated, developed and changed. Most school effectiveness researchers also believe that the factors that they have identified are, in large part, under the schools' control.

How, then, can these positions be squared with the findings on stability? We have two preliminary suggestions. The first is to look for clear patterns of change amongst the data available – even a 'high stability' correlation may conceal some improving/deteriorating schools. The second is to combine this with a search for trends over longer periods of time. A trend, however, requires a minimum of 3 years' data, something which very few studies of school effectiveness to date have had available.

Framework III: the search for improvement

To establish appropriate estimates of schools' improvement over time a number of components must be brought together. These, in our view, include:

- measures of outcomes and prior attainment on individual pupils;
- data from 3 or (preferably) more years;
- a multi-level statistical analysis;
- an orientation towards examining the data for systematic changes in schools' performance over time.

As far as we can see, none of the previous studies have combined all four of these requirements at the same time.

Figure 11.3a outlines the patterns for schools which are consistently improving or deteriorating. It has been assumed that there

Table 11.1 Previous studies of the stability of school effects

	Author(s) of study	Country	Age-group	Years	Main control*	Reported level of stability[†]
1	Willms and Raudenbush (1989)	Scotland	Secondary	1980 1984	Prior attainment and SES	High
2	Nuttall, Goldstein, Prosser and Rasbash (1989)	England	Secondary	1985–7	Prior attainment	High
3	Sime and Gray (1991)	England	Secondary	1985–7 1983 1984 1990 1991	Prior attainment	High High High
4	Rutter, Maughan, Mortimore and Ouston (1979)	England	Secondary	1974 1976	Prior attainment	Reasonable
5	Mandeville (1988)	USA	Primary	1985 1986	SES	Low to reasonable
6	Tymms and Fitz-Gibbon (1990)	England	Post-16 (16–19)	1983–9	Prior attainment	Low to reasonable[§]

7 de Blok and Hoeksma (1993)	Netherlands	Primary	1987–91	SES	Reasonable
8 Teddlie and Stringfield (1993)	USA	Primary	1983–5 1989 1990	SES	Not clear¶
9 Bosker and Guldemond, (1991)	Netherlands	Secondary	1973 1974 1975	Prior attainment	High
10 de Jong and Roeleveld (1988)	Netherlands		‡	SES	Reasonable
11 Rowan and Denk (1982)	USA	Elementary	1975 1976 1977	Prior attainment	Low

SES = socio-economic status.

* Studies 1, 2, 3 and 7 used multi-level statistical techniques.

† 'High' = correlations of 0.9 and above; 'reasonable' = between 0.5 and 0.9; 'low' = less than 0.5.

‡ Not listed in the source cited.

§ Based on subject departments as the unit of analysis rather than schools.

¶ Because of the 'outlier' pairs design of this study it is not strictly comparable to the others listed in the table. There were also other changes in the nature of the data collected which make clear comparisons over time difficult to establish. The authors themselves report that 4 schools were 'stable effective', 4 were 'stable ineffective', 5 'improving' and 3 'declining', although they do not say whether these latter schools started from a base of being 'effective' or 'ineffective'.

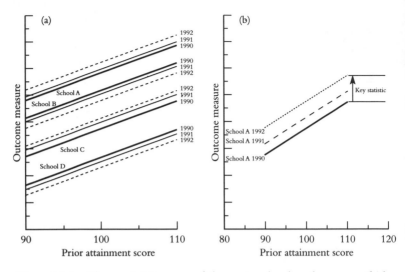

Figure 11.3   Change. (a) Patterns of change in school performance; (b) key statistic of change for school A.

are small changes from year to year although it should be stressed that, at this stage, this is just an assumption. Figure 11.3b focuses on just one of the schools, School A, which is consistently improving. The 'key statistic' in relation to school improvement relates to these changes from year to year. We have not been able to identify the size or existence of such trends from the previous literature.

In Figure 11.1 the important comparisons were between the more effective schools (A and B) and the less effective ones (C and D). Figure 11.3 suggests a more complex picture. School A is of interest because it is effective and improving over time. School D is of interest because it is ineffective and deteriorating over time. But School C is also of interest, because it is ineffective but improving over time, as is School B, which is still relatively effective but deteriorating.

In brief, the focus on improvement reveals a variety of different patterns which need to be understood. There are five basic types. These are: (1) an effective school which is improving; (2) an effective school which is deteriorating; (3) an ineffective school which is improving; (4) an ineffective school which is deteriorating; and (5) effective and ineffective schools which are neither consistently improving nor consistently deteriorating. Obviously, with data over longer periods of time, other 'types' might also emerge.

There is clearly something to be learnt from the experiences of schools falling into all these various types. Unfortunately the previous literature (summarized in Table 11.1) offers few insights. The Louisiana project (Teddlie and Stringfield 1993) comes closest to offering tentative explanations. However, its research design inevitably makes these both fragile and largely speculative. Ineffective schools which are improving (type (3)) represent a particularly important focus for further research. Such schools would, of course, have been neglected in most earlier studies.

There are several ways in which a school's effectiveness might change over time. The main possibilities are outlined in Figure 11.4. The first is that improvement and deterioration approximate to linear processes – schools get uniformly better or worse by roughly equal amounts each year. A second is that the process starts off slowly and then accelerates, and a third is that the process starts off rapidly and then decelerates. There are clearly other possibilities as well, including schools which fluctuate in their effectiveness from year to year.

There is a further aspect which we have so far avoided considering but which could be an important way in which schools start the process of improvement. Most of our discussion has been in terms of the typical (or median) pupil in a school; we have ignored the possibility of differential effectiveness. It may well be the case, however, that a school increases its effectiveness by first working with one particular group of pupils rather than others.

Figure 11.5 outlines two possibilities. The first is the case of a school which initially boosts its effectiveness with respect to its higher-attaining pupils. The second depicts a school which has initially worked on its lower-attaining pupils. Clearly reciprocal patterns could occur with respect to deteriorations in effectiveness (although we have not shown them here).

First steps towards estimates of school improvement

We are in the fortunate position of possessing contemporary data which permit us to make preliminary estimates of the incidence and extent of changes in schools' effectiveness over time.

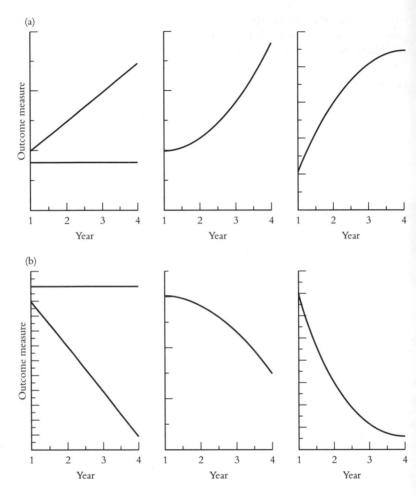

Figure 11.4 Different patterns of change over time. (a) Patterns of improvement; (b) patterns of deterioration.

Data

The data were drawn from all the institutions in a single LEA with over 30 secondary schools. For each of 3 years information was available at the pupil level on: (1) GCSE exam scores (converted into a points score for each pupil with 7 for a grade A, 6 for a B and so on); (2) a finely-differentiated measure of prior attainment taken

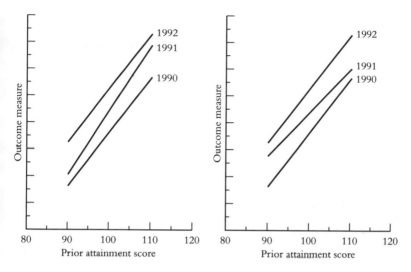

Figure 11.5 Differential slopes in school improvement.

shortly prior to transfer to secondary school 5 years previously; (3) gender; and (4) several other items of information including free school meals (although as this latter variable was not available for the first of the 3 years it was not employed in the analyses reported here). In 1990 a 20 per cent sample was drawn of all pupils in Year 11 of the authority's schools; in 1991 and 1992 the nominal sample size was increased to cover all Year 11 pupils.

Analysis

A series of multi-level analyses were conducted on the data using the ML3 package (see Prosser *et al.* 1992). A standard two-level model was employed with year fitted as a dummy variable (an alternative, in this case, to fitting a three-level model). The amounts and structure of the variance explained were very similar to those emerging in earlier studies as the various variables available had good explanatory power (see Chapter 6). There was some evidence of differential slopes between schools across the 3 years although, as these were not broken down for separate years, they are not considered further here. Full details of the technical analysis are available elsewhere (see Gray *et al.* 1995).

Table 11.2   Distribution of 'school effects' over 3 years

Size of effect in GCSE points	1990	1991	1992
Highest two schools (effective)	+4	+5	+6
	+3	+4	+5
Upper quartile	+1	+2	+2
Median	0	0	0
Lower quartile	−1	−2	−2
Lowest two schools (ineffective)	−3	−4	−4
	−4	−5	−6
(Standard deviation of residuals)	(1.7)	(2.1)	(2.5)

GCSE points scores were established as follows: each grade in a GCSE subject at grade A = 7 points; grade B = 6 points; C = 5 points; D = 4 points; E = 3 points; F = 2 points; G = 1 point; ungraded or absent = zero points.

Based on a multi-level model which utilized information on pupils' gender, school attended, prior attainment (and its mathematical power transformation), examination performance and year of entry into examinations. At school level contextual variables representing pupils' average prior attainment (and its square) were incorporated.

Estimated for pupils at the 50th percentile in each school. All points scores have been rounded to the nearest whole number.

It should be remembered that 'school effects' are defined here as the residuals, i.e. that part of the variation which is not explained by the controls for prior attainment, etc.

Results

The results of the analysis as regards differences in school effectiveness (more strictly the residuals) are reported in Table 11.2 for each of the 3 years. For example, in 1990 the median pupil in the single most effective school achieved 4 more exam points than would have been predicted from knowledge of their prior attainment and other characteristics, whilst the 'same pupil' in the least effective school achieved 4 points less than predicted. There was, in other words, a difference of around 8 exam points; the gap between pupils at schools at the upper and lower quartiles was a good deal smaller at around 2 points. These estimates are very much in line with previous estimates we have reported and with those from other studies (see Chapter 6).

Generally speaking, the results for 1991 and 1992 confirmed the

Table 11.3 Correlations between 'unadjusted results' and 'school effects' over 3 years

	1990	1991	1992
Correlations between schools' unadjusted results			
1990	–	–	–
1991	0.84	–	–
1992	0.81	0.90	–
Correlations between school effects			
1990	–	–	–
1991	0.99	–	–
1992	0.87	0.88	–

Based on estimates for pupils at the 50th percentile.

evidence from 1990 (see Table 11.2). The range between the most and least effective schools was around two grade C passes at GCSE per pupil; between the upper and lower quartiles it was between 2 and 4 points.

Table 11.3 presents the correlations between schools' 'raw', unadjusted results for each of the adjacent years. It will be clear that with these correlations ranging between 0.8 and 0.9 there was some movement over the course of the 3 years.

Table 11.3 also presents the correlations between the 'school effects' (residuals) for adjacent years. These were all around 0.9 confirming the high levels of stability reported in some previous research in Table 11.1. These correlations were all higher than those for the unadjusted results. In general, schools do not appear to have varied very much in their effectiveness from one year to the next. None the less, there were some variations and it is these we now consider.

Table 11.4 shows the extent to which individual schools improved or deteriorated over the periods 1990–1, 1991–2 and 1990–2. Several points are worthy of note. The largest increase was just under 3 exam points, and the largest decrease just over 2 exam points; more typical changes averaged around 1 point either way. If we compare these estimates with those concerning differences in effectiveness in Table 11.2 it is clear that they are, in comparison, a good deal smaller. It would take several years of *consistent* improvement for an ineffective school to become an effective one, even assuming

Table 11.4   The distribution of school improvement: increases and decreases in 'school effects' over 3 years

Size of change in GCSE points	1990–1	1991–2	1990–2
Highest increase	+0.9	+2.8	+2.9
Increase at upper quartile	+0.5	+1.0	+1.0
Median	0	0	0
Decrease at lower quartile	−0.4	−1.0	−1.0
Highest decrease	−1.0	−2.0	−2.3

These are indicative estimates for heuristic purposes obtained by subtracting the residual score for each school for 1990 from the residual for 1991 and so on. A positive remainder indicates a school which was improving; a negative remainder a school which was deteriorating.

it always made year-on-year increases at or near the highest levels reported in the table. As the figures in the third column (1990–2) indicate, however, no school in practice made increases that approached these levels; the biggest increase over the period was around 3 points.

Just under one in five of the schools changed their performance by an average of 2 or more points per pupil over the period covered by our surveys (see Table 11.5). We chose this level of change as representing something of substantive significance. It is equivalent to all the pupils in a school increasing their performance by one grade (say from a grade D to a grade C) in one subject each year. These changes were, of course, over and above any general 'improvements' that occurred across most or all schools in the sample or which occurred in individual schools as a direct result of changes in their intakes; both these kinds of changes were taken into account in the statistical modelling. In over four out of five schools the changes were smaller than 2 points or, in some cases, non-existent (see Table 11.5).

We allocated each school to one of three groups using statistical criteria to determine whether they were 'effective', 'ineffective' or performing 'around predicted levels'. A school which fell into the 'effective' category was performing above the upper quartile cut-off in Table 11.2; a school in the 'ineffective' category was performing below the lower quartile cut-off; schools performing 'around predicted levels' fell somewhere between these two points. These are quite stringent criteria for judging effectiveness/ineffectiveness. Most schools fell into the third group.

Looking in greater detail at the schools which experienced changes of more than 2 points, four schools improved their performance and two deteriorated (see Table 11.5). One of these four improving schools moved from performing 'around predicted levels' (or just below) into the 'effective' grouping over the period of the study. Only one of the four schools made equal amounts of progress each year. The other three made considerably greater progress in the second year than the first, suggesting an 'accelerating' pattern (see Figure 11.4).

Table 11.5 is also interesting for the patterns it does not reveal. Neither of the 'ineffective' schools improved their position whilst the greater majority of schools fluctuated a little in their performance without changing their overall positions.

In brief, the number of schools in the study which were clearly changing in terms of their effectiveness (either by improving or deteriorating) appeared to be rather modest; the greater majority remained (more or less) stable.

Some caveats

Some caveats are in order. The first and most obvious one is that 3 years' data only just constitute a trend. Data from further years are highly desirable and possibly essential – a school which has improved at least 4 years on the run is a better target for investigation. However, anyone who has assembled data for just a 1-year study will recognize the logistical challenges this presents.

Second, whilst multi-level models are clearly the most appropriate statistical method, we are still short of practical understanding about how they work with data over time. To date we lack the consistent body of findings associated with the recent reanalyses of research on school effectiveness. The estimates of between-year variation look consistent with earlier work but there is not much to compare them with.

Third, the size of the changes we are referring to as 'improvements' is quite small, at least when compared with the estimates for differences in schools' effectiveness we have been familiar with. The 'robustness' with which individual schools are identified as

Table 11.5 Changes in school effectiveness during the study (1990–2)

Position in 1990	Effective	Position in 1992 around predicted levels	Ineffective
Schools whose effectiveness changed by 2 or more points over the period (6 schools)			
Effective	1 school remained effective and also improved	No schools	No schools deteriorated a lot
Around predicted levels	1 school improved to become effective	4 schools changed but remained within band (2 improved, 2 declined)	No schools
Ineffective	No schools improved a lot	No schools	No schools
Schools whose effectiveness changed by less than 2 points over the period (28 schools)			
Effective	1 school remained effective	2 schools deteriorated a little	Not applicable
Around predicted levels	No schools	23 schools did not change their position	No schools
Ineffective	Not applicable	No schools	2 schools remained ineffective

A school was defined as 'effective' or 'ineffective' if its residual score fell 1.4 standard deviations above or below the mean. In 1990 this translated into a points score of plus or minus 2.4 GCSE points; in 1992 the equivalent figure was plus or minus 3.5 GCSE points.

changing may vary when the specifications of the model are changed.

Fourth, we have ignored, for the moment, the existence of differential slopes on the pragmatic grounds that this further complicates an already complicated story. In three or four schools this *may* be a significant issue. Clearly more work on sorting out the implications of their existence in the sample needs to be undertaken.

Our final caveat is a more general one. We have focused here on just one aspect of pupils' achievements. As Hargreaves (1984) reminds us forcibly there are at least three others (relating to pupils' capacities to apply knowledge, their personal and social skills, and their motivation and commitments) which we have, for the moment, neglected and which are not necessarily correlated with exam results. A full account of school improvement would take changes in these into account as well.

Explaining improvements

Which factors might begin to explain the changes we have observed? The literature offers a variety of plausible candidates. With only a small number of schools clearly improving/deteriorating, however, it is possible that a search for common factors across the sites is doomed. A 'situated' understanding of change may be required. The position is further complicated by the fact that we know only a little about which 'stage' we are tapping into in each school's 'natural history'. None the less, the existing research offers some pointers and it is to a brief consideration of these that we now turn.

If we were to go into schools at the present time and ask heads and teachers for their explanations their responses would, we suspect, focus on prioritizing achievement gains as captured by the outcome measure, namely exam results. There are a variety of pressures in the system contributing to this narrowing of focus. We would expect schools to describe both general strategies and particular tactics.

Amongst the strategies at departmental level might be the reviewing and setting of (fresh) targets, the careful monitoring of pupils' progress, particularly in relation to coursework, and the provision of regular feedback to pupils on their development. At secondary school level we might anticipate moves to increase the total numbers of exams entered, the monitoring of differences between departments in their entry policies, changes in the time allocated to different subjects and, in some cases, the identification of particular pupils and groups of pupils for additional support. Gender differences may be an important dimension here.

We might also expect more use of tactics such as changing syllabuses and examination boards and the encouragement of higher-attaining pupils to increase their total tallies by continuing the occasional option they might otherwise have dropped. Some of those approaches are discussed briefly elsewhere (Hedger and Raleigh 1992) and it would be interesting to know whether they can yield more than 'one-off' returns. Scheerens (1992) would probably describe all of them under the heading 'determination to achieve better results'.

Coping strategies

Researchers of school improvement have tended to look at other potential explanations of change alongside these. Seeking to explain why school principals who had reported 'great improvements' in their students' academic achievements had been successful, Louis and Miles (1992) invoked the concept of 'coping' strategies. They concluded that:

> Active problem-coping efforts are extremely central in successful implementation. Passive avoidance, procrastinating, 'doing business as usual', and shuffling people from job to job do not work, if they are the only strategies used. They must be accompanied by 'deep' coping strategies such as vision-building and sharing, rolling planning, substantial restaffing, increasing school control over the environment, empowering people and redesigning the school organization.
>
> (Louis and Miles 1992: 281)

These are, of course, far from being minor considerations. 'Coping' strategies go to the centre of a school's organization. It is of interest, therefore, that although this 'factor' was the most important of those Louis and Miles identified, it none the less failed to explain large parts of the variation in principals' reported outcomes regarding student achievement.

Cultural explanations

Other researchers of school improvement have sought to expand on the 'cultural' explanations also offered by school effectiveness researchers. In a rare study of an ineffective school Reynolds and Packer (1992), for example, describe a number of barriers to school improvement, including a lack of familiarity amongst staff in discussing educational matters and a 'behind closed doors' mentality, which resulted in a variety of defensive, 'anti-change' positions. It is to counter such difficulties that Fullan and Hargreaves (1992) counsel leaders of school improvement strategies to understand the culture of their schools, promote collaboration amongst staff and 'guide' rather than 'direct' the general thrusts of school development strategies. Building greater staff commitment and new approaches to staff development are central themes of other studies as well (Brighouse 1991; Fullan 1992). Whether such strategies can deliver within the same time-scales as the 'head-on' approaches described earlier, however, remains debatable. Much of the school improvement literature may, in practice, be about working for change in the longer term.

Quality of teaching

Some recent research on school effectiveness has suggested that differences between classrooms and departments may be as important as differences between schools (Creemers 1992; Tymms and Fitz-Gibbon 1990). Classroom-level studies usually try to grapple with issues surrounding the quality of teaching and the nature of pupils' responses. It may be that the schools which have begun to make sustained progress have found renewed ways of raising such issues directly amongst teachers. Indeed, some departments may have taken ownership of the process more substantially than others.

Changes in leadership

Finally, there is a tradition of research which emphasizes the importance of changes in leadership as the engine-room of improvement. This is an explanation which Teddlie and Stringfield (1993) frequently invoke in their case studies of improving Louisiana primary schools. Leadership issues are also behind many of the factors identified in the inner London study (Mortimore *et al*. 1988). Changing the head is something which is frequently cited by LEA personnel as a key factor, although our understanding of what precisely new leaders do is more limited. Leadership may need to be explored in terms of its particular effects in each of the areas outlined above.

Concluding comment

The study of change has been a thorn in the side of school effectiveness researchers for much of the past decade. We have argued that it requires some reorientation as regards familiar and well-established relationships. Researchers of school improvement, by contrast, have tried to deal with a messier world in which 'movement' is an accepted fact. The challenge for both paradigms is to test out their assumptions within each other's frameworks.

12

THE CHALLENGE OF TURNING ROUND INEFFECTIVE SCHOOLS

Introduction

In September 1994 Fairfax Community School in Bradford was reported to be 'the first casualty among local authority schools of the new inspection system launched by the Office for Standards in Education' (*The Guardian*, 7 September 1994). Senior education officers within the authority had recommended it be closed.

The previous autumn the school had been visited by OFSTED inspectors, who had produced a series of strongly worded criticisms as well as recommendations for its improvement. Unusually, the school had also featured in a High Court case when a group of (mainly Bangladeshi) parents had tried unsuccessfully to get their children places at other schools in the area. A second visit by OFSTED inspectors during the summer of 1994 had 'found little improvement and made further criticisms'.

The acting headteacher was said to be 'shocked and horrified by the [closure] decision. The staff's hard work seemed to have been ignored and wasted.' A leader of the Bangladeshi community meanwhile was reported as saying: 'if this means all other schools have to improve their standards, it will have been justified. The parents feel that it shows their stand was right.'

In the same article a second school, St Mark's Church of England comprehensive in Hammersmith and Fulham LEA, was reported to have been 'condemned by OFSTED inspectors as a failing school'. The inspectors said that 'a plan drawn up by the head and governors after an adverse report in December 1993 had not improved teaching'.

A mere fortnight after their initial recommendations, Bradford LEA had had second thoughts about closing Fairfax, stepping back from their initial decision (*BBC Breakfast TV News*, 20 September 1994). The school had the chance to fight on.

Both cases underline how high the improvement stakes have become. Ineffective schools, which fail to improve rapidly, run the risk of being simply closed down. Rarely can knowledge about how to improve have been at more of a premium.

Some case studies of change in 'ineffective' schools

In fact there is very little research, especially in the UK, which is explicitly about 'turning round' so-called 'ineffective' schools. This is not to say that no research has been done on this topic but rather that, in the search for the correlates of effectiveness, the correlates of ineffectiveness have been assumed to be the same. It is by no means clear, however, that they are. How an 'ineffective' school improves may well differ from the ways in which more effective schools maintain their effectiveness.

Most of the work which has been undertaken to date has been in the form of case studies and it is to some of these that we now turn.

Charismatic leadership on the 'wrong side of the tracks'

The story of improvement at George Washington Carver High School in Atlanta is told in Lightfoot's study *The Good High School* (1983, Chapter 1). It is the first of six case studies she presents of 'good' American schools and the only one relating to an inner-city area. Its claim to a place in the book rests on the extent to which a new leader had secured sufficient changes within a relatively short space of time to bring the school back from the brink. Lightfoot clearly felt that such a school deserved a place in her catalogue of excellence as much as, if not more than, more traditional examples.

The school's story of change revolved around just one figure, the new principal, Dr Norris Hogans. Hogans was in his late forties, a former American football player:

> powerful in stature and character, he dominated the school . . .
> a man of great energy he walked about the campus in perpetual motion, looking severe and determined, always carrying his walkie-talkie. Through the walkie-talkie he barked orders and made enquiries. His requests sounded like commands. There was an immediacy about him, an unwillingness to wait or to be held back.

Atlanta's school superintendent, Dr Alonzo Crim, had turned to Hogans when he had contemplated closing the school which was, at the time, '. . . an ugly reminder of the deterioration, chaos and unrest that plagues many big-city schools' (Lightfoot 1983: 31 and *ff*). Crim saw Hogans as 'a diamond in the rough, a jock who made good . . . and a man who learnt and grew every day'. In Crim's view Hogans had done a good job in a short space of time (just 3 years): 'he had gotten the kids to listen [and] disrupted the inertia'.

Opinions about Hogans amongst the staff were more mixed.

> Everyone agreed he was powerful. Some viewed his power as the positive charisma and dynamic force required to turn an institution around and move it in a new direction. These enthusiasts recognized his abrupt, sometimes offensive style, but claimed that his determined temperament was necessary to move things forward. They willingly submitted to his autocratic decisions because they viewed his institutional goals as worthy and laudable.

His detractors, on the other hand, had been around in the school for long periods of time and were used to policies which had permitted considerably more autonomy. Now they 'tended to keep their complaints to themselves, forming a covert gossip ring and passively resisting [Hogans'] attempts to make changes by preserving their own inertia'.

Lightfoot felt there were three key thrusts to Hogans' interventions: (1) the need for discipline; (2) the need for a new image for the school; and (3) the need for better and closer links with the community. 'Discipline and authority had become the key to gaining control of the change process.' Hogans believed passionately that the school:

> ... must provide the discipline, the safety and the resources that students were not getting at home and that it must demand something from them ... A chaotic school setting and a permissive atmosphere could only lead to ruin and failure so there was a preoccupation with rules and regulations at Carver ... Visible conformity, obedience and a dignified presence were critical concerns.

Reflecting in a concluding chapter on why Carver might deserve the accolade of 'excellence', Lightfoot was clearly concerned to present both the pros and the cons. On the positive side she identified several areas where Carver had made 'great strides'. 'School people focused on the measurable, visible indices of progress: steady attendance rates, fewer disciplinary problems, a decline in acts of vandalism to property, and more jobs filled upon graduation.' On some other 'standards of goodness', however, such as the '... more psycho-social, less measurable qualities of civility, poise and ambition' she was less certain. And on a number of indices which '... reflected the substance of education including curricular design and structure, and pedagogical processes', Carver lagged behind many other Atlanta high schools. Many of the staff were committed to tackling 'the educational malaise' but '... the school had a long way to go before it could claim that most of its students were receiving a good education'. The school had '... progressed from terrible to much better' and it was this progress which was impressive. But, in the round, it had only achieved the '... minimal standards of goodness which [she] envisioned as a first stage of movement towards higher goals'.

'Hostility and conflict' on the road to change

Most case studies of improving schools report that some improve-ment (eventually) occurred. In our view such studies, biased as they tend to be towards the change efforts that worked, probably give too rosy an impression of how much change can take place over relatively short periods of time. More work on the myriad efforts which probably 'failed' is required.

The few pieces of research which report attempts to tackle this issue suggest that we may be looking at a rather different set of factors from those which emerge in the successful cases. In all-too-brief accounts of a project which failed to turn around an ineffective Welsh school Reynolds (1991) and Reynolds and Packer (1992: 178–82) argue that the 'deep structures' of ineffective schools may have been inappropriately ignored.

A variety of factors were observed to be at stake in the school Reynolds worked in. Individual teachers, he suspected, were projecting their own deficiencies as teachers on to the children or the communities from which they came, claiming that the latter were the reason for the school's ineffectiveness. They 'clung on' to past practices, arguing that things had always been done the way they were doing them. They had, at the same time, built up defences to keep out threatening messages from outsiders. They were reluctant to attempt change 'for fear that it might fail and were convinced that change was someone else's job, not theirs'. They sought 'safety in numbers', retreating into a ring-fenced mentality. Finally, the staff were organized into strongly demarcated sub-groups, with sometimes hostile relationships between them.

Reynolds goes on to describe some of the issues he encountered which the 'school improvement literature had given [him] no warning about'. Attempts to get the staff to discuss the educational problems facing the school, rather than the personal deficiencies of individual children, often resulted in 'increased interpersonal conflicts amongst staff, a breakdown of some pre-existing relationships and much interpersonal hostility'. An attempt to get teachers to understand the nature of pupils' experiences by shadowing them during the course of a morning or afternoon produced a situation in which many staff '. . . realised for the first time the incompetence of their colleagues, having experienced it at first hand rather than merely encountering it through rumour or innuendo'.

The account offered is not uniformly pessimistic. Eventually some of the change efforts began to penetrate the school's management structures, encouraging more openness and sharing on the part of the management team. These changes, in turn, influenced the staff who began to 'solidify in terms of interpersonal relationships'. None the less, there were casualties including, in this particular case, the headteacher who retired from a nervous breakdown.

Eventually the school emerged through these processes as a 'more

effective institution ... more able to handle the complex interpersonal difficulties that school improvement brings'. Summing
up, Reynolds concluded that '... knowledge of the rational–
empirical paradigm encountered irrationality, emotionality, abnor-
mality and what can only be called personal and group disturbance'
(Reynolds and Packer 1992: 182).

This Welsh account opens up the dark side of school improvement efforts and exposes the naive optimism on which much of
the current literature is premised. In particular it encourages
us to read the major studies with a more discerning eye whilst
paying greater attention to what they do not say as well as what
they do.

A recent British 'success story'?

The story of change at Newall Green High School on the Wythenshawe estate in Manchester is told in the OFSTED study, *Improving
Schools* (OFSTED 1994c). The school serves one of the most
disadvantaged areas of Manchester with high rates of unemployment in the locality. The extent of its 'improvement' appears to offer
significant messages for all those involved in providing for the
educationally disadvantaged.

At the time when the school was inspected a wide variety of issues
apparently required attention. These included:

> ... improvement in the quality of classroom experience; greater
> use of assessment to set expectations and to raise standards;
> adoption of a wider range of teaching styles; improvement in
> the effectiveness of departmental management; reorganisation
> of support for low-attaining pupils; improvement in voca-
> tional and educational guidance; and the continued develop-
> ment of the transitional arrangements between primary and
> secondary school.
>
> (OFSTED 1994c: 9)

Standards of achievement, at least as measured by public examinations, were low: only 6 per cent of the year group (some eight or
nine pupils) were obtaining five or more A–C passes.

The most striking thing about the school's subsequent experience
was the very short period from the time of the first inspection within
which, it is claimed, the improvements took place. First inspected

in October 1991 and revisited just over a year later (in January 1993) '. . . there was no mistaking the fact that the issues identified in the inspection had been addressed and that this was an improved and improving school; there were clear advances on many fronts' (OFSTED 1994c: 10).

Amongst the 'tangible improvements' HMI cited was the increase in pupils gaining five or more A–C passes at GCSE. From 6 per cent in 1991 it had jumped to 18 per cent by 1993 representing, as HMI observed, 'a three-fold improvement in two years' (OFSTED 1994c). In some departments the changes had been 'astonishing'. In Science, for example, there had been 'a five-fold improvement' in the grades obtained over the 2 years and History had also secured very considerable gains. Improvements were not confined to those taking exams either: 'In 1992–93 53 per cent of entrants had a reading age below nine years [but] by Christmas every child had improved measurably and some had made enormous gains.' At the same time 'unusual methods' for handling the processes of transition from primary to secondary school had produced 'unmistakable improvements in pupils' attitudes, confidence and motivation to learn' (OFSTED 1994c: 11). Commenting on the school's ethos, 'an area where the measurement of improvement by objective yardsticks is most difficult', HMI identified a 'brightening, school-wide picture' of 'better relationships, better behaviour, better attendance and better attitudes'.

The report went on to ask 'what was special about the way this school achieved the improvements?' It identified five main areas in which there had been significant developments. The first was in relation to school development planning. 'Successive plans had built carefully on earlier ones, rearranging priorities, ensuring continuity and progression, and the rescue of any neglected or uncompleted initiatives.' The second was the 'regularity with which various kinds of review were undertaken'. These took place between the SMT and faculty heads; between faculty heads and individual teachers; and between subject teachers and individual pupils. The third was in the 'sharing of aspirations and criteria for success'. This had included making pupils aware of what constituted progress in their work and developing innovative arrangements for pupils' transition from primary to secondary school. The fourth related to quality control. 'The school understood the need to monitor its work, to maintain momentum and to keep standards up' through a wide variety of arrangements. Fifth, and finally, there was the 'hard work and dedication' the school staff had put in.

Important changes were undoubtedly taking place at Newall Green between the time of the first inspection and the second. Whether they were as substantial as the report suggests seems, however, more doubtful. School development planning, for example, has some potential but no previous studies have envisaged success on the scale reported here. And other institutions have sought to bring about changes in the ways teachers review their work and counsel students but again with more limited success.

It may, of course, be that Newall Green was already successful in certain key respects and that the 'improvements' described were consequently developed over the following year from already solid foundations. Returning to the original inspection report, there are signs that, whatever the list of areas identified as requiring further action, much was already going well in the school. Indeed, at the time of the first inspection 'standards of work were satisfactory or better in three-quarters of lessons seen' (a figure, we note, that was around the national average for all schools), 'relationships in the classroom [were] generally very good', 'behaviour around the school [was] courteous and orderly' and teachers already 'worked hard to provide a stimulating environment for learning'. Finally, the school was 'well led' by the headteacher and deputies who gave 'a clear sense of direction and purpose' through 'concise and realistic' aims and objectives which 'linked effectively with the school development plan and faculty/departmental schemes of work' (Newall Green 1991: *iv*). Indeed, with the benefit of hindsight, the only features of the school that seem out of place within a general story of success were: (1) the extremely low exam results (which were rather generously described in the initial report merely as being 'below the national and Manchester averages'); and (2) the attendance of Year 11 pupils.

None the less there is a problem in interpreting what caused what. If all these positive features were already in place at the time of the first inspection, then it is more difficult to see how the particular factors identified in the case study made the 'extra difference' that brought about the considerable improvements which were noted. If school development planning, for example, was already an established part of school practice (as it seems to have been), then it must have been some additional and notable aspect of the increasingly targeted plan(s) that made the *additional* difference. If relationships in the classroom were already 'generally good' then teachers would surely have had difficulty in improving them much further; and if teachers already 'worked hard', then they would have had to work still harder.

Another possible explanation is that, at the time of the first inspection, the school had undertaken much of the groundwork needed for improvement to flourish but had not yet seen the more tangible benefits which began to emerge shortly afterwards. On another tack, the study does not rule out the possibility that the improvements in measured performance could have been brought about by other means. The better results in GCSE might, for example, have come about through the school targeting a rather small number of 'borderline' pupils and giving them extra help to get them over the five A–C hurdle, as has happened in a considerable number of other schools nationally. Starting from a very low base one can make considerable progress in percentage terms by improving the performance of rather small numbers of pupils. And on the question of whether the school succeeded in improving the attendance of boys in Years 10 and 11 (a concern that was singled out for comment in the first inspection) the account is simply vague.

The purpose of this critique is not to suggest that there were *no* important changes at Newall Green over the period between the two inspections. We doubt, however, whether the school's experience was typical of improvement efforts in similar schools. A sense of realism about what schools can be expected to achieve over periods as short as a year is required. If a 'failing' school's fate is to be judged simply by the distance the most successful have travelled then most will be damned.

What's in it for teachers?

Most studies agree that, by one means or another, teachers' enthusiasm and commitment to change must be captured. The task of mobilizing them, however, may be more difficult in some circumstances and cultures than in others. For example, in her study, *Teachers' Workplace*, Rosenholtz (1989) identifies two kinds of schools at opposite ends of a continuum. One group she describes as 'high consensus' schools. In these principals and teachers 'appeared to agree on the definition of teaching and their instructional goals occupied a place of high significance' (Rosenholtz, 1989: 206–8). There were numerous other ways in which the teachers in these schools created an educative environment. 'They seemed attentive to instructional goals, to evaluative criteria that gauged their success, and to standards for student conduct that enabled teachers to teach and students to learn.' In low-consensus schools, by contrast, 'few teachers seemed attached to anything or anybody, and they were more concerned with their own identity than a sense of shared community'. Teachers in such schools talked of 'frustration, failure, tedium, though not in their own person; they managed to transfer those attributes to the students about whom they complained, themselves remaining complacent and aloof'. In these latter schools 'no-one, not even the principals, lay claim to the responsibility for helping struggling teachers improve'. Again, by way of contrast, 'in learning-enriched settings an abundant spirit of continuous improvement seemed to hover school-wide because no-one ever stopped learning to teach'.

Rosenholtz's attempt to capture the spirit of these two ideal-types led her to characterize them as 'stuck' and 'moving' schools, terms which have proved sufficiently illuminative for them to have achieved wider adoption since then. Teachers from 'moving' schools held an ideology that was 'the reverse of fatalism – everything was possible'. Teachers in 'stuck' schools, on the other hand, created environments in which they were 'unfree'. 'Boredom, punitiveness and self-defensiveness resulted.' To free themselves from 'their distressing work' they took days off, with obvious consequences for their schools and their colleagues. Unfortunately the study has little to say directly about schools which actually improved over the course of time but the implications would appear to be largely self-evident. Improvement efforts which duck the question of what's in them for teachers are likely to fail.

Searching for some broader lessons

How much improvement can schools be expected to achieve in the medium term? One of the leading North American contributions is Louis and Miles' (1992) study *Improving the Urban High School*. In it they try to trace the longer-term outcomes in over one hundred schools which implemented 'effective school' programmes during the mid- to late 1980s.

The basic tenets of such programmes have usually been summarized in five- or seven-point plans. These have tended to emphasize the importance of such factors as: (1) strong administrative leadership; (2) the creation of a safe and orderly climate for teaching and learning; (3) an emphasis on the acquisition of basic academic skills; (4) the generation of higher teacher expectations; and (5) constant monitoring of pupils' performance. Interventions along these lines were pioneered in New York by Ron Edmonds (1979) in the late 1970s and early 1980s, although the extent to which they have been firmly grounded in the research evidence has since been questioned (see, for example, Ralph and Fennessey 1983).

Louis and Miles contacted participating schools several years after they had embarked on their reform programmes. Principals in each school answered a variety of questions put to them by the researchers. Of particular interest are the principals' assessments of the outcomes.

Most change was claimed in the areas of student attitudes and behaviour. Half the principals (49 per cent) reported 'greatly improved' outcomes in terms of student behaviour whilst over four out of ten (43 per cent) reported 'greatly improved' student attitudes. Just under four out of ten (38 per cent) reported 'greatly improved' student attendance. However, only a small minority (12 per cent) reported 'great improvements' in the employment of their students upon graduation and a similarly small minority (15 per cent) reported that student dropout rates were 'greatly improved'. These findings would suggest that it is relatively easy to improve the things which are directly under the schools' control but more difficult in some other respects.

The final area considered in the research was the central one of student achievement. It is reasonable to suppose that all the programmes sought improvements in this area as one of their main objectives. Only one in four (24 per cent) principals, however, reported that student achievement had 'greatly improved'. The majority were frank enough to report only modest improvements. Taken as a whole the study reminds us forcibly of the extent to which schools have to struggle for progress without guarantees of success.

The detailed case studies Louis and Miles provide of individual schools which claimed to have improved are sufficiently varied to offer little prospect of common findings across cases. In their quantitative review of the data from interviews with the principals, however, one major factor survived their statistical analyses and emerged as influential. This was the schools' capacity for what they termed 'deep coping'. It is interesting that this notion has some of the social–psychological dimensions Reynolds identified in his study. Whether it is an empirically-realizable concept, however, is more doubtful. Amongst the features Louis and Miles identified as examples of 'deep coping' were: 'vision-building and sharing, rolling planning, substantial restaffing, increasing school control over the environment, empowering people and redesigning the school organization' (Louis and Miles 1992: 281). Each of these seems to us, however, to represent a substantial agenda in its own right. To simply sweep them into a single factor, as Louis and Miles attempted to do, is to take the process of simplification a stage too far.

We suspect the attempt to distil the 'lessons' of school improvement into a rather small (and manageable) number of 'factors which work' is unlikely to be convincing as anyone who has attempted to follow Fullan's comprehensive reviews of the change process will testify. As Fullan himself has remarked: 'It is so easy to underestimate the complexities of the change process' (Fullan 1991: 350).

Some common elements of the change process

At the same time, any attempt to identify 'key factors' in the change process is likely to mushroom rapidly. In our own reading of the literature, however, there were only a handful which survived across context and circumstance.

First, there is the question of timescales. These are best summarized as medium-to-long-term. Hardly any studies have seen time in terms of months.

Second, there is the question of ownership. For improvement to take off, a body of staff within a school need to agree amongst themselves (and with 'the management') that there is 'a problem' which needs to be tackled, that there are some strategies which could be explored and that they will search out the solutions for a while.

Third, there is the question of prioritizing. For the space to be created for a significant body of staff energy to be targeted towards change, some 'problems' need to be identified as more important than others. By their nature, however, schools seem to be organizations in which it is difficult to focus and prioritize – one concern invariably seems to compete with another.

These three dimensions will strike many as being rather obvious. We would merely observe that they would appear to have challenged, at times, even the most experienced school leaders. There is also an additional factor at play in 'ineffective' schools. If we believe the research the skills that are required to bring these key factors into play are likely to be in short supply. Time and resources are often seen as fully committed already; views about what the staff see as the problems and are willing to take on will vary; and the capacity to prioritize is seen as lacking. First, teachers will need to be convinced – and then pupils (Rudduck 1991). It is no surprise, therefore, that a common piece of advice about how to get things moving in such circumstances has been to 'do and then plan', hoping, in the process, that something will take root. As Louis and Miles put it:

> In 'depressed schools' one of the few ways of building commitment to a reform programme is for successful action to occur that actualises hope for genuine change. Effective action by a small group often stimulates an interest in planning rather than vice versa.
>
> (Louis and Miles 1992: 204)

Coordinating such change efforts frequently challenges the leadership of 'effective' schools; in 'ineffective' schools the problems posed may prove insurmountable.

Closure: the unthinkable alternative?

In the UK we are very reluctant to close schools down; it also happens to be rather difficult to do this. However, if we allow ourselves, for a moment, the possibility of a 'symbolic' closure leading to the formation of a 'new' school it becomes much easier to see how the various factors which have been identified in the school improvement literature might be allowed to flourish. We undertake this exercise cautiously and for heuristic purposes, mindful that it is usually the institutions which need 'fixing' rather than the individuals (teachers and pupils) who inhabit them. Teachers should not be made to suffer for problems which are beyond their influence.

First, there is the question of staffing. A new headteacher in a 'new' school is probably in a much better position to build a senior management team and teaching staff who are prepared to work together within a collaborative culture. The current practice of simply replacing the headteacher (and other staff as and when 'natural wastage' allows) merely places the same 'problems' in another set of hands. Few can single-handedly rise to the challenge.

Second, there is the possibility of creating a new vision of what the school might be about whilst sharing it with the school's community. In a new institution the need to deconstruct one set of messages and concerns whilst, simultaneously, fostering another is lessened; people expect there to be some changes.

Third, there is the prospect of mounting a mutually consistent set of curriculum practices. Traditions associated with the teaching of different subjects may linger on. With the whole approach up for review, one is likely to be in a better position to break through the varying and uneven patterns pertaining within different departments.

Fourth, there is the possibility of deploying resources in different ways. It is a feature of most school improvement efforts that they are perched on the backs of staff whose goodwill is, almost certainly, stretched already. Within a new institution there is the possibility of some re-examination of prevailing assumptions about resourcing.

The most likely outcome for any newly created institution is that it would start life as a school of 'average effectiveness'.

Although there is much interest amongst policy-makers in the problems of closing 'ineffective' schools, there is not much prospect of them doing so as a direct response to the problems posed by research on school improvement. 'School closure' will, doubtless, continue to be a last resort when all other efforts have failed – a long, drawn-out and painful experience for all concerned.

Betting on change

In the early to mid-1990s a number of school improvement projects were launched in the UK, each in its different way claiming to build directly upon previous research. Such projects are of interest in so far as they represent different 'bets' on the importance of the various starting points we have discussed.

The largest to date is, undoubtedly, *Improving School Effectiveness* launched by the Scottish Office Education Department and involving some 60 Scottish schools (see MacBeath and Mortimore 1994). Three candidates for action have, in the Scottish view, emerged.

One is the process of school development planning. This is an area which has been given some prominence in recent reports by Scottish HMI (SOED 1990). There has been a good deal of interest in the potential of planning processes in schools in recent years (see Hargreaves and Hopkins 1991) although, as yet, only limited direct evidence that it brings about significant improvements in children's learning (Caldwell and Spinks 1992).

Another thrust is a concern to improve schools' 'culture and ethos', a theme which has dominated earlier research on school effectiveness and of whose importance Bryk *et al.*'s most recent study (1993) of Catholic high schools powerfully reminds us. The conditions within which educational activities are conducted are seen as generating crucial conditions for learning. By working on teachers' and pupils' expectations of the learning environment the project hopes to make the development of school cultures more tangible in their contribution to pupils' learning.

The third area concerns the view that the methods of teaching and learning that schools are employing need to be examined and possibly changed. This is the most challenging and potentially controversial of the three concerns. Interventions in the classroom have hitherto seldom been undertaken as part of school improvement efforts. It is also likely to be the one with the greatest pay-off from successful intervention.

The *Schools Make A Difference* (SMAD) project launched by the Hammersmith and Fulham LEA in 1993 is another example of a school improvement project in action, albeit on a somewhat smaller scale than the Scottish one. The main aim has been 'to lay the foundations for raising student levels of attainment, achievement and morale' in eight secondary schools within the authority (see Stoll *et al.* 1994). One of the original schools involved was St Mark's, which we noted earlier had been severely criticized by OFSTED's inspectors.

SMAD is of particular interest because it has been relatively well resourced, albeit over a relatively short, 2-year period. Like an earlier project in Sheffield LEA (Rudduck and Wilcox 1988) the project team has paid particular attention to ensuring staff 'ownership' of the action. Much of what the schools have been doing will seem familiar: sharing theories about change, views of school culture, value-added approaches to measuring progress and the need for some monitoring and evaluation. But there are also some elements which suggest a more fundamental and innovative review of prevailing practices has taken place: course-work clinics outside school time for pupils taking public exams, mentoring of Year 8 students in relation to their literacy skills and the formation of a group of teachers in one school to act as 'critical friends' in each other's classrooms.

Another project which has claimed considerable success in raising achievement is the *Two Towns School Improvement Project* in Staffordshire (reported in *The Times Educational Supplement*, 5 June 1994, and Barber *et al.* 1994). The head of one school is quoted as saying that prior to the project 'the school had gone through a hasty reorganisation and was on a downward spiral . . . staff were demoralised and credibility was declining'. The head had taken over shortly before the project had begun and its involvement had helped to remotivate the school. She partly attributed the school's improving staying-on rates, falling truancy rates and better exam results (up over 3 years from 19 per cent achieving five or more A–C passes to 26 per cent) to the project's influence.

These three projects do not exhaust the range of initiatives. Others of which we have some personal knowledge have started in Birmingham, Bradford, Lewisham, Nottinghamshire and Shropshire; and there are doubtless many more.

Establishing the extent of 'real change'

When industrial psychologists first began to experiment with the conditions of the workplace they believed that it was the specific initiatives they had introduced which made the difference. It was only later that they discovered so-called 'Hawthorne effects'. Most changes made some difference to workers' productivity – but not for very long. Their experiences prompt the question whether the 'successes' claimed by improvement projects, especially in 'ineffective' schools, are just a more sophisticated version of Hawthorne effects played out in educational settings?

There are several ways in which we could guard against this possibility. The first is the need to scrutinize external reviews closely. They may capture the issues but they should be treated, initially at least, as only one account of what needs to be fixed; insiders' views need to be treated equally seriously. We have to find better ways of 'listening in' on a school's 'discussions' about change. Who saw things this way? What was and wasn't on the agenda? What ideas got tossed around and thrown out? And, crucially, whose view(s) of the 'problems' eventually prevailed?

Second, we need better accounts of what actually went on. Over 20 years have passed since the early studies of implementation taught us that what gets planned and what gets put into practice can differ, sometimes alarmingly. How far did the initiative penetrate and influence classroom practice? Did anyone, for example, broaden their repertoire of teaching styles? Did anyone eventually succeed in shifting their dominant pedagog(ies)? And could any of them explain how? Much of this evidence is likely to be qualitatively based but could be powerfully complemented by some quantitative evidence as well.

Third, we need to keep reminding ourselves of the importance of taking the longer view, by which we mean considerably more than a 12-month period. The educational world is full of initiatives (and their attendant evaluations claiming 'success') which were still up-and-running 3 months after the funding and/or the energy were withdrawn but which disappeared a short while later. The only really longer-term follow-up we have of TVEI, for example, suggests that a project's survival chances are not always that good (Williams and Yeomans 1993). It is hard to keep momentum going and rather too easy to help an initiative change direction and fade away. We must expect to plough our way through numerous cases which claim to have been successful to find those which probably have.

In conclusion

We began by asking whether the existing evidence on how to improve 'ineffective' schools pointed the way ahead. The traditions of research conducted within the school effectiveness paradigm encouraged us in our belief that there might be some 'common messages'. In the event we encountered two stumbling blocks. The first was the rather small number of studies from which to generalize. Most are not specifically about how 'ineffective' schools improve but about the more general processes of improvement *per se*. We still suspect that there are problems and barriers to change which are specific to 'ineffective' schools but which the research has not teased out as yet. The second was more fundamental. As Hargreaves (1994: 54) has noted: 'faith in generalized and scientifically known principles of school effectiveness has begun to be superseded by commitments to more ongoing, provisional and contextually sensitive processes of school improvement'.

The national and international press towards 'raising achievement' is something that can engage the professional commitment of teachers. It is potentially a powerful enough rallying cry to allow schools to review their routine ways of going about things. Ultimately a school's staff are and feel accountable of their pupils, who must eventually leave capable of taking their place with confidence in the world beyond. The commitment to 'raising achievement' (broadly construed) could be one expression of the 'visible ideology' which Lightfoot discovered in all her 'excellent' schools; and it evokes the professional 'inspiration' that Bryk argued animated his. It can encourage teachers to explore the possibilities of real change. However, as Rosenholtz (1989: 216) warns us, 'there is no easy formula . . . there are [only] clues and guidelines'. Teachers will have to interpret the clues and adapt the broad guidelines in the light of the demands of their own setting and situation. 'The success of any given strategy depends in large part upon its context' (Rosenholtz, 1989) and the sensitivity with which each individual institution can, as Richardson (1973: 330) put it, 'creatively reconcile its newness and its oldness', relinquishing some of the pull of the past in the endless pursuit of understanding and improvement.

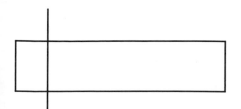

REFERENCES

Ainscow, M. (ed) (1991) *Effective Schools For All*. London: David Fulton.

Aitkin, M. and Longford, N. (1986) Statistical issues in school effectiveness. *Journal of the Royal Statistical Society*, Series A, 149: 1–42.

Audit Commission (1989) *Assuring Quality in Education*. London: HMSO.

Auld, R. (1976) *William Tyndale Junior and Infant School's Public Enquiry*. London: ILEA.

Ball, S. (1981) *Beachside Comprehensive*. Cambridge: CUP.

Ball, S. (1990) *Politics and Policy-Making in Education*. London: Routledge.

Barber, M., Collarbone, P., Cullen, E. and Owen, D. (1994) *Raising Expectations and Achievement in City Schools: The Two Towns School Improvement Project*. University of Keele.

Barnes, A. (1983) Undergoing a formal inspection – what it was like. *Education*, 20 May: 391–2.

Barnes, A. (1984) HMI inspection: what happens next? *Education*, 164(13): 257–8.

Beare, H., Caldwell, B. J. and Millikan, R. H. (1989) *Creating an Excellent School: Some New Management Techniques*. London: Routledge.

Blakey, L. and Heath, A. (1988) Differences between comprehensive schools: some preliminary findings for fifteen schools. In D. Reynolds and P. Cuttance (eds) (1992) *School Effectiveness: Research, Policy and Practice*. London: Cassell.

Blok, H. de, and Hoeksma, J. B. (1993) The stability of the school effect over time: how stable were differences between primary schools in the performance of their pupils. *Tijdschrift voor Onderwijsresearch*, 18(6): 331–42.

Bosker, R. J. and Guldemond, H. (1991) Interdependency of performance indicators: an empirical study in a categorical school system. In S. Raudenbush and J. D. Willms (eds) *Schools, Classrooms and Pupils*. San Diego, CA: Academic Press.

Bosker, R. J. and Scheerens, J. (1989) Criterion choice, effect size and stability: three fundamental problems in school effectiveness research. In B. Creemers and D. Reynolds (eds) *School Effectiveness and School Improvement*. Lisse: Swets and Zeitlinger.

Brighouse, T. (1991) *What Makes A Good School?* Stafford: Network Educational Press.

Browne, S. (1979) The accountability of HM Inspectorate. In J. Lello (ed) *Accountability*. London: Ward Lock, pp. 35–44.

Bryk, A., Lee, V. and Holland, P. (1993) *Catholic Schools and the Common Good*. Cambridge, MA: Harvard University Press.

Caldwell, B. J. and Spinks, J. M. (1988) *The Self-Managing School*. Basingstoke: Falmer Press.

Caldwell, B. J. and Spinks, J. M. (1992) *Leading the Self-Managing School*. Basingstoke: Falmer Press.

Cannell, J. J. (1987) *Nationally-Normed Elementary Achievement Testing in America's Public Schools: How All 50 States Are Above the National Average*. Daniels, WV: Friends of Education.

Chubb, J. E. and Moe, T. M. (1990) *Politics, Markets and America's Schools*. Washington, DC: The Brookings Institution.

CIPFA (1988) *Performance Indicators in Schools: A Contribution to the Debate*. London: Chartered Institute of Public Finance and Accountancy.

Clift, P. S., Nuttall, D. L. and McCormick, R. (1987) *Studies in School Self-Evaluation*. Basingstoke: Falmer Press.

Coleman, J. S. *et al.* (1966) *Equality of Educational Opportunity*. Washington, DC: US Office of Education, US Govt Printing Office.

Coleman, P. and Larocque, L. (1990) *Struggling to be 'Good Enough': Administrative Practices and School District Ethos*. Basingstoke: Falmer Press.

Coopers & Lybrand (1988) *Local Management of Schools*. London: HMSO.

Cox, C. B. and Dyson, A. E. (1969a) *Fight for Freedom: A Black Paper*. London: The Critical Quarterly Society.

Cox, C. B. and Dyson, A. E. (eds) (1969b) *Black Paper Two: The Crisis in Education*. London: The Critical Quarterly Society.

Cox, C. B. and Dyson, A. E. (eds) (1970) *Black Paper Three: Goodbye Mr Short*. London: The Critical Quarterly Society.

Creemers, B. P. M. (1992) School effectiveness, effective instruction and school improvement in the Netherlands. In D. Reynolds and P. Cuttance (eds) *School Effectiveness: Research, Policy and Practice*. London: Cassell.

Cuttance, P. (1988) Intra-system variation in the effectiveness of schools. *Research Papers in Education*, 2(3): 180–216.

Cuttance, P. and Goldstein, H. (1988) A note on national assessment and school comparisons. *Journal of Education Policy*, 3: 197–202.

Dean, J. (1994) *What Headteachers and Teachers Think About Inspection*. Slough: EMIE, NFER.

Dearing, R. (1993) *The National Curriculum and Its Assessment: Interim Report*. London: School Curriculum and Assessment Authority.

DES (1977) *Ten Good Schools: A Secondary School Enquiry*. London: HMSO.

DES (1987) *Report by Her Majesty's Inspectors on LEA Provision and the Quality of Response in Schools and Colleges in England 1986*. London: Department of Education and Science.

DES (1988a) *Secondary Schools: An Appraisal by HMI*. London: HMSO.

DES (1988b) *Task Group on Assessment and Testing: A Report* (the Black Report). London: Department of Education and Science.

DES (1989a) *Standards in Education 1987–88: The Annual Report of HM Senior Chief Inspector of Schools Based on the Work of HMI in England*. London: Department of Education and Science.

DES (1989b) *School Indicators for Internal Management: An Aide-Mémoire*. London: Department of Education and Science.

DES (1989c) *The Use Made by Local Education Authorities of Public Examination Results*. London: Department of Education and Science.

DES (1990a) *Standards in Education 1988–89, The Annual Report of HM Senior Chief Inspector of Schools*. London: Department of Education and Science.

DES (1990b) *Report by HM Inspectors on Hackney Free and Parochial Church of England Secondary School*. London: Department of Education and Science.

DFE (1992a) *Choice and Diversity: A New Framework for Schools*, Cmnd 2021. London: HMSO.

DFE (1992b) *Framework for the Inspection of Schools*, Paper for Consultation. London: HMSO.

DFE (1993) *Inspecting Schools: A Guide to the Inspection Provisions of the*

Education (Schools) Act 1992 in England, Circular 7/93. London: Department for Education.

DFE (1994a) *The Parent's Charter*. London: Department for Education.

DFE (1994b) *The Parent's Charter: Publication of Information about Secondary Schools*, Circular 14/94. London: Department for Education.

Driver, R. (1989) The Construction of Scientific Knowledge in School Classrooms. In R. Miller (ed) *Doing Science: Images of Science in Science Education*. Basingstoke: Falmer Press.

Edmonds, R. (1979) Effective schools for the urban poor. *Educational Leadership*, 37: 15–27.

Eisner, E. W. (1991) *The Enlightened Eye*. New York: Macmillan.

Elliott, J. and Ebbutt, D. (1986) How do HMI judge educational quality? *Curriculum*, 17(3): 130–40.

Fitz-Gibbon, C. T. (ed) (1990) *Performance Indicators*. Clevedon: Multilingual Matters.

Fitz-Gibbon, C. T. (1992) School effects at A-level: genesis of an information system? In D. Reynolds and P. Cuttance (eds) *School Effectiveness: Research, Policy and Practice*. London: Cassell.

Fullan, M. (1982) *The Meaning of Educational Change*. New York: Teachers College Press.

Fullan, M. (1991) *The New Meaning of Educational Change*. London: Cassell.

Fullan, M. (1992) *Successful School Improvement: The Implementation Perspective and Beyond*. Buckingham: Open University Press.

Fullan, M. and Hargreaves, A. (1992) *What's Worth Fighting For in Your School? Working Together for Improvement*. Buckingham: Open University Press.

Goldstein, H. (1984) The methodology of school comparisons. *Oxford Review of Education*, 10: 69–74.

Goldstein, H. (1987) *Multi-level Models in Educational and Social Research*. London: Griffin.

Goldstein, H. *et al.* (1993) A multi-level analysis of schools' examination results. *Oxford Review of Education*, 19(4): 425–33.

Goodlad, J. (1984) *A Place Called School: Prospects for the Future*. New York: McGraw-Hill.

Gray, J. (1981a) A competitive edge: examination results and the probable limits of secondary school effectiveness. *Educational Review*, 33(1): 25–35.

Gray, J. (1981b) Towards effective schools. *British Educational Research Journal*. 7(1): 59–69.

Gray, J. (1982) *Making More Sense of Examination Results*. Milton Keynes: Open University, Block 6 of Course E364, Curriculum Evaluation and Assessment in Educational Institutions.

Gray, J. (1989) Multi-level models: issues and problems emerging from their recent application in British studies of school effectiveness. In R. D. Bock (ed) *Multi-level Analysis of Educational Data*. New York: Academic Press, pp. 127–45.

Gray, J. and Jesson, D. (1987) Exam results and local authority league tables. In A. Harrison and J. Gretton (eds) *Education and Training UK 1987*. Newbury: Policy Journals, pp. 31–41.

Gray, J. and Jesson, D. (1989) The impact of comprehensive reforms. In R. Lowe (ed) *The Changing Secondary School*. Basingstoke: Falmer Press, pp. 72–98.

Gray, J. and Jesson, D. (1991) The negotiation and construction of performance indicators. *Evaluation and Research in Education*, 4(2): 93–108.

Gray, J. and Jones, B. (1983) Towards a framework for interpreting schools' examination results. Reprinted in R. Rogers (ed) *Education and Social Class*. Basingstoke: Falmer Press, pp. 51–7.

Gray, J. and Sime, N. (1988) Findings from the National Survey of Teachers in England and Wales. In *Discipline in Schools: Report of the (Elton) Committee of Enquiry*. London: HMSO.

Gray, J. and Wilcox, B. (1995) In the aftermath of inspection: the nature and fate of inspection report recommendations. *Research Papers in Education*, 10(1): 1–18.

Gray, J., Jesson, D., Goldstein, H. and Hedger, K. (1995) A multi-level analysis of school improvement: changes in schools' performance over time. *School Effectiveness and School Improvement*, 6(2).

Gray, J., Jesson, D. and Jones, B. (1986) The search for a fairer way of comparing schools' examination results. *Research Papers in Education*, 1(2): 91–122.

Gray, J., Jesson, D., Pattie, C. and Sime, N. (1990) *Education and Training Opportunities in the Inner City*. Sheffield: Department of Employment Research and Development Series No. 51.

Gray, J., McPherson, A. and Raffe, D. (1983) *Reconstructions of Secondary Education: Theory, Myth and Practice in Scotland Since the War*. London: Routledge and Kegan Paul.

Great Britain Statutes (1992) *Education (Schools) Act 1992*. London: HMSO.

Hansard (1979) *Parliamentary Debates*, 5 November. London: HMSO, p. 100.

Hare, D. (1989) Cycles of hope and despair, *The Guardian* (weekend section), 3 June: p. 5.

Hargreaves, A. (1994) *Changing Teachers, Changing Times*. London: Cassell.

Hargreaves, D. H. (1984) (Chair) *Improving Secondary Schools*. London: Inner London Education Authority.

Hargreaves, D. H. (1990) Accountability and school improvement in the work of LEA inspectors: the rhetoric and beyond. *Journal of Education Policy*, 5(3): 230–9.

Hargreaves, D. H. and Hopkins, D. (1991) *The Empowered School: The Management and Practice of Development Planning*. London: Cassell.

Heath, A. and Clifford, P. (1980) The seventy thousand hours that Rutter left out. *Oxford Review of Education*, 6: 1–19.

Heath, A. and Clifford, P. (1981) The measurement and explanation of school differences. *Oxford Review of Education*, 7: 33–40.

Hedger, K. (1992) Seen it; been there; done it: the analysis of GCSE examination results in Shropshire. *Management in Education*, 6(1): 29–33.

Hedger, K. and Raleigh, M. (1992) GCSE examination results: improvement of: route 1. *Curriculum Journal*, 3(1): 53–62.

Hexter, J. H. (1971) *The History Primer*. London: Allen Lane.

HMI (1977) *Ten Good Schools*, Matters for Discussion, No. 1. London: HMSO.

HMI (1988) *Rating Scales and HMI Exercises, Working Instruction 27/87*. London: Department of Education and Science.

HMI (1991) *Aspects of Education in the USA: Indicators in Educational Monitoring*. London: HMSO.

HMI (1992) *Education in England 1990–91: The Annual Report of HM Senior Chief Inspector of Schools*. London: Department of Education and Science.

Jencks, C. *et al.* (1972) *Inequality: A Reassessment of the Effects of Family and Schooling in America*. New York: Basic Books.

Jenkins, V. (1987) *School Effectiveness and School Change: The IBIS Approach*. Paper presented to the Annual Conference of the British Educational Research Association, Manchester Polytechnic.

Jesson, D. and Gray, J. (1991) Slants on slopes: using multi-level models to investigate differential school effectiveness and its impact on pupils' examination results. *School Effectiveness and School Improvement*, 2(3): 230–47.

Jong, U. de, and Roeleveld, J. (1988) Openbaar en bijzonder onderwijs: een constant verschil? NSAV-paper, quoted in R. J. Bosker and J. Scheerens, in B. Creemers and D. Reynolds (eds) *School Effectiveness and School Improvement*. Lisse: Swets and Zeitlinger.

Kilgore, S. and Pendleton, T. (1986). In M. Aitkin and N. Longford, *Journal of the Royal Statistical Society*, Series A, 149: 1–42.

Knight, C. (1990) *The Making of Tory Education Policy in Post-War Britain: 1950–1986*. Basingstoke: Falmer Press.

Lawton, D. and Gordon, P. (1987) *HMI*. London: Routledge and Kegan Paul.

Lello, J. (1979) *Accountability in Education*. London: Ward Lock.

Levine, D. U. and Lezotte, L. W. (1990) *Unusually Effective Schools: A Review and Analysis of Research and Practice*. Madison, WI: National Center for Effective Schools Research and Development.

Lightfoot, S. L. (1983) *The Good High School: Portraits of Character and Culture*. New York: Basic Books.

Longford, N. T. (1986) VARCL: interactive software for variance component analysis. *Professional Statistician*, 5: 28–32.

Louis, K. S. and Miles, M. B. (1992) *Improving the Urban High School: What Works and Why*. London: Cassell.

MacBeath, J. and Mortimore, P. (1994) *Improving School Effectiveness: A Scottish Approach*. Paper presented to the Annual Conference of the British Educational Research Association, Oxford.

Mandeville, G. K. (1988) School effectiveness indicators revisited: cross-year stability. *Journal of Educational Measurement*, 25: 349–66.

Maychell, K. and Keys, W. (1993) *Under Inspection*. Slough: NFER.

McPherson, A. F. (1992) *Measuring Added Value in Schools*, Briefing No. 1. London: National Commission on Education.

McPherson, A. F. and Willms, J. D. (1986) Certification, class conflict, religion and community: a socio-historical explanation of the effectiveness of contemporary schools. In A. C. Kerckhoff (ed.) *Research in Sociology of Education and Socialisation*. Greenwich, CT: JAL.

Miles, M. B. and Huberman, A. (1984) *Qualitative Analysis*. London: Sage Publications.

Miles, W. J. W. (1982) The inspectorial role of HMI with a case study analysis of the full inspection, unpublished MEd dissertation. Birmingham University.

Mortimore, P., Sammons, P., Stoll, L., Lewis, D. and Ecob, R. (1988) *School Matters: The Junior Years*. Wells, Somerset: Open Books.

Murnane, R. J. (1987) Improving education indicators and economic indicators: the same problems? *Educational Evaluation and Policy Analysis*, 9(2): 101–16.

Nebesnuick, D. (1991) *Promoting Quality in Schools and Colleges*. Slough: EMIE, NFER.

Newall Green (1991) *Newall Green High School: A report by HMI*. London: DES (reference 67/92/SZ).

Nixon, J. and Rudduck, J. (1993) The role of professional judgement in the local inspection of schools. *Research Papers in Education*, 8(2): 135–48.

Nuttall, D., Goldstein, H., Prosser, R. and Rasbash, J. (1989) Differential school effectiveness. *International Journal of Educational Research*, 13(7): 769–76.

Oakes, J. (1987) *Conceptual and Measurement Issues in the Construction of School Quality*. Santa Monica, CA: Rand Corporation.

Oakes, J. (1989) School context and organisation, in R. J. Shavelson, L. M. McDonnell, and J. Oakes, (eds) *Indicators for Monitoring Mathematics and Science Education*. Santa Monica, CA: Rand Corporation, pp. 40–65.

OFSTED (1992a) *Framework for the Inspection of Schools: Paper for Consultation*. London: OFSTED.

OFSTED (1992b) *The Handbook for the Inspection of Schools*. London: OFSTED.

OFSTED (1993a) *Corporate Plan 1993–94 to 1995–96: Improvement Through Inspection*. London: OFSTED.

OFSTED (1993b) *The Handbook for the Inspection of Schools*. London: OFSTED.

OFSTED (1994a) *The Handbook for the Inspection of Schools*. London: OFSTED.

OFSTED (1994b) *A Focus on Quality*. London: OFSTED.

OFSTED (1994c) *Improving Schools*. London: HMSO.

Paterson, L. and Goldstein, H. (1991) New statistical methods for analysing social structures: an introduction to multi-level models. *British Educational Research Journal*, 17(4): 387–93.

Peters, T. (1987) *Thriving on Chaos: Handbook for a Management Revolution*. London: Pan Books.

Plewis, I. (ed) (1981) *Publishing School Examination Results: A Discussion*. Bedford Way Papers. London: Institute of Education, University of London.

Powell, A., Farrar, E. and Cohen, D. (1985) *The Shopping Mall High School*. Boston, MA: Houghton Mifflin.

Preece, P. (1989) Pitfalls in research on school and teacher effectiveness. *Research Papers in Education*, 4(3): 47–69.

Prosser, R., Rasbash, J. and Goldstein, H. (1992) *ML3 Software for Three-Level Analysis: User's Guide for V2*. London: Institute of Education, University of London.

Purkey, S. C. and Smith, M. S. (1983) Effective schools: a review. *Elementary School Journal*, 83(4): 427–52.

Ralph, J. and Fennessey, J. (1983) Science or reform? Some questions about the Effective Schools Model. *Phi Delta Kappan*, 64(10): 689–94.

Ranson, S., Gray, J. and Hannon, V. (1987) Citizens or consumers? Policies for school accountability. In S. Walker and L. Barton (eds) *Changing Policies, Changing Teachers: New Directions for Schooling?* Milton Keynes: Open University Press.

Ranson, S., Gray, J., Jesson, D. and Jones, B. (1986) Exams in context: values and power in educational accountability. In D. L. Nuttall (ed) *Assessing Educational Achievement*. Basingstoke: Falmer Press.

Rasbash, J., Prosser, R. and Goldstein, H. (1989) *ML2 Users Guide:*

Software for Two-level Analysis. London: Institute of Education, University of London.

Raudenbush, S. and Bryk, A. (1986) A hierarchical model for studying school effects. *Sociology of Education*, 59: 1–17.

Raudenbush, S. and Willms, J. D. (1991) *Schools, Classrooms and Pupils: International Studies of Schooling from a Multi-Level Perspective*. San Diego, CA: Academic Press.

Reynolds, D. (1976) The delinquent school. In M. Hammersley and P. Woods (eds) *The Process of Schooling*. London: Routledge and Kegan Paul.

Reynolds, D. (1991) Changing ineffective schools. In M. Ainscow (ed) *Effective Schools For All*. London: David Fulton.

Reynolds, D. and Cuttance, P. (eds) (1992) *School Effectiveness: Research, Policy and Practice*. London: Cassell.

Reynolds, D. and Packer, A. (1992) School effectiveness and school improvement in the 1990s. In D. Reynolds and P. Cuttance (eds) *School Effectiveness: Research, Policy and Practice*. London: Cassell.

Reynolds, D., Hopkins, D. and Stoll, L. (1993) Linking school effectiveness and school improvement. *School Effectiveness and School Improvement*, 4(1): 37–58.

Reynolds, D., Sullivan, M. and Murgatroyd, S. J. (1987) *The Comprehensive Experiment*. Basingstoke: Falmer Press.

Richardson, E. (1973) *The Teacher, the School and the Task of Management*. London: Heinemann.

Riddell, S. and Brown, S. (eds) (1991) *School Effectiveness Research: Its Messages for School Improvement*. Edinburgh: HMSO.

Rorty, R. (1991) *Objectivity, Relativism and Truth*. Cambridge: Cambridge University Press.

Rosenholtz, S. (1989) *Teachers' Workplace: The Social Organization of Schools*. New York: Longman.

Rowan, B. and Denk, C. E. (1982) *Modelling the academic performance of schools using longitudinal data: an analysis of school effectiveness measures and school and principal effects on school-level achievement*. Instructional Management Program Publication. San Francisco, CA: Far West Laboratories, quoted in D. Willms and S. Raudenbush, (1989) *Journal of Educational Measurement*, 26: 209–32.

Rudduck, J. (1991) *Innovation and Change: Developing Involvement and Understanding*. Buckingham: Open University Press.

Rudduck, J. and Wilcox, B. (1988) Issues of ownership and partnership in school-centred innovation. *Research Papers in Education*, 3(3): 157–79.

Rumbold, A. (1989) *The Times Educational Supplement*, 8 December.

Rutter, M., Maughan, B., Mortimore, P. and Ouston, J. (1979) *Fifteen*

Thousand Hours: Secondary Schools and Their Effects on Children. London: Open Books.

Salford LEA (1991) *Management Generic Pointers* (Draft), *Reporting Practice*. Salford: Education Department.

SCAA (1994) *Review of the National Curriculum* (The Dearing Review), Draft Proposals. London: School Curriculum and Assessment Authority.

Scheerens, J. (1990) School effectiveness research and the development of process indicators of school functioning. *School Effectiveness and School Improvement*, 1(1): 61–80.

Scheerens, J. (1992) *Effective Schooling: Research, Theory and Practice.* London: Cassell.

SCIA (1990) *Evaluating the Achievement of Schools and Colleges: Performance Indicators in Perspective.* Woolley Hall, Wakefield: Society of Chief Inspectors and Advisers.

Scottish Office Education Department (SOED) (1990) *The Role of School Development Planning in School Effectiveness.* Edinburgh: HMSO.

Scottish Office Education Department (SOED) (1992) *Using Ethos Indicators in Secondary School Evaluation.* Edinburgh: Scottish Office Education Department.

SHA (1980) You cannot treat exams as important and then try to suppress the results. *The Times Educational Supplement*, 12 December: 2.

Shepard, L. A. (1989) *Inflated test score gains: Is it old norms or teaching the tests?* Paper presented to the American Educational Research Association Annual Conference, USA: San Francisco.

Sime, N. and Gray, J. (1991) *Struggling for improvement: some estimates of the contribution of school effects over time.* Paper presented to the Annual Conference of the British Educational Research Association, Nottingham.

Smith, D. and Tomlinson, S. (1989) *The School Effect: A Study of Multiracial Comprehensives.* London: Policy Studies Institute.

Smith, M. S. (1972) The basic findings reconsidered. In F. Mosteller and D. P. Moynihan (eds) *On Equality of Educational Opportunity.* New York: Random House.

Stoll, L. and Fink, D. (1992) Effective school change: the Halton approach. *School Effectiveness and School Improvement*, 3(1): 19–41.

Stoll, L., Myers, K. and Harrington, J. (1994) *Linking school effectiveness and school improvement through action projects.* Paper presented to the Annual Conference of the British Educational Research Association, Oxford.

Suffolk LEA (1990) *Suffolk Criteria for School Evaluation.* Ipswich: Suffolk County Council.

Teddlie, C. and Stringfield, S. (1993) *Schools Make a Difference: Lessons*

Learned From a Ten-Year Study of School Effects. New York: Teachers College Press.

Tymms, P. and Fitz-Gibbon, C. T. (1990) *The stability of school effectiveness indicators.* Paper presented to the Annual Conference of the British Educational Research Association, Newcastle.

Wightman, T. (1986) *The Construction of Meaning and Conceptual Change in Classroom Settings: Case Studies in the Particulate Theory of Matter.* Leeds University: Children's Learning in Science Project.

Wilby, P. (1983) An inspector calls. *The Sunday Times*, 5 June.

Wilcox, B. (1989) Inspection and its contribution to practical evaluation. *Educational Research*, 31(3): 163–75.

Wilcox, B. (1992) *Time-Constrained Evaluation: A Practical Approach for LEAs and Schools.* London: Routledge.

Wilcox, B., Gray, J. and Tranmer, M. (1993) LEA frameworks for the assessment of schools: an interrupted picture. *Educational Research*, 35(3): 209–19.

Williams, R. and Yeomans, D. (1993) The fate of TVEI in a pilot school: a longitudinal case study. *British Educational Research Journal*, 19(4): 421–34.

Willms, J. D. (1985) The balance thesis: contextual effects of ability on pupils' O grade examination results. *Oxford Review of Education*, 11: 33–41.

Willms, J. D. (1986) Social class segregation and its relationship to pupils' examination results in Scotland. *American Sociological Review*, 51: 224–41.

Willms, J. D. (1987) Differences between Scottish Education Authorities in their examination attainment. *Oxford Review of Education*, 13: 211–37.

Willms, J. D. (1992) *Monitoring School Performance: A Guide for Educators.* Basingstoke: Falmer Press.

Willms, J. D. and Raudenbush, S. (1989) A longitudinal hierarchical linear model for estimating school effects and their stability. *Journal of Educational Measurement*, 26: 209–32.

Witte, J. F. and Walsh, D. J. (1990) A systematic test of the Effective Schools Model. *Educational Evaluation and Policy Analysis*, 12: 188–212.

Woodhouse, G. and Goldstein, H. (1988) Educational performance indicators and LEA league tables. *Oxford Review of Education*, 14: 301–20.

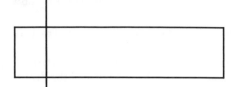

SUBJECT INDEX

NAME INDEX

TOTAL QUALITY MANAGEMENT AND THE SCHOOL

Stephen Murgatroyd and Colin Morgan

The management team within the school are currently faced with a great deal of pressure to achieve a range of 'performance' expectations in a climate of increasing uncertainty, financial stringency and competition. Total Quality Management is a framework and set of practical resources for managing organizations in the 1990s. Based on sound principles and a strong body of experience, Total Quality Management provides a school-based management team with the tools they need to become highly effective in meeting the goals of their stakeholders, and in creating a place that teachers want to work in.

This book is the first to fully examine the practice of Total Quality Management in the context of schooling. It looks, for instance, at the nature of a school's strategic management in the context of growing competition and expectations for performance; and at the positioning of the school in terms of vision and mission. It considers the setting of 'outrageous' or exceptional goals to create momentum and alignment and explores the nature of high performing teams within the school. It discusses commitment-building as part of the new quality culture and involving stakeholders in the daily management of the school.

It is practical and well illustrated with case vignettes and examples of Total Quality Management in action. It is based on the experience of two senior academic practitioners who have both carried out extensive work in school management and development.

Contents
Making sense of schooling in the 1990s – Choosing a generic strategy – Definitions of quality and their implications for TQM in schools – A model for TQM in the school – Vision, ownership and commitment – Customers and processes as the basis for schooling – Outrageous goals and the task of continuous improvement – Teams, team performance and TQM – Daily management tools for effective TQM – Implementing TQM in the school – Postscript – References – Index.

240pp   0 335 15722 X (Paperback)

SUCCESSFUL SCHOOL IMPROVEMENT
THE IMPLEMENTATION PERSPECTIVE AND BEYOND

Michael G. Fullan

The focus on implementation – or what actually happens in practice when innovations or reforms are attempted – is barely twenty years old. This book examines this powerful concept by demonstrating its use in a variety of policy and program applications. In addition to tracing the evolution of the knowledge bases on implementation over the last twenty years, the different chapters present case studies of its use on such diverse topics as (a) the implementation of microcomputers in classrooms, (b) curriculum implementation models in school districts, (c) the role of the principal, (d) the relationship between staff development and innovation, and (e) the larger role of teacher education and education reform. Taken together the chapters provide insights into successful change processes, and develop strategies for bringing about innovation in education more effectively.

Contents
Critical introduction by Michael Huberman – Successful school improvement and the implementation perspective – The implementation of microcomputers in schools: a case study – The school district and curriculum implementation – The role of the principal and school improvement – Staff development, innovations and institutional development – Beyond implementation: teacher development and educational reform – References – Index.

144pp   0 335 09575 5 (Paperback)   0 335 09576 3 (Hardback)